POWER
PRECISION

Also by Alan Sontag

THE BRIDGE BUM

POWER PRECISION

A REVOLUTIONARY
BRIDGE SYSTEM FROM A
WORLD CHAMPION PLAYER

By
ALAN SONTAG

WILLIAM MORROW AND COMPANY, INC.

NEW YORK   1979

Library of Congress Cataloging in Publication Data

Sontag, Alan.
    Power precision.

    1. Contract bridge—Bidding.   I. Title.
GV1282.3.S625   795.4'152   78-27250
ISBN 0-688-03472-1

BOOK DESIGN   CARL WEISS

Printed in the United States of America.

First Edition

1   2   3   4   5   6   7   8   9   10

To my parents
ROSE and LOUIS SONTAG

ACKNOWLEDGMENTS

I want to thank Oswald Jacoby, Jim Jacoby, Al Roth, Kathy and C. C. Wei, and of course Peter Weichsel.

CONTENTS

SESSION II

Trump . . . How Opener Asks for Controls after
Learning Distribution . . . A Bridge "Superstition" . . .
Additional Sequences Beginning with One Club–Two
Clubs . . . Meaning of Responder's Bid of Two Dia-
monds over Opener's One Club . . . How Opener
Clarifies Responder's Hand . . . Bidding More Im-
portant than Enlightened Card Play . . . Wisdom of
Not Conceding Contracts . . . The All-Important Club
Structure Now Complete

SESSION III

Diamonds . . . How to Ask for Queens . . . Two-Heart Opening Bid . . . Sequences that Begin with Two Hearts . . . Two-Spade Opening Bid . . . Sequences that Begin with Two Spades . . . Two No Trump Opening Bid . . . Two No Trump Sequences

The Beckers . . . Age No Hindrance to Great Play . . . Exact Bidding . . . Sion-Jacobus . . . Wonder and Wonder Woman . . . A Life Master in Less than One Year . . . A Correct Guess . . . They Make Costly Error . . . The Question of Whether to Play Fast . . . Hamman-Larsen . . . World Bridge Federation Rankings . . . Hating to Lose . . . An Important Slam . . . The Value of Pretending

Each Three-Bid and Four-Bid Analyzed . . . Possible Sequences after Each Three-Bid and Four-Bid . . . Extra Value Because of Special Meaning of Three-Club Opening Bid

Kasle-Guiver . . . A Great Bridge Teacher . . . Another Example of Standard American's Weakness . . .Trent-Radin . . . A Speeding Ticket . . . Peter Finds Right Opening Lead . . . Linhart-Gorfkle . . . The Basketball Player . . . Cheating . . . Bidding Three, Making Five . . . Moss-Bramley . . . An Unusual Arrangement . . . Momentum for the Final Session . . . Results at the Three-Quarters

---

SESSION IV

Silverman-Pender . . . Searching for Heirs . . . An Ice-Skating Champion . . . One-Club Opening Bid in

INTRODUCTION

by

PETER WEHCHSH

ALAN SONTAG AND I HAVE A LOT IN COMMON. WE BOTH love bridge, play it for a living, and believe it is the best game in the world. Many of the happiest moments of my bridge career have been shared with Alan, and some of the saddest. We won the 1975 *London Sunday Times* tournament, flew to Paris the next day, rented a car and drove to Germany, and spent two solid weeks drinking good beer. Another time we lost an important tournament on the last hand when Alan rescued the opponents from a one no trump contract I had doubled. They were destined to go down two tricks. Alan went down one. I threw the cards at him, but he really should have been strangled.

I was nervous when Alan first told me he was going to write about the system. System books are usually dry, sterile, packed with jargon. I did not want what we had invested so many years to make dynamic to read that way. Our system is a series of intricate concepts, each complete of itself, and it had to be presented with that in view.

Bidding has become very scientific. Primitive methods will no longer suffice. Most people will improve their bidding by adopting just one of the concepts presented in the book. The more that are learned, the greater will be the improvement. Really serious players will want to learn everything. Some of the system is quite difficult, some is not, but mastering it is decidedly worth the effort.

The book has another major merit. I know of no other work that details a bidding system and at the same time showcases it in action—the true test—against the world's greatest players in one of the world's toughest tournaments.

Finally, I loved reliving that 1977 Cavendish Calcutta, the richest bridge tournament ever played up to that time. No bridge event has ever been sketched so colorfully and completely.

Despite all we have shared, however, I still can't trust Alan. He promised he would never mention, much less write about, our grand slam bidding disaster in the Calcutta.

SESSION I

1

THE AUCTION

I WILL NEVER BECOME ACCUSTOMED TO BEING SOLD. I CAN'T say that I understand what real slaves went through, but I do know it is a strange feeling to stand on an auction block, being examined like a side of beef. It was stranger still because the entire affair, which took place in New York City, was filmed on French National Television, Channel One in France. I was dressed in silk and velvet, the setting was impressive, almost opulent, but there was no getting around the reality that I was up for sale to the highest bidder.

Auctioneer Mike Moss was the happiest person in the house. He winked at me and Peter Weichsel, sixth of the forty bridge partnerships to be sold, as we prepared to be scrutinized by prospective buyers. So far the winning bids had been higher than even Moss's optimistic expectations. Along with everyone else, he had been stunned when the *opening bid* on the first partnership offered for sale—current World Champions Ira Rubin and Fred Hamilton—was $7,000. It was clear to me, even before this partnership was ultimately sold for $9,800, that the bridge tournament in which I was about to compete would offer the largest cash prize in the history of the game.

The occasion was the auction for the third annual Cavendish Bridge Calcutta. A Calcutta is an exotic form of gambling that has been popular in Europe for years, but is just beginning to catch on in the United States. Several hundred potential buyers—high rollers, hustlers, rich people, even bridge players who had formed syndicates for this event so they could join the bidding—took part in the Cavendish Calcutta auction. Except for expenses connected with running the tournament and a donation of more than $10,000 to the Children's Cancer Fund, the total amount of money bid on the forty partnerships was placed into a pool to be divided among the owners of the top eight finishers. That pool was being flooded.

Calcutta rules enable the players to buy back up to half of themselves from the winning bidder. Most players, including myself and Peter, took advantage of this buy-back provision. Since we were all betting on ourselves, there was a guarantee that the competition would be intense. How much more effort, for example, would athletes expend if failure to win not only cost them prize money, but money out of their own pockets as well?

Professional athletes are paid whether they win or lose. Such is not the case in a Calcutta. Peter and I would lose money if we did not finish near the top.

A partnership's winnings were dependent on more than just its final placing in the tournament. The Calcutta would consist of four separate bridge sessions contested over two days, and money would be divided among the top four scorers in each session as follows: $3,000 for first, $2,000 for second, $1,000 for third, $1,000 for fourth. A partnership conceivably could win $12,000 in session prizes alone, a huge payday for bridge players but not a great deal compared to what the tournament winners would take from the Calcutta Pool: after Rubin and Hamilton sold for $9,800, sponsors of the event began predicting a first-place payoff of $50,000. That figure might be commonplace for tennis and golf pros, but is straight out of fantasy fiction for bridge players. I decided that I really did not mind being sold by Mike Moss.

The auction started at 10 P.M. on May 6, 1977, in the main card room of the exclusive Cavendish Club, where earlier in the evening players and bidders had enjoyed cocktails and a sumptuous meal featuring dishes named after bridge champions. The Chicken Supreme was named for Broadway Billy Eisenberg, the coffee for Omar Sharif, and there was even a salad named for Peter Weichsel and me. I was too keyed up to eat any of it. Peter Weichsel and I had won this tournament the previous year—the prize money had been about half—and winning twice in a row against such an elite field was considered virtually impossible.

"I wouldn't bid a nickel on you two," said a friend of mine, Mike Becker. Mike Becker is also a great bridge player.

"Why's that?" I asked. I was annoyed.

"Winning the Cavendish twice in a row," said Mike, "is like a golfer winning the Masters twice in a row. Do you know how many times that has happened?"

"Tell me."

"Look it up."

I did look it up. Only Jack Nicklaus ever won the Masters two years in a row.

A casual observer at the Cavendish Club on the night of the auction might have thought he was attending a formal dinner for some retiring senior diplomat. Everyone wore evening clothes or tuxedos. Ice tinkled in finely cut glasses. People talked in whispers. I was startled by a waiter who suddenly materialized behind me, his footsteps muffled by the thick red carpet. If I had not been so impressed by what was going on I would have been tempted to laugh. Here was a group of gamblers, quick-buck artists, and bridge experts, all of them looking forward to making a killing through a card game. I caught a glimpse of World Champion Ira Rubin, known to bridge players as "The Beast" because of the loud and devastating abuse he often heaps on erring partners. Rubin was talking quietly with a lady.

After Ira Rubin and Fred Hamilton were auctioned for

$9,800, James Jacoby (the nationally syndicated bridge columnist) and Dave Berkowitz (no relation to the Son of Sam) sold for $8,100, Bob Wolff and Jim Hooker for $3,700, Bob Hamman and Kyle Larsen for $8,000, and Vic Mitchell and Bill Roberts for $3,100. Then Peter and I stood up in the big card room, cleared now of its dishes and silverware, under its high white ceiling and bright fluorescent lights. This was the room where the tournament would later be played. It reminded me of a great cavern.

Auctioneer Mike Moss was at his best in front of the French television cameras. "Weichsel and Sontag," he huckstered as we shuffled our feet and looked embarrassed. "How can you assign a price tag to players of this quality?" he asked, and then provided an answer. "To show my respect for these champions," Moss said, "I'm going to start the bidding myself with eight thousand dollars."

Mike Moss looked relieved when someone bid more. Eventually, for $10,000, Peter and I became the property of a high roller who had come all the way from the West Coast to find out about this new form of gambling called a Calcutta.

I had two contradictory emotions during the bidding. On the one hand I wanted the partnership to be sold for as little as possible, because then it would cost us less to buy part of ourselves back. On the other hand I wanted us to sell for as much as possible because that would be gratifying and demonstrate that we were held in high esteem.

The auction lasted for about two hours. Mike Moss kept it moving at a brisk pace. The action was similar to horse betting except that here it was human beings who were being handicapped. The only partnership among the forty that sold for more than $10,000 was Broadway Billy Eisenberg and Jimmy Cayne, $10,100. The lowest priced pair went for $1,500. The total amount of money bid was $191,300, assuring $50,400 for first place and $36,000 for second.

I thought Peter and I had an excellent chance to take first money, which was almost double what it had been the year before. At that time there had been $97,000 in the Calcutta

Pool with $27,580 going to the winners. The highest priced pair in that Calcutta sold for $4,800. Future Calcuttas, I imagined, would offer incredible amounts of money.

When the auction was over and everyone was milling about, I bumped into four-time World Champion Broadway Billy Eisenberg, also winner of the world backgammon championship. Eisenberg is short and cocky, walks like a duck and thinks like a computer, and has an exceptional memory bank. In the previous year's Calcutta, Eisenberg and his partner Jimmy Cayne finished second to Peter and me, and Billy had not forgotten. "This year," he said, bobbing and weaving like a boxer, "we finish first. You might get second."

"Your nightlife is affecting your judgment," I told him. There is a reason Billy's nickname is Broadway.

"No, sir," Billy said. "Why, it's even written in the stars that we're going to win."

Billy is deep into astrology, among other pursuits. I did not see how the stars could help him, but who knew? I did know that our bidding system, which took seven years to develop, was a weapon even stars and stargazers like Billy Eisenberg would have difficulty overcoming. But I did not want to argue with Billy so I asked him about his tennis game.

As in the two previous years of the Calcutta, heavy security precautions were in force. Players were not allowed to make their bids orally because they might be able to convey illegal information to their partners through voice inflections. Instead, bidding boxes were used and all bids were printed on cards. The cards had an additional value in an international tournament such as this, where players spoke different languages.

I think everyone was in favor of the security precautions. Of course, anyone who objected was not going to speak up. The bridge world had been rocked by a number of cheating scandals, and nobody wanted one of these repeated in a showcase, televised event offering more than $190,000 in prize money.

The Cavendish Calcutta was a duplicate tournament and

its scoring system was based on International Match Points (IMPs). Since forty partnerships were competing, each hand would be played twenty different times. A partnership's score would be calculated by comparing its results against the results of nineteen other partnerships playing in the same direction. This form of scoring placed a premium on accurate game and slam bidding. A single hand could result in an avalanche of IMPs. There could be drastic switches in a partnership's position in the standings.

The IMP table was cut off at 17 IMPs for this tournament. A partnership could win or lose at most 17 IMPs against any one partnership on any one hand. Thus, it was possible to win 17 IMPs against nineteen other pairs playing in the same direction, or a maximum of 323 IMPs per deal.

Here is an example of the scoring system: if Rubin and Hamilton, playing North-South, made three hearts, and all of the other North-South pairs made only two hearts, Rubin and Hamilton would win one IMP from each of those North-South pairs for a total of 19; all of the other North-South pairs would have a score of minus one IMP. This is the IMP table that was in effect for the Cavendish Calcutta:

TOTAL POINTS	IMPs	TOTAL POINTS	IMPs
0–10	0	370–420	9
20–40	1	430–490	10
50–80	2	500–590	11
90–120	3	600–740	12
130–160	4	750–890	13
170–210	5	900–1090	14
220–260	6	1100–1290	15
270–310	7	1300–1490	16
320–360	8	1500 and up	17

Altogether the Calcutta would be comprised of three hands against each of thirty-nine different partnerships, 117 hands in all played over four sessions. Thirty hands would be played during each of the first three sessions, twenty-seven in the final session. It would be a grueling event against a world-class field.

Players from nine different countries were represented in the Cavendish Calcutta. Eleven of the players were current or former World Champions. Five of the best women players in the world were in the field. Some players were in their seventies and already bridge legends. Another, Robert Levin, was a brilliant teenage college sophomore. Here is a list of the entire field, given in the order in which they were auctioned:

PARTNERSHIP	COUNTRY	AUCTION PRICE
Ira Rubin-Fred Hamilton	U.S.A.	$ 9,800
James Jacoby-David Berkowitz	U.S.A.	$ 8,100
Bob Wolff-Jim Hooker	U.S.A.	$ 3,700
Bob Hamman-Kyle Larsen	U.S.A.	$ 8,000
Vic Mitchell-Bill Roberts	U.S.A.	$ 3,100
Peter Weichsel-Alan Sontag	U.S.A.	$ 10,000
Paul Heitner-John Lowenthal	U.S.A.	$ 4,100
Irving Rose-Maurice Esterson	England	$ 6,500
Kathy and Mike Cappelletti	U.S.A.	$ 4,000
Steve Sion-Marc Jacobus	U.S.A.	$ 5,100
George Rapee-John Solodar	U.S.A.	$ 6,200
Jeff Westheimer-Amos Kaminsky	U.S.A.	$ 3,700
B. J. and Steve Becker	U.S.A.	$ 5,000
Mike Moss-Bart Bramley	U.S.A.	$ 4,500
Howard Schenken-Peter Leventritt	U.S.A.	$ 4,600
Judi Radin-Paul Trent	U.S.A.	$ 5,300
Steve Robinson-Kit Woolsey	U.S.A.	$ 6,300
Jacqui Mitchell-John Roberts	U.S.A.	$ 3,400
Lou Bluhm-Larry Gould	U.S.A.	$ 5,200
Harold Guiver-Gaylor Kasle	U.S.A.	$ 3,800
Jack Blair-Robert Levin	U.S.A.	$ 4,100
Omar Sharif-Leon Yallouze	Egypt-France	$ 5,500
Ken Cohen-Walt Walvick	U.S.A.	$ 4,200
Peter Nagy-Eric Kokish	Canada	$ 5,600
Estee Griffin-Sergio Barbosa	U.S.A.-Brazil	$ 1,500
Ron Blau-Martin Ginsberg	U.S.A.	$ 3,900
Joe Silver-Fred Hoffer	Canada	$ 4,000

PARTNERSHIP	COUNTRY	AUCTION PRICE
Peter Pender-Neil Silverman	U.S.A.	$ 6,700
Jim Linhart-Ken Gorfkle	U.S.A.	$ 2,600
Dr. Sam Marsh-Larry Blum	U.S.A.	$ 1,600
Sam Stayman-Matt Granovetter	U.S.A.	$ 4,300
Dr. Francis Vernon-David Berah	Venezuela	$ 3,100
Michael Rosenberg-Zia Mahmoud	Scotland-Pakistan	$ 5,200
Vic Goldberg-George Mittelman	Canada	$ 3,300
Henry Bethe-Ron Rubin	U.S.A.	$ 3,600
Gail Moss-Ahmed Hussein	U.S.A.-Egypt	$ 1,500
Lou Reich-Jay Merrill	U.S.A.	$ 4,700
Mike Becker-Alan Greenberg	U.S.A.	$ 3,200
Tim McPhail-Baron Wolf Lebovic	Canada	$ 2,200
Billy Eisenberg-Jimmy Cayne	U.S.A.	$ 10,100
TOTAL		$191,300

The field in the Cavendish Calcutta was one of the strongest ever assembled for a single tournament. But none of the partnerships used the same bidding system Peter Weichsel and I had developed. If the system was as advanced as we believed, we had an advantage—even before the tournament started—over every other pair in the event.

Peter and I had been playing bridge at a championship level for ten years and in that time we experimented with many different bidding systems: Kaplan-Sheinwold; Roth-Stone; ACOL; Animal ACOL; Schenken Club; Mitchell Diamond; E.H.A.A. (Every Hand An Adventure—a really horrible system, but fun to play); the Strange Diamond (another too atrocious to describe); Eastern Scientific; the Blue Club; Canary Club; the Solar System (this never got off the ground); the Little Major (invented by the great Terence Reese); the Roman Club; Romex; the U.A.I. Club; Marmic; Relay; Goren; Culbertson; Vanderbilt Club; Roth Club; Precision; Super-Precision; and Standard American.

Some people believe an expert can win using any system. This simply is not true. A player employing an inferior or outmoded bidding system—and bidding is 80 percent of the game—is at an enormous disadvantage. Of the many systems

Peter and I played and studied—except possibly E.H.A.A., the Strange Diamond, and the Solar System—each contained many excellent ideas, but they had faults. Together we decided to take the best ideas from each system and mold them into something new and better. We believe we have accomplished this.

This book will explain the system, compare it to others, and demonstrate its effectiveness in action.

2

OPENING BIDS

THE SIMPLEST AUCTIONS OFTEN BECOME CONFUSING FOR partnerships. What partners need is a bidding language both can understand. The immortal Ely Culbertson described an effective bid as "one that describes your hand or asks a question that partner will easily understand."

Opening bids are extremely important. An incorrect or misleading opening bid can set a partnership on a disastrous course from which it might never recover. The Weichsel-Sontag opening bids are designed to convey the maximum possible information at the minimum possible level. By keeping the bidding low whenever possible a partnership will avoid many contracts that cannot be made while allowing sufficient bidding space to explore game and slam opportunities.

There are about twenty-one opening bids with Weichsel-Sontag:

1. One Club. Strong, artificial, and forcing. This is *the* most important bid in the system. Simply by learning the one-club structure, a partnership will have a formidable advantage over opponents using any other methods. The one-club bid is made with most hands containing 16 or more high-

card points. There are three exceptions: one no trump, two diamonds, and two no trump.

In 1978 I was watching an early round of the Vanderbilt. A partnership on the team that was destined to win the event held the following cards:

NORTH (Soloway)	SOUTH (Goldman)
♠ A K 8 3	♠ 10 9 7 6 2
♥ A J 7 4 2	♥ 3
♦ A Q 9 6	♦ K 10 7 4
♣ Void	♣ J 6 2

SOLOWAY	GOLDMAN
1 ♥	Pass

Paul Soloway and Bobby Goldman were former World Champions. Their bidding on this hand was inaccurate, but most players in the world would bid precisely as they did. Not only had they missed an excellent small slam contract in spades, but a lay-down game contract was lost when one heart was passed out. Soloway and Goldman are two of the best players in the world, but any beginner with a rudimentary understanding of our one-club opening would have bid the hand better.

Soloway and Goldman were fortunate this hand did not come up in a later match when the opposition was stronger. They might not have won the event.

Anyone using the W-S (Weichsel-Sontag) club system would have bid the hand as follows:

NORTH	SOUTH
1 ♣	1 ♦
1 ♥	1 ♠
2 ♠	4 ♠
5 ♦	6 ♠
Pass	

2. One Diamond. The catchall bid in the system. It shows 12 to a poor 16 high-card points, usually denies a five-card

major, and can be made with as few as one diamond.

3. One Heart. At least five hearts and 11 to 16 high-card points.

4. One Spade. At least five spades and 11 to 16 high-card points.

5. One No Trump. A balanced hand (no voids or singletons) and 15 to 17 high-card points. Opener might have a five-card major.

6. Two Clubs. Opener has 11 to 16 high-card points and usually six clubs. Possibly there is another suit with four or five cards.

7. Two Diamonds. Shows one of three holdings: (1) a weak two-bid in hearts (6 to 12 points and a good six-card heart suit); (2) a strong hand containing 4-4-4-1 distribution with any singleton and 16 to 24 high-card points; or (3) a strong, balanced hand of 26 to 27 high-card points.

The *first* time Peter and I played together was in 1971 in Phoenix in the Life Masters Men's Pairs. We won the event by an enormous margin. Before the event, however, many of the finest players in the country told us we had no chance using our club system. Without our two-diamond opening bid, we would have missed an ice-cold five-club contract in Phoenix. We held:

NORTH (Weichsel)	SOUTH (Sontag)
♠ A 10 3 2	♠ Q
♥ A	♥ 10 4 3
♦ K Q 6 5	♦ 8 7 2
♣ A K 9 8	♣ 7 6 5 4 3 2

NORTH	SOUTH
2 ♦	2 ♥
3 ♦	5 ♣
Pass	

Most partnerships in Phoenix, not playing our two-diamond opening bid, languished in contracts of one club or one diamond. We were able to reach an easy game contract because Peter's three-diamond response told me he had exactly 4-1-4-4 distribution and 20 to 24 high-card points. With the ace of diamonds in front of the K Q, and trump breaking 2-1, we actually made six clubs.

8. Two Hearts. Four spades, five hearts, any other minor suit distribution; or, four spades, four hearts, and four or five clubs. In either case, hand has 12 to 15 high-card points.

9. Two Spades. A weak two-bid in spades (6 to 12 high-card points) with a strong six-card spade suit.

10. Two No Trump. A balanced hand with 24 or 25 high-card points.

11. Three Clubs. Any seven-card suit headed by the A K Q, but very little else.

12. Three Diamonds. Depending on the vulnerability, the bid shows as little as seven diamonds headed by the Q J, or as much as seven diamonds headed by the A K J 10.

13. Three Hearts. The same as three diamonds, but the long suit is hearts.

14. Three Spades. Also the same as three diamonds, but the long suit is spades.

15. Three No Trump. Eight clubs or eight diamonds and very little else. Usually denies the ace in the long suit.

16. Four Clubs. A strong four-heart opening bid that shows less than 16 high-card points and the ability to win eight or nine tricks.

17. Four Diamonds. The same as four clubs, except it shows a strong four-spade opening bid.

18. Four Hearts. A weak four-heart opening. Opener has a poor hand but seven or eight hearts.

19. Four Spades. The same as four hearts, except the length is in spades.

20. Four No Trump. Blackwood, asking for partner's aces.

21. All Other Opening Bids. Natural, and indicate this is where opener wants to play the hand. Responder may raise only if he has a trump fit plus aces.

* * *

I first learned a club system in 1970 in two hours during an automobile trip from Manhattan to Chicopee, Massachusetts, to play in a regional tournament. The team I was on reached the semifinals of the event and I have played a club system at every opportunity ever since.

Parts of the W-S club system are difficult to learn. Most is not. And learning even a portion of the system will improve the play of almost every partnership.

3

THE BEGINNING

Take it easy on us, Billy."

I had just walked up to the table where we had been assigned to play our first opponents in the Cavendish Calcutta. Billy Eisenberg was already there and, unbelievably I thought, doing deep knee bends.

A few minutes later, at 1:30 P.M., May 7, 1977, Cavendish Club manager Tom Smith announced, "Ladies and gentlemen, please take your seats. It's game time."

The huge card room, it seemed like the Grand Canyon with carpets, was packed with intent bridge players, jittery gamblers, the French television crew, and curious people pushing and shoving for a better position from which to watch the bridge spectacular. Peter brushed a drop of sweat from his nose. The big room was noisy and chaotic and filled with smoke.

Billy Eisenberg looked like a cat about to pounce. Worse, he gave the impression of knowing something I did not. I decided he was just his usual cocky self—which meant this four-time World Champion would be very hard to beat—and made up my mind not to let him upset me.

"I taught you boys how to play this game," Billy tried.

"Nonsense," I said, although in a way it was true. In 1963 and 1964 Billy owned the Players Club in Valley Stream, New York, and a whole new generation of bridge players developed out of it. At that time Billy was already an expert, recognized as the best young player in the East, and he was generous with his time and advice.

Billy had been a member of the World Champion Dallas Aces, a team founded by multimillionaire Ira Corn for the specific purpose of returning the World Championship to the United States. Billy was instrumental—along with teammates James Jacoby, Bob Wolff, Bob Hamman, Bob Goldman, and Mike Lawrence—in accomplishing just that. Ira Corn's support and backing did a great deal to restore this country's preeminence in the game. However, Corn was a conservative businessman, the president of the big Michigan General Corporation, and it was inevitable his life-style would clash with that of the flamboyant Eisenberg. Billy was asked to leave the team, which hurt the team more than Billy.

I was delighted that our first opponents were Cayne and Eisenberg. They were among four or five partnerships that I considered our main competition, although in reality the field was so filled with talent that conceivably any partnership could win. I believed that playing these two right at the start would provide a good gauge of how we could expect to do.

Jimmy Cayne, a forty-three-year-old investment banker, did not on the surface seem to be a perfect partner for the mercurial Eisenberg. At the bridge table Cayne reminds me of Rocky Marciano, always attacking, and occasionally the person he attacks is his own partner. One time I made a mistake when I was his partner and I thought the torrent of abuse would never stop. I figured if he did that with Billy Eisenberg, who could not be tamed even by Ira Corn's bankroll, there would be an eruption.

Despite appearances, Cayne and Eisenberg were a well-matched partnership. They once even lived together for a year, which is not a bad idea if you want to compete successfully at the highest level of the game. Teamwork is definitely what is needed for success at bridge. What melded the Cayne and Eisenberg partnership was ambition and strong competitive instincts. For some reason, they were also friends.

In 1974 in the Canary Islands Jimmy Cayne accomplished a rare and brilliant double. He was second in the World Mixed Pairs and second in the World Mixed Teams. "It was a disaster," he told me.

The room was so crowded that it was difficult to move about. Shoving seemed to be the best way. Peter Weichsel's parents were on hand and I was concerned for their comfort. Peter's father is a pediatrician, both are Jewish refugees from Hitler's Germany, and they are extremely proud of their son's many accomplishments. I thought they might be uncomfortable because of the jammed conditions and the irritating smoke, but they seemed to enjoy the atmosphere and excitement.

"Okay," Peter said with determination, and picked up his first hand.

I picked up my cards, but before looking at them I gave them a little shuffle and consciously forced everything but bridge out of my mind. This was no friendly game.

On the first hand Cayne and Eisenberg slightly misjudged their values and stopped at two spades when it was an easy matter to make four. With our bidding system Peter and I would have reached the game.

Billy was steaming. I knew how much he wanted to win this tournament and a bad result on the very first hand was the last thing he wanted. I picked up the second hand:

NORTH (Weichsel)
♠ Q 7 5 3
♥ 10 5 2
♦ 8 7
♣ K Q 8 6

WEST (Eisenberg)
♠ 8 6 2
♥ 9 8 7
♦ 9 6 5 4
♣ 10 9 3

EAST (Cayne)
♠ A K 9
♥ K J 4 3
♦ Q J 10 2
♣ 7 2

SOUTH (Sontag)
♠ J 10 4
♥ A Q 6
♦ A K 3
♣ A J 5 4

East-West vulnerable. The bidding:

WEST	NORTH	EAST	SOUTH
			1 ♣
Pass	1 ♦	Pass	1 no trump
Pass	2 ♣	Pass	2 ♦
Pass	3 no trump	Pass	Pass
Pass			

My one-club opening bid, as described in the previous chapter, was strong, artificial, and forcing, and promised a minimum of 16 points. Peter *had* to respond, even if the highest card in his hand was a five. Although the minimum for a one-club opening bid is 16, the maximum can be almost anything.

The beauty of the one-club opening bid is that it is the lowest possible bid, and therefore provides the greatest space necessary to explore game and slam possibilities, without climbing to catastrophic heights. The one-club opening bid is so simple, so inexorably logical, that I find it impossible to understand why so few experts use it. The idea was first propounded by Harold Vanderbilt in 1929 (modern bridge itself was invented in 1925), was improved on by the Chinese theoretician C. C. Wei in the early 1960s, was further improved by the immortal Italian Blue Team, and has been perfected even more by Peter and me.

On the diagrammed hand, Peter's one-diamond response to my one club was artificial and showed 0 to 8 high-card points. My one no trump rebid told him I had 18 or 19 high-card points and balanced distribution. His two clubs was a Stayman inquiry asking if I had a four-card major. My two diamonds denied such a major. Peter ended the auction with three no trump, *knowing* that we had a minimum of 25 high-card points. Peter literally *knew*. It is so important to know in a game unfortunately often dominated by guesswork.

As declarer, I had no trouble making *four* no trump.

"My grandmother could have bid that hand," said Billy.

"You're not supposed to talk at the table," I said.

Billy was right, however. His grandmother could have bid that hand. A hand I do not think she could have bid took place in a "Challenge the Champs" contest sponsored by *The Bridge World* magazine. Peter and I were matched in a bidding contest against Bob Goldman and Mike Lawrence of the Dallas Aces. The following hand took place in that contest, and what happened to Goldman would be repeated in that early round of the 1978 Vanderbilt.

NORTH (Lawrence)	SOUTH (Goldman)
♠ A Q J 7	♠ 10 5
♥ Void	♥ 10 8 6 3
♦ A Q 9 6 3	♦ 10 2
♣ A K 9 4	♣ Q J 10 7 2

Neither side vulnerable. The bidding:

LAWRENCE	GOLDMAN
1 ♦	Pass

SONTAG	WEICHSEL
1 ♣	1 ♦
1 ♠	2 ♣
4 ♥	5 ♣
6 ♣	Pass

"This deal," said *The Bridge World,* "is likely to be cited for years to come as an illustration of the advantage of a club system. North's hand is a nightmare for standard bidders—a huge, unbalanced hand just took weak, and too awkward, for a forcing opening. The one-bid clearly risks just what happened here—an odds-on six clubs played in one diamond."

I know of no other partnership in the world that would have reached six clubs on this hand, yet, given our bidding system, it was automatic. Peter and I are not smarter than Lawrence or Goldman, or any other world-class partnership, but we do have a superior method of bidding.

Al Roth is perhaps the greatest bidding theorist of all time. I once asked him why he did not use a club system. "It's too good," he answered, "and it's too simple. It takes away from an individual's creativity."

Maybe so. But for people who want to play the game well, and win consistently, it really is the only way to go. It was Edmond Hoyle (1679–1769) of "According to Hoyle" who wrote a book titled *A Short Treatise on the Game of Whist, Containing the Laws of the Game, and Also Some Rules Whereby a Beginner May, With Due Attention to Them, Attain to the Playing it Well.*

"Playing it Well" is the only way to approach anything.

I was grateful as I picked up my third and final hand against Cayne and Eisenberg that my name was not Omar Sharif. My stomach hurt because the card room was so packed with people that I was squeezed against the table. It was a struggle to move my elbow to lay the cards on the table, and the smoke, with which the Cavendish's air-conditioning could not cope, was causing my eyes to hurt and water.

But it had to be worse for Sharif. He was the real star of the show, most of the casual spectators wanted to be near him, and the French television crew was recording every time he sneezed. Between hands people asked for his autograph. Reporters hovered over his shoulder and jotted notes about each hand he played. I wondered if an athlete in any other sport could maintain composure under similar stress and pressure. However, Sharif was performing to his ability, something I never could have done. In fact, as the results would later reveal, he was playing great bridge.

But there was a different drama at our table. Billy Eisenberg looked grim. Jimmy Cayne was wadding up a handkerchief. They were behind and I knew what was going on in their minds: they were telling themselves that the tournament was young, there were plenty of hands to catch up, and it was no time to start taking desperate gambles.

No players are more dangerous than Cayne and Eisenberg when they are behind in the late stages of a tournament. In this sense I was happy the Calcutta was young. Cayne and Eisenberg seem to summon some inner resource near the end of an event that results in brilliant play. The year before, backed against the wall in the final session, they charged from tenth place to second and might have caught Peter and me if there had been ten additional hands.

On the third hand Billy opened with light values (subminimum by his standards) and Jimmy Cayne, with a fair hand in a competitive auction, correctly judged that three clubs was the maximum that could be made. Some partner ships overbid the hand to three no trump and went down. Cayne and Eisenberg scored a few IMPs from us on this hand, but overall we had the best of them.

"It's been a pleasure," I said to Billy as I got up to move to the next table. I was razzing him, hoping to goad him into mistakes against future opponents. Actually, it was amateurish on my part; four-time World Champions should not be trifled with. But for some reason Billy rose to the bait.

"You think it's over already?" He bristled.

"It's over for you," I said. "Good luck in Caracas, though." Billy was flying to Venezuela after the Cavendish for another Calcutta.

Peter and I shouldered our way to the next table. I tripped over someone's foot and was saved from falling by a spectator. "Take it easy," he said. "Go slow." It was good advice.

Our second opponents were Baron Wolf Lebovic and Tim McPhail of Canada. Lebovic, originally from Budapest, even looked like a baron. He was dressed in expensive clothes, was small but composed and impressive (I have found that rich people usually exude a confidence that I envy but seldom feel), and had impeccable manners. He stood up as we were about to sit down.

"Mr. Sontag," he said. "Mr. Weichsel. I've been reading about how well you've been doing. It's a pleasure to compete against you."

"Thanks," I said.

What could I say? Lebovic seemed to be from a different world than the pressure cookers that were Billy Eisenberg and Jimmy Cayne. He and McPhail had sold for only $2,200, which meant they were not among the favorites. Such is the nature of bridge, however, that this seemingly kind and gentle man aroused my suspicions. Was he trying to catch us off guard? Lull us to sleep?

Lebovic's suit must have cost five hundred dollars. I knew he was a Canadian builder who had a Rolls-Royce Commarch that reportedly had a bed in the backseat. I saw the Rolls-Royce one day in Montreal. It was magnificent but I did not get close enough to confirm the bed.

"Would you like a cigar?" Lebovic asked.

I did not know how to react to this man. Billy Eisenberg would have offered a knife with the suggestion that I stab myself.

"I'd like that," I said.

"It's a real Havana," he said.

It was a real Havana. I blinked and looked at Lebovic. Fifty thousand dollars was at stake and I did not want to like him.

Lebovic's partner, Tim McPhail, reminded me of a social worker I once knew. He was polite and always smiling. If I did something outrageous, I imagined McPhail would nod understandingly. I was sure that if we were introduced at a party I would like him. Winning the tournament was not as important to Lebovic and McPhail as it was to Peter and me.

I had to prepare myself differently for this partnership than I had for Cayne and Eisenberg. I stuffed Lebovic's cigar in my pocket and reminded myself that he would not be in the tournament if he did not possess excellent credentials. Many fine partnerships who wanted to be in the event had been bypassed.

I picked up the fourth hand of the Calcutta.

The hand was a made-to-order Weichsel-Sontag system hand and illustrative of the strength of our opening bids:

NORTH (Weichsel)
- ♠ 4
- ♥ K
- ♦ A 9 8 7 2
- ♣ A K J 10 4 2

WEST (Lebovic)
- ♠ K J 5
- ♥ Q J 8 7 4
- ♦ K Q 6 3
- ♣ 7

EAST (McPhail)
- ♠ Q 9
- ♥ A 10 6 5 3
- ♦ J 10 4
- ♣ 9 8 6

SOUTH (Sontag)
- ♠ A 10 8 7 6 3 2
- ♥ 9 2
- ♦ 5
- ♣ Q 5 3

North-South vulnerable. The bidding:

WEST	NORTH	EAST	SOUTH
	2 ♣	Pass	2 ♠
Pass	3 ♦	Pass	5 ♣
Pass	Pass	Pass	

Many experts believe that the two-club opening bid in a club system is its weakest point. I used to agree with this reasoning, but no more. Peter and I have experimented with this bid for a long time and we now believe we have the finest two-club structure in the game.

In the diagrammed auction, most of the partnerships in the Calcutta arrived at either three or four clubs or three or four spades. But game in clubs is an *excellent* contract, and in fact we were able to make it. Four spades was easily defeated.

Peter's two-club opening bid showed a full opening with a good six-card club suit, and a hand that possibly contained another four- or five-card suit. Obviously, the hand was not strong enough for our forcing one-club opening. Obvious, also, after just one bid, I had an excellent idea of what Peter's hand contained.

In Standard American bidding, the most widely used system in the United States, the normal player in the diagrammed hand would bid one club and his partner would have no idea whether he had a minimum opening of 12 to 15 points, an intermediate hand with 16 to 18 points, or a very strong hand with 19 to 21 points. Also, the opening bidder might have as few as three clubs.

Peter's two-club bid narrowed the high-card structure and guaranteed that clubs were his longest suit. The purpose of bidding is to convey the most accurate possible information to the partner. Peter's two-club bid was clearly superior to Standard American's one club and set the stage for the bidding that came later, enabling us to arrive at the game contract.

On the diagrammed hand, using Standard American, the bidding could very well, and sometimes did during the Calcutta, proceed as follows:

WEST	NORTH	EAST	SOUTH
	1 ♣	Pass	1 ♠
Pass	2 ♣	Pass	2 ♠
Pass	3 ♦	Pass	4 ♣
Pass	Pass	Pass	

Partnerships bidding this way went wrong because South was not sure of the strength and distribution of the North hand, and South could not appreciate how strong his 6 points were. As South, I was able to understand (not because I am smarter, but because our system is superior) the power of my 6 points in the context of the two-club opening bid and the auction. My two-spade response to the two-club opening bid was non-forcing and showed at least five spades. If Peter liked spades, he could bid three spades or raise to game. If not, he could pass or rebid clubs; on rare occasions he could introduce another suit if he had the maximum two-club bid with strong distribution. His three-diamond bid showed five diamonds to go with the six clubs. I jumped to five clubs because I had excellent club support, a singleton in diamonds, and the spade ace.

Even though McPhail made the best opening lead, a trump, Peter made five clubs by ruffing two diamonds in dummy and eventually establishing his fifth diamond.

Only four of the Calcutta's 117 hands had been played, but I knew we were off to a wonderful start: if we were not in the lead, we were at least near the head of the hunt. On two of the three hands against Cayne and Eisenberg we had scored well, and we had done the same on the first hand against Lebovic and McPhail. There was nothing that could have been done against Cayne's inspired refusal to go beyond three clubs.

I fingered Lebovic's Havana, wondering if I should smoke it on the spot. It seemed a waste of a good cigar. The only time I smoke is during duplicate tournaments, and then only in protection against other smokers. Somehow the smoke is more endurable if I'm contributing to it. I was still considering lighting that marvelous Havana when Lebovic, smiling, offered me a light with a gold lighter. Lebovic had won several important events, including the 1967 Blue Ribbon Pairs with the great Sammy Kehela, but he was so gentlemanly—so unlike players like The Beast (Ira Rubin), The Crab (Walter Walvick), The Stripe-tailed Ape (John Lowenthal), The Mouth (Mike Moss), and The Whale (Paul Heitner)—that I continued to wonder what he was doing in this tournament.

It was 2:15 this May 7 when I picked up my fifth hand of the afternoon, and second against Lebovic-McPhail. Soon, as the bidding developed, I deeply wished that Peter and I were holding the East-West cards:

WEST (Lebovic)	EAST (McPhail)
♠ K Q 7	♠ A 10 3 2
♥ 2	♥ A K 5 4
♦ A K Q 10 8 4	♦ J
♣ 10 9 7	♣ A J 5 2

Neither side vulnerable. The bidding:

WEST	EAST
1 ♦	1 ♥
2 ♦	3 no trump
Pass	

This bidding was a sad commentary about the level certain bridge "experts" attain. An easy small slam had been missed. Even worse was the fact that eighteen of the twenty world-class partnerships playing East-West with these cards also bid three no trump. This is how Peter and I would have bid the hand:

WEST	EAST
1 ♦	1 ♥
3 ♦	3 ♠
4 ♠	5 ♣
5 ♦	5 ♥
5 ♠	5 no trump
6 ♦	6 no trump
Pass	

The key in our auction would have been the rebid of three diamonds. Since we did not open the bidding with one club, the jump to three diamonds would show 14 or 15 high-card points and a good six- or seven-card diamond suit. In Standard American bidding, the West hand could not rebid three diamonds because it lacked the necessary high-card count (17–18). The Weichsel-Sontag system does not contain such a restriction: jumps and reverses are encouraged when the suit quality and distribution are extraordinary.

The only problem Peter and I would have with this hand would be to stay away from seven no trump which, by the way, can be made, but requires a favorable spade distribution. But bidding and making six no trump is easy. All of the bids we would have made after three diamonds were cue bids showing the aces and kings in the suits bid and searching for the best possible contract.

In the third and final hand against Lebovic and McPhail they bid five clubs and went down one.

The round against Lebovic and McPhail had been success-ful for us. When I said good-bye to Lebovic, I really was thinking that justice had been served by trouncing them. That Rolls-Royce cost $90,000. Peter and I needed the prize money more than he did.

"It was fun," Lebovic said as we were leaving.

Our third opponents, we discovered after a bumpy trip through the spectators (I was concerned about Peter's parents, who followed us from table to table), were George Mittelman and Victor Goldberg of Toronto, Canada. I nodded a greeting at them and Mittelman asked how it was going for us.

George Mittelman is a friend of mine. He often stays at my apartment in New York, and I have been a guest in his large home in Toronto. Mittelman used to loan me money, which I surprised him by repaying, but there were times when I felt an obligation to do more for him. My opportunity came when a bridge player—who would know more about this sort of thing than a bridge player?—gave me a hot tip on the stock market: buy into Empire Life Insurance Com-pany of Alabama. The stock was only six dollars a share and Roy Rogers was on the board of directors. I relayed this in-formation to Mittelman, who immediately mailed a money order to me from Canada to invest for him. I bought a few shares for myself.

The next time I looked the stock was selling for three dollars. I called my bridge friend and asked what was going on.

"It's only temporary," he said. "A slight drop before the big skyrocket. Do you know about averaging?"

"What does it mean?"

"It means you should buy more shares. With averaging, the stock only has to go to four-fifty and you'll be even."

"What's this about a lawsuit?" I asked. "Something about one member of the board of directors suing another?"

"A good sign. Shows there's competitiveness. Would Roy Rogers lend his name to a failure?"

"Of course he wouldn't."

I thought about Roy Rogers, averaging, and that encouraging lawsuit, and finally I called George Mittelman. "I think we should invest more," I said.

"The stock is cheaper now," he said.

"Right," I said. I had not thought of that. I also had not learned (it might have made a difference) that Roy Rogers' real name was Leonard Slye.

Mittelman mailed more money which became less money and ultimately no money as the lawsuit drained away company funds and Empire Life slid off the board. I hoped, as we prepared to play Mittelman, that he had forgotten.

Victor Goldberg, Mittelman's partner, was a reasonable player but a cut below the best. I thought that if they finished high in the standings it would be because to an extent Mittelman had carried Goldberg. One top-notch partner usually is not enough.

The more I studied Mittelman and Goldberg, the more confident I was that we would score heavily against them. There were little signs. Goldberg was nervous and his hands shook. Mittelman was criticizing him for what had happened during a previous round.

A partnership that quarrels during the actual play of a tournament (as opposed to one that quarrels afterward, which may be healthy) is not likely to score well. Peter and I have an agreement that we will never fight about our play during the actual event.

On the first hand against Mittelman-Goldberg I made a bid I usually would not risk. Here was the hand:

NORTH (Mittelman)
♠ K
♥ A J 8 4
♦ A 7 5 3
♣ A 10 6 2

WEST (Sontag)
♠ Q J 10 9 3
♥ 10 9 7 5
♦ K 10 8
♣ 5

EAST (Weichsel)
♠ A 8 7 4
♥ 6
♦ J 9 6 4 2
♣ K Q 9

SOUTH (Goldberg)
♠ 6 5 2
♥ K Q 3 2
♦ Q
♣ J 8 7 4 3

No one vulnerable. The bidding:

WEST	NORTH	EAST	SOUTH
Pass	1 ♦	Pass	1 ♥
1 ♠	3 ♥	4 ♠	5 ♥
Pass	Pass	Pass	

Mittelman and Goldberg went down three tricks. Most East-West partnerships never got into the bidding with our cards. However, if we had played four spades, and if North-South had not found their diamond ruffs, we would have been able to draw trump, establish the diamond suit, and make the four-spade contract. As it was, Goldberg's bid of five hearts was ill-judged and resulted in a substantial loss for his side.

My one-spade overcall was not part of any system, including Weichsel-Sontag, but it proves that on occasion a player must judge his opponents and use his common sense.

Mittelman and Goldberg had not been playing well and this seemed the ideal time to force them to make a high-level competitive decision. Also, the hand demonstrates the power of the spade suit: if they were going to overrule us, they would have to go to the next suit level, i.e., five clubs, diamonds, or hearts.

Mittelman and Goldberg bid four spades on the next hand and went down two tricks. On the final hand we competed over their strong no trump opening and bought a contract for three spades, which we just made.

We had done well and I wanted to crack a joke about Empire Life, but it would have made everyone angry, including Peter. Also, there was not going to be much that was amusing from here on. We had played only three of our thirty-nine opponents and, waiting ahead, itching to tear us apart, were many of the most skilled and formidable players the game had ever known.

4

ONE DIAMOND OVER
ONE CLUB

ONE CLUB—ONE DIAMOND SEQUENCE

THE *only* NEGATIVE RESPONSE TO THE ONE-CLUB OPENING bid is one diamond. Game *must* be reached after any response but one diamond. Since this is understood, a partnership may use as many bids as it wants to reach the proper contract, often a slam. Neither partner has to worry about the other passing in the middle of an auction.

The negative one-diamond response shows 0 to 8 high-card points.

ONE CLUB—ONE DIAMOND—
ONE HEART SEQUENCE

When opener bids one heart during the one club—one diamond sequence, he has one of two types of hands: (1) at least five hearts, with or without another suit, and it may mean a minimum one-club opening or it may be game-forcing; (2) a very strong balanced hand of at least 20 points.

OPENER	RESPONDER
1 ♣	1 ♦
1 ♥	

Regardless of whether opener has Number 1 or Number 2 type of hand, the one-heart rebid is unconditionally forcing on responder, and he may make one of four bids:

1. One Spade. This is the expected response and occurs 95 percent of the time. It is a waiting bid. Responder wants opener to clarify his hand on the next bid.
2. One No Trump. A balanced hand with 7 or 8 points.
3. Two of Any Suit. Shows a weak six- or seven-card suit with no other four-card suit. The hand cannot contain a card higher than a queen, and only one of these.
4. Three of Any Suit. Shows a semisolid suit, six or seven in length, headed, for example, by K Q J or A Q J.

Except for the one-spade response, which is artificial and forcing, opener may want to pass the other bids. However, usually the bidding will have gone as follows:

OPENER	RESPONDER
1 ♣	1 ♦
1 ♥	1 ♠

This sequence is valuable because it is flexible and exact. Bids with multiple meanings increase the limited vocabulary of bridge and provide partnerships with information that otherwise might not be conveyed. At a recent sectional Swiss Team-of-Four in New York, Peter and I held the following cards:

NORTH (Weichsel)	SOUTH (Sontag)
♠ A K 9	♠ 8 6 3
♥ A Q 4 2	♥ 9 3
♦ A J 8 3	♦ 7 5
♣ K 5	♣ J 10 7 6 4 2

WEICHSEL	SONTAG
1 ♣	1 ♦
1 ♥	2 ♣
Pass	

Our opponents bid differently:

NORTH	SOUTH
2 no trump	Pass

Two clubs was cold, yet without our club system the contract would have been impossible to reach. Two no trump was defeated three tricks. Standard American, especially with very strong balanced hands, is cumbersome and wastes far too much room describing high-card points, and often there is little or no feedback from partner.

Over the one club—one diamond—one heart—one spade sequence, opening bidder can make one of seven responses.

1. One No Trump. A balanced hand with 20 or 21 high card points.

2. Two Hearts. Six hearts and probably no other four-card suit.

3. Two Clubs, Two Diamonds, or Two Spades. Natural and non-forcing. They show hearts as well as the suit bid.

4. Two No Trump. Shows unlimited strength and forces to at least a game. Opener's hand is strong, balanced, and contains at least six of the top eight cards (Aces and Kings).

5. Three Clubs or Three Diamonds. Natural and forcing. Shows hearts plus the suit bid.

6. Three Hearts. Shows a very good heart suit, 8½ to 9 playing tricks, and is non-forcing.

7. Three Spades. Forcing. Shows more hearts than spades (usually 6-5).

Only three of the bids by opener over responder's one spade are forcing: two no trump, a jump in a minor, and three spades. With the other bids, responder must evaluate his hand in relation to what opener has shown and determine whether to try for game, bid a game, bid his own suit, or pass. Responder will most frequently be faced with a decision when opener bids one no trump.

OPENER	RESPONDER
1 ♣ (at least 16 points)	1 ♦ (0 to 8 points)
1 ♥ (one of two hands)	1 ♠ (waiting bid)
1 no trump (20 to 21 high-card points)	

In this situation responder has many bids available to investigate the proper contract: Stayman, Jacoby Transfers, minor suit relays. Of course, responder may also pass.

ONE CLUB—ONE DIAMOND—
ONE SPADE SEQUENCE

One spade by opener is natural, non-forcing, and shows five spades with 16 to 19 points (occasionally this bid can be made with four spades).

OPENER	RESPONDER
1 ♣	1 ♦
1 ♠	

These are the twelve possible responses to one spade:

1. Pass. Responder has 0 to 4 high-card points and probably no three-card spade support.

2. One No Trump. Natural, non-forcing, shows 5 to 8 high-card points and denies three spades.

3. Two of a New Suit. Natural, non-forcing, shows at least five cards in the suit bid, 3 to 8 points, and denies three spades.

4. Two Spades. Three or more trump, 4 to 7 points (not necessarily high-card points).

5. Two No Trump. Bad three-card spade support, 4-3-3-3 distribution, good 7 or 8 high-card points.

6. Three Clubs. Three-card spade support, an unspecified singleton, and 7 or 8 high-card points.

7. Three Diamonds. Natural, non-forcing, shows a semi-solid diamond suit.

8. Three Hearts. Shows three-card spade support, five or more hearts, and 7 or 8 high-card points. The bid is non-forcing.

9. Three Spades. Also non-forcing. Shows four-card trump support and 7 to 9 points (if 9 points, at least one would be distributional).

10. Three No Trump. Forcing. Balanced hand, four- or five-card trump support, 8 or 9 points (one point would be a doubleton). Opener now bids four spades or tries for a slam.

11. Four Clubs, Four Diamonds, Four Hearts. Four-card trump support, singleton in suit bid, 9 to 11 points (distributional), and forces to four spades or a slam try.

12. Four Spades. Opener must pass. Shows length in spades and a weak distributional hand.

These twelve bids provide such a vivid picture of responder's hand that opener should have little difficulty reaching the correct final contract.

ONE CLUB—ONE DIAMOND— ONE NO TRUMP SEQUENCE

One no trump by opening bidder is non-forcing and shows 18 or 19 high-card points with a balanced hand. Opener may have a five-card major.

OPENER	RESPONDER
1 ♣	1 ♦
1 no trump	

Responder may bid as follows:

1. Pass. Shows 0 to 5 high-card points and probably denies a five-card major or a six-card minor.

2. Two Clubs. Stayman (asks opener to bid a four-card major if he has one, or else two diamonds). Opener should bid hearts first if he has both majors.

3. Two Diamonds. Jacoby Transfer (forces opener to bid at least two hearts). Shows five or more hearts and 0 to 8 points. Opener usually bids only two hearts, but on some rare hands may want to show he has maximum high-card strength and excellent heart support. He would do this by bidding three hearts, which shows four trump and 3-4-3-3 distribution. Opener might also bid two spades, three clubs, or three diamonds, which would show four trump and a doubleton in the suit bid. Two no trump by opener would show an excellent 19-point hand and three good hearts.

4. Two Hearts. Jacoby Transfer and identical to two diamonds except the long suit is spades.

5. Two Spades. Forces opener to bid two no trump and responder will clarify his hand on the next bid in one of four ways: (1) three clubs, showing 0 to 5 points and at least 5-5 distribution in the minors—opening bidder either passes or chooses three diamonds; (2) three diamonds, showing 5 to 8 points and at least 5-5 distribution in minors—opening bidder appraises his own cards and decides whether to try for a minor suit game, a minor suit part-score, or three no trump; (3) three hearts or three spades, showing 5-4 distribution either way in the minors, a singleton in the suit bid, and 5 to 8 points—opener will probably go to game, either in no trump, one of the minors, or the non-bid major suit; or (4) three no trump, showing 5-4 distribution either way in the minors, two weak doubletons in the majors, and 6 to 8 points —opener may pass three no trump if he is strong in the majors, or bid a minor suit at the four or five level.

6. Two No Trump. Forces opener to bid three clubs. Responder will clarify on next bid in one of three ways: (1) pass, wants to play three clubs; (2) three diamonds, wants to

play three diamonds; or (3) three of a major, showing 5 to 8 high-card points, a void in the suit bid, four in the other major, and 5-4 distribution in the minors.

7. Three Clubs. Shows 4-4-4-1 with a black singleton, and 5 to 8 high-card points. Three diamonds by opener asks for the singleton. Responder bids three hearts to show a spade singleton, three spades to show a club singleton.

8. Three Diamonds. The same as three clubs except a red singleton. Opener bids three hearts to learn the singleton. Three spades shows a diamond singleton, three no trump a heart singleton.

9. Three Hearts. Shows a six- or seven-card club suit, no other four-card suit, 7 or 8 high-card points.

10. Three Spades. The same as three hearts except the long suit is diamonds.

11. Three No Trump. Opening bidder must pass. Bid shows a balanced hand with 6 to 8 points.

12. Four Diamonds. A Texas Transfer to four hearts. Responder wants the game played at four hearts, but he wants the stronger hand concealed.

13. Four Hearts. Texas Transfer to spades.

14. Four Spades. Shows long, weak minors, 6-6 distribution, and asks opening bidder to choose.

All responses to the one club—one diamond—one heart— one spade—one no trump auction are the same as with the one club—one diamond—one no trump auction, and Forcing Stayman is used over both these auctions.

OPENER	RESPONDER
1 ♣	1 ♦
1 ♥	1 ♠
1 no trump	2 ♣
2 of any new suit	Any new suit is forcing

OPENER	RESPONDER
1 ♣	1 ♦
1 no trump	2 ♣
2 of any new suit	Any new suit is forcing

Some of the responses listed after the one club—one diamond—one no trump auction seldom arise, but when they do the partnership who knows them will be prepared when no one else is. For example, in the seven years Peter and I have been playing together, the one club—one diamond—one no trump—four spades auction has never come up. I saw a hand played once, however, that convinced me the sequence should be added to our system. The hand was played by Barbara Rappaport and Al Roth, the best mixed partnership in the country:

NORTH (Roth)	SOUTH (Rappaport)
♠ A J 5	♠ 2
♥ Q 9 6 3	♥ Void
♦ A K 7 4	♦ Q J 8 6 5 3
♣ A 9	♣ Q J 10 8 7 2

ROTH	RAPPAPORT
1 no trump	5 ♣
Pass	

Barbara made six clubs. Actually, all that is needed to make seven diamonds is a successful club finesse. Al Roth is probably the best bridge bidding theorist alive, yet he and Barbara had no way to show a hand with two long weak minor suits. If the hand ever arises between Peter and me, and I hope it does, we would bid as follows:

NORTH	SOUTH
1 ♣	1 ♦
1 no trump	4 ♠
6 ♦	Pass

This is hardly an elegant auction but it is effective. A Grand Slam that depends on a finesse is not the right contract.

ONE CLUB—ONE DIAMOND— TWO CLUBS SEQUENCE

Two clubs is non-forcing, shows 16 to 21 high-card points, and reveals that clubs are the longest suit.

OPENER	RESPONDER
1 ♣	1 ♦
2 ♣	

These are responder's possible bids:

1. Pass. Less than 6 points and no good suit.

2. Two Diamonds. Artificial bid. Six to 8 high-card points and asks opener to bid naturally.

3. Two Hearts. Five or six hearts and 5 to 8 high-card points.

4. Two Spades. Five or six spades and 5 to 8 high-card points.

5. Two No Trump. Six to a bad 8 high-card points, balanced hand, denies a four-card major. Opener may pass.

6. Three Clubs. Shows 5 to 8 high-card points and club support. Denies a five-card major.

7. Three Diamonds, Three Hearts, Three Spades. All show good six-card suits in the suit bid, such as K Q J, K Q 10, A Q 10, A Q J, K J 10, and are forcing to at least four clubs. Game is likely.

8. Three No Trump. Balanced hand, good 8 high-card points, stoppers in at least two suits other than clubs.

9. Four Clubs. Excellent club support and 8 to 10 points (including distributional values).

10. Four Diamonds, Four Hearts, Four Spades. Excellent club support, void or singleton in suit bid, 8 to 10 points (including distributional values).

Opener may rebid on any of these responses if he chooses, but only Bids #2, #7 and 10 are forcing.

ONE CLUB—ONE DIAMOND—
TWO DIAMONDS SEQUENCE

Two diamonds is non-forcing, shows 16 to 21 high-card points and that diamonds is the long suit.

OPENER	RESPONDER
1 ♣	1 ♦
2 ♦	

Here are the bids responder can make:

1. Pass. Less than 6 points and no good suit.
2. Two Hearts. Five or six hearts and 4 to 8 high-card points.
3. Two Spades. Five or six spades and 4 to 8 high-card points.
4. Two No Trump. Six or 7 high-card points and a balanced hand. Denies a five-card major but asks opener to bid a four-card major.
5. Three Clubs. Five or six clubs and 5 to 8 high-card points.
6. Three Diamonds. No five-card major, 5 to 8 points and diamond support.
7. Three Hearts, Three Spades. Both show a good six-card suit in the suit bid, force to at least four diamonds, and game is likely.
8. Three No Trump. Balanced hand, 8 high-card points, stoppers in at least two suits other than diamonds.
9. Four Diamonds. Excellent diamond support and 8 to 10 points (including distributional values).
10. Four Clubs, Four Hearts, Four Spades. Excellent diamond support, singleton in suit bid, 8 to 10 points (including distributional values).

Only Bids #7 and 10 are forcing.

ONE CLUB—ONE DIAMOND—
TWO HEARTS SEQUENCE

Two hearts shows an old-fashioned strong two-bid in hearts and is unconditionally forcing to at least game. Opener may have a very strong (21 or more points) distributional hand with hearts; or a strong, balanced hand with five or six hearts; or a two-suiter with five or six hearts and another four-card suit. If opener has hearts with another five-card suit, he would use a different sequence: one club—one diamond—one heart —one spade—three clubs (or diamonds or spades).

OPENER	RESPONDER
1 ♣	1 ♦
2 ♥	

These are the responses over two hearts:

1. Two Spades. At least five spades and 5 to 8 points. Denies three hearts. Opener rebids hearts if that is his only suit, or bids his other suit, or bids two no trump if his hand is balanced.
2. Two No Trump. A doubleton in hearts and 7 to 8 balanced points. The ideal two no trump bid would show two kings and a queen, or two queens and a king, with none of the honors in hearts. Opener now bids naturally.
3. Three Clubs. An artificial, negative response showing 0 to 5 points and no heart support. Opener will respond, and even if his response is not a game bid partner must bid again even if he has 0 points.
4. Three Diamonds. Shows 5 to 8 points and at least five diamonds headed by an A, K, or Q J. Denies good heart support and opener now bids naturally.
5. Three Hearts. Shows 5 to 8 points, at least three hearts, and responder may have another suit because his first obliga-

tion is to show heart support. Opener now cue bids an ace or bids his second suit looking for slam.

6. Three Spades. Shows 5 to 8 high-card points, a singleton spade, and good heart support. Opener cue bids looking for a slam.

7. Three No Trump. The bid, in this sequence, does not exist.

8. Four Clubs, Four Diamonds. A singleton in the suit bid and four-card heart support with 5 to 8 high-card points. Opener now bids naturally.

9. Four Hearts. A very weak hand with at least four-card heart support but no aces, kings, singletons, or voids. Responder must have a doubleton. Opener almost always passes since he would need virtually a slam in his own hand to make anything more.

Peter and I are fond of the one club—one diamond—two hearts sequence. We were on the winning team in the 1975 Von Zedtwitz Double Knockout and this sequence helped us establish a large lead going into the last quarter of the final match against a team that included Sam Stayman and Vic and Jacqui Mitchell. This was the hand:

NORTH (Weichsel)
- ♠ 10 7 6
- ♥ Q 9 5
- ♦ 8 4 2
- ♣ K J 3 2

SOUTH (Sontag)
- ♠ A 8
- ♥ A K J 10 8
- ♦ K Q
- ♣ A Q 9 5

WEICHSEL	SONTAG
Pass	1 ♣
1 ♦	2 ♥
3 ♥ (5 to 8 points, at least three hearts)	4 ♣ (either a four-card suit or cue bid of ace)
5 ♣ (four-card club suit to one high honor and no outside aces)	6 ♣
Pass	

I knew we were missing the ace of diamonds and almost surely the king of spades. Had I bid six hearts, we could only have taken eleven tricks. With clubs as trump, however, the twelfth trick would eventually come from a spade ruff in Peter's hand. The success of this contract depended only on a 3-2 trump break, almost a 68 percent chance. We were able to bid the slam in the right suit because we knew we had a 4-4 fit in clubs. Most partnerships using Standard American would probably have ended up in a heart game or slam. They would not have known for sure about the guaranteed four clubs to an honor in the North hand, and might have thought the five clubs was a cue bid showing the king and one other club. To show a doubleton club honor Peter would have cue bid four no trump, which also would show four hearts to an honor and no outside aces.

ONE CLUB—ONE DIAMOND— TWO SPADES SEQUENCE

Two spades is a strong opening two-bid in spades and is unconditionally forcing, with one exception, to at least game. Opener may have a very strong distributional hand with at least 21 points and spades as the only suit; or a balanced hand with five or six spades; or a two suiter with spades and any other four- or five-card suit.

OPENER	RESPONDER
1 ♣	1 ♦
2 ♠	

These are the responses over two spades:

1. Two No Trump. A balanced hand with 7 or 8 points and a doubleton spade. Ideally, responder has two kings and a queen, or two queens and a king.

2. Three Clubs. Artificial and negative. Shows 0 to 5 points and no spade support. If opener rebids spades at the three level, and responder has 0 to 3 points, responder may pass.

This is the *one* exception mentioned previously where game does not have to be reached.

3. Three Diamonds. At least five diamonds headed by A, K, or Q J and 5 to 8 points. Denies good spade support.

4. Three Hearts. At least five hearts and 5 to 8 points. Denies three spades.

5. Three Spades. Shows 5 to 8 points, at least three spades, and responder may have another suit.

6. Three No Trump. No such bid exists in this sequence.

7. Four Clubs, Four Diamonds, Four Hearts. Four-card spade support, 5 to 8 high-card points, singleton in suit bid.

8. Four Spades. A very weak hand with at least four-card spade support but no aces, kings, singletons, or voids. Responder must have at least one doubleton.

ONE CLUB—ONE DIAMOND— TWO NO TRUMP SEQUENCE

Two no trump shows 22 or 23 points in a balanced hand.

OPENER	RESPONDER
1 ♣	1 ♦
2 no trump	

Here are the possible responses to two no trump:

1. Three Clubs. Stayman, asks opener to bid a four-card major. Shows 3 to 8 high-card points. If opener has two four-card majors, he bids the best one. If he has no four-card major, he bids three diamonds. If responder's next bid after Stayman is four of either minor, it is a forcing bid showing five or six cards in that suit and an unspecified four-card major. If opener bids a major in response to Stayman, and responder bids the other major, it is an artificial slam try in opener's major suit and the rest of the bidding would be natural. If opener denies a four-card major by bidding three diamonds and responder

then bids a major suit, responder is showing four cards in the suit bid and five in the other major. He is effectively re-transferring to his partner so the strong hand will be declaring if an eight-card fit exists.

2. Three Diamonds. Jacoby Transfer to three hearts. Shows 0 to 8 points and at least five hearts. Responder will clarify on next bid. If opener's hand contains outstanding heart support, he may bid more than three hearts. He may bid four hearts, or even a new suit—three spades, four clubs, four diamonds—which would be a cue bid showing the ace in the suit bid plus excellent four-card heart support and a top hand in aces and kings. Responder may reject this slam try by retreating to four hearts.

3. Three Hearts. Jacoby Transfer to spades with the same structure as three diamonds.

4. Three Spades. Shows slam or game interest in both minor suits. Opener may reject by bidding three no trump, over which responder may still bid again. A major suit cue bid by responder would show a singleton or void in the suit bid. Responder may also bid a strong minor over three no trump.

5. Four Clubs. Shows slam interest in one of the minors. Responder has 6 to 8 high-card points and six or seven cards in one of the minors. Opener may bid in one of four ways: (1) four diamonds, which shows no slam interest in either minor; (2) four hearts, showing slam interest if the suit is clubs; (3) four spades, showing slam interest if suit is diamonds; and (4) four no trump, showing slam interest in both minors.

6. Three No Trump. Ends the auction.

7. Four Diamonds. Modified Roman Redwood, an ace-asking bid. A response of four hearts shows 0 or three aces; four spades shows one or four aces; four no trump shows two aces.

8. Four Hearts, Four Spades. Slam try showing good six-card suit in suit bid. Opener may pass.

9. Four No Trump. Natural and a slam try.

The great English player and writer Terence Reese bemoaned the increasing artificiality of bidding. Artificial bidding is becoming more popular but what Reese overlooked—as he himself discovered—is that it is also much more effective.

Reese, before seeing the light, pontificated that what was needed was a "Geneva Convention" to end the proliferation of bids that were being developed. As a spoof, Reese invented a system called "The Little Major" that was almost completely artificial. A club meant a heart, a diamond meant a spade, a heart showed a very strong hand or 2 to 6 points, a spade showed the minors, two no trump was a weak preempt in a minor; in short, it was "1984" where everything meant something else.

Reese wrote about his put-on, made jokes about it, discoursed lengthily to anyone who would listen about the absurdity of the new breed of bridge players and their "Newsspeak." Back-to-basics was what was needed, Reese insisted.

But something strange happened. Reese began to see merit in "The Little Major." Could it be possible, he wondered. Increasingly what had started as a joke to Reese now seemed to him a superior method of bidding.

Terence Reese ended up using "The Little Major" in the 1965 World Championships in Buenos Aires.

ONE CLUB—ONE DIAMOND— THREE CLUBS SEQUENCE

Three clubs shows a strong, natural two-bid with clubs as the long suit and it is forcing.

OPENER	RESPONDER
1 ♣	1 ♦
3 ♣	

These are the responses to three clubs:

1. Three Diamonds. Artificial and negative. Shows 0 to 4

points and no club support. Opener bids another suit if he has one, or perhaps bids four clubs or three no trump.

2. Three Hearts. At least five hearts and 5 to 8 high-card points. Responder might have three clubs.

3. Three Spades. The same as three hearts, except the long suit is spades.

4. Three No Trump. Natural and shows scattered values in other suits besides clubs with 5 to 8 high-card points. If opener now bids four hearts or four spades, the bid is natural and shows a four-card suit. Responder may pass, raise the suit, take the auction to four no trump, or bid clubs.

5. Four Clubs. At least three clubs, there may be another suit, and 5 to 8 points. Opener now cue bids his aces or a second suit looking for slam. Any bid by responder over the slam try—except five clubs—is a return slam try.

6. Four Diamonds, Four Hearts, Four Spades. Show singleton or void in the suit bid plus four-card trump support and 4 to 8 high-card points. Opener now cue bids his first round controls.

7. Four No Trump. The bid does not exist in this sequence.

8. Five Clubs. A very weak hand with four- or five-card club support but no aces, kings, singletons, or voids. However, responder does promise at least one doubleton. With 3-3-3-4 distribution, responder should bid three diamonds because three no trump may prove to be an easier contract than five clubs.

ONE CLUB—ONE DIAMOND—
THREE DIAMONDS SEQUENCE

Three diamonds shows a strong, natural two-bid with diamonds as the long suit.

OPENER	RESPONDER
1 ♣	1 ♦
3 ♦	

Responder may bid as follows:

1. Three Hearts. Artificial and negative, 0 to 4 points, poor diamond support. Possibly responder has hearts, but it is unlikely.

2. Three Spades. Natural, 5 to 8 points, at least five spades, possibly three-card diamond support.

3. Three No Trump. Natural, shows scattered support for everything except diamonds, 6 to 8 points.

4. Four Clubs. Natural, good five or six clubs, 5 to 8 points.

5. Four Diamonds. At least three diamonds, 5 to 8 points, may have another suit. Opener now cue bids his aces or a second suit looking for slam. Any bid responder makes over the cue bid—except five diamonds—is a return slam try.

6. Four Hearts. Natural, 5 to 8 high-card points, five or six good hearts.

7. Four Spades. A singleton or void in spades, four-card diamond support, 5 to 8 high-card points.

8. Four No Trump. Singleton or void in hearts, four-card diamond support, 5 to 8 high-card points.

9. Five Clubs. Singleton or void in clubs, four-card diamond support, 5 to 8 high-card points.

10. Five Diamonds. A very weak hand with four- or five-card diamond support but no aces, kings, singletons, or voids. Responder promises at least one doubleton. With 3-3-4-3 distribution, responder would bid the negative three hearts because three no trump may prove easier to make than five diamonds.

ONE CLUB—ONE DIAMOND—
THREE HEARTS SEQUENCE

Three hearts shows exactly nine tricks in hearts.

OPENER	RESPONDER
1 ♣	1 ♦
3 ♥	

With this sequence, responder should raise to game if he has an ace, a king, good trump, or ruffing value. Of course, responder may pass three hearts. Any new suit responder bids over three hearts is a cue bid showing slam interest. Any jump in a new suit would show shortness in the suit bid and at least two kings, or an ace and a king, with at least three hearts.

ONE CLUB—ONE DIAMOND— THREE SPADES SEQUENCE

Three spades, depending on a partnership's agreement, can have one of two meanings: it can show a nine-trick hand in spades; or it can show a very strong minor suit (must have both minors) hand containing at least 6-5 distribution—this forces responder to the four level of his preferred minor. A typical holding for this second kind of three-spade bid would be a singleton spade, a singleton heart, A K J 10 x x in diamonds, and A K J x x in clubs.

OPENER	RESPONDER
1 ♣	1 ♦
3 ♠	

If three spades means a nine-trick hand (in spades), responder should bid the same way he would if opener had bid three hearts. However, if three spades has the secondary meaning, responder would bid four hearts or four spades to show the ace in that suit and demonstrate interest in slam. Four of a minor would show little interest in game. Five of a minor would show good trump support and no outside aces. If responder jumps to four no trump, he has no major suit aces but two key honors in opener's minor suits: a key honor would be an ace, king, or queen. Three no trump would be natural and to play by responder.

ONE CLUB—ONE DIAMOND—
THREE NO TRUMP SEQUENCE

Three no trump is a natural bid indicating that is where opener wants to play the hand. Because of the negative one-diamond response and his own holdings, opener knows there is no slam. Three no trump shows 18 to 21 high-card points, a solid six- or seven-card minor, and stoppers in at least two other suits. A likely distribution for this bid would be 2-2-2-7 or 3-2-2-6.

OPENER	RESPONDER
1 ♣	1 ♦
3 no trump	

Responder almost always passes this bid.

ONE CLUB—ONE DIAMOND—
FOUR OF A MINOR SEQUENCE

There are no such sequences in the W-S system.

ONE CLUB—ONE DIAMOND—
FOUR OF A MAJOR SEQUENCE

Four hearts or four spades are natural bids showing that is where opener wants to play the contract. Because of the negative one-diamond response, opener knows there is no slam. Four hearts or four spades shows at least a seven-card suit and 16 to 19 points.

OPENER	RESPONDER
1 ♣	1 ♦
4 ♥ or 4 ♠	

Responder must pass this bid unless he has two aces.

ONE CLUB—ONE DIAMOND—
FOUR NO TRUMP SEQUENCE

Four no trump shows exactly 31 high-card points and a balanced hand.

OPENER	RESPONDER
1 ♣	1 ♦
4 no trump	

If responder has a queen, he should bid five no trump. With two queens, six no trump. With an ace, six no trump. With an ace and a queen, seven no trump.

This covers the sequences that begin with one club—one diamond, an auction that occurs very frequently. It is an easy sequence to master. Its simplicity makes it powerful.

5

MIDDLE OF THE FIRST

CONCENTRATION IS ALWAYS A PROBLEM DURING A BRIDGE tournament, especially one like the Cavendish Calcutta where the room is crowded and the noise level is high. I sometimes tell myself to concentrate so often that I find myself concentrating on concentrating and not on the cards.

I figured a plot was afoot to destroy what little concentration I had when I saw who our fourth opponents of the first session of the Calcutta were.

"Going to win again this year?" Mike Cappelletti asked me pleasantly.

"What?" I said. My eyes were out on stalks. Kathy Cappelletti, Mike's wife and bridge partner, has legs that remind me of Betty Grable on a World War II poster. She was wearing a miniskirt.

"How's your wife?" Mike Cappelletti asked Peter.

"What?" said Peter. Kathy Cappelletti's legs are incredible.

I realized I should say something. Peter was behaving like an animal. "How's your form?" I asked Kathy.

"What?" said Mike Cappelletti.

"I mean at bridge."

I would make a recommendation to the American Contract

Bridge League (ACBL) that people like Kathy Cappelletti be banned from tournaments for the good of the game, but I realize it would reflect poorly on me and, besides, she is a whiz at the bridge table. So is her husband, Mike.

Kathy and Mike Cappelletti have won many important bridge tournaments, including the 1967 Summer National Mixed Teams. They also were second in the 1967 Fall National Mixed Pairs and second in the 1973 and 1977 Blue Ribbon Pairs, the most prestigious Match Point event in the United States. Their victories in sectional and regional tournaments are too numerous to list. Both are outstanding players and that rarest of bridge combinations, a successful husband-and-wife partnership.

The Cappellettis live in Washington, D. C. Mike is a lawyer with the Federal Trade Commission and Kathy is a para-legal aide. Mike is just under 6 feet tall, quiet, polite, a casual dresser. Kathy is 5 feet 7 inches, extremely pretty, and always wears a dress or skirt. They have two children, a boy and a girl.

Washington, D. C., is not only a hotbed of political activity, but of bridge as well. Mike once met Ahmed Osman, the Moroccan ambassador to the United States, and they began to play bridge together quite often and became friends. In 1974 Mike and Kathy were playing in the World Pairs Championship in the Canary Islands and they ran into Osman. He was now the Prime Minister of Morocco and a genuine bridge addict. He invited Kathy and Mike to visit his country when the tournament was over. It was too good an offer to turn down.

Kathy and Mike were met at the Rabat airport by a chauffeured Citroën Maserati. "What a beautiful automobile!" Kathy said.

The next morning the car was sitting outside the hotel where the Cappellettis were staying. It seems that in Morocco if a guest indicates he likes something, that something is his for the duration of the visit.

The Cappellettis enjoyed a memorable two weeks in Morocco, all compliments of Osman. It was not an unusual occurrence for champion bridge players, who often receive attractive offers from wealthy people who enjoy playing with them. Mike and Kathy became friendly with Osman's wife, a princess whose hobby was hunting Kodiak bears.

We picked up the first hand. I had reason to fear the Cappellettis. They used a club system, different from ours and perhaps not as effective, but far more potent than the primitive Standard American. It was their club system that enabled them to bid an excellent vulnerable small slam in clubs that cost us more than 200 IMPs. Only one other pair bid this slam:

NORTH (Weichsel)
- ♠ K J 10 8 5
- ♥ Q 9 7 2
- ♦ Q 10
- ♣ 6 4

WEST (K. Cappelletti)
- ♠ 7
- ♥ 8 4 3
- ♦ K 6 3
- ♣ Q 10 9 7 5 2

EAST (M. Cappelletti)
- ♠ A 9
- ♥ A K J 5
- ♦ A 8 2
- ♣ A K J 3

SOUTH (Sontag)
- ♠ Q 6 4 3 2
- ♥ 10 6
- ♦ J 9 7 5 4
- ♣ 8

East-West vulnerable. The bidding:

WEST	NORTH	EAST	SOUTH
	Pass	1 ♣	Pass
1 ♦	Pass	2 no trump	Pass
3 ♠	Pass	4 ♣	Pass
5 ♣	Pass	6 ♣	Pass
Pass	Pass		

The key bid was Kathy's three spades, promising game or slam interest in one or both of the minor suits. The slam depended on Mike Cappelletti's establishing the heart suit for three tricks. After drawing trump, Mike maximized his chances in hearts by cashing the ace and king, crossing to the dummy with a spade ruff, and leading up to his jack of hearts.

"Nicely bid," Peter said. He meant it. Peter had not lost his desire to win, but he admired the power of a club system and the way the Cappellettis had handled the auction. This is how most partnerships bid the hand:

WEST	NORTH	EAST	SOUTH
		2 ♣	Pass
2 ♦	Pass	2 no trump	Pass
3 no trump	Pass	Pass	Pass

On the second hand against the Cappellettis, Peter and I bid a non-vulnerable three no trump contract and made it. On the third and final hand they stretched to a 23-point four-spade contract that failed by one trick. Nevertheless, they had the best of us, thanks to their big score on the slam contract.

"Not so good," Peter said.

"We haven't made a mistake," I said. I knew our showing against Mike and Kathy Cappelletti had dropped us out of the lead, if indeed we had ever held it, and I was trying to encourage Peter. Often he is the strong member of our partnership, lifting my spirits when things go wrong, showing optimism when probably none is merited, but this time he needed help and I hoped I could provide it. Bridge is truly a *partnership* game. An individual, no matter how brilliant, is virtually helpless at bridge without a strong partner.

Next we sat down to play George Rapee and John Solodar. Physically they were a mismatched pair. Solodar was 6 feet 4 inches, Rapee was 5 feet 4. George was sixty-two, John was thirty-seven. Mentally, however, both were giants, and together they formed one of the strongest partnerships in the world.

"Not exactly ideal conditions," I said to Rapee.

"Would you rather nobody came?" he said. He had a point.

George Rapee, a three-time World Champion, represented the United States in the *first* Bermuda Bowl, in 1950, the U. S. winning the World Championship. Of all people who have ever played the game, Rapee has the best record of anyone who has competed in the major national team championships. He has compiled a magnificent record of 21 firsts and 16 seconds in the prestigious Spingold, Vanderbilt, and Reisinger team championships. Known as "The Little Giant of Bridge," Rapee would be my nominee for the best-dressed American bridge player. Rapee, a lawyer, is a very generous person. I have been in restaurants several times with him and exceptional quickness is needed to beat him to the check. George has frequently footed tabs for less affluent bridge players who otherwise would not have been able to attend a national tournament.

John Solodar, Rapee's partner, is a good-looking graduate of Columbia University. Solodar, teamed with Rapee, finished second in the 1976 Spingold in Salt Lake City. Among his many triumphs was the Life Masters Men's Pairs with Henry Bethe in 1968. If Peter Weichsel, one of the absolute best players in the world, were not my partner, I would try to establish a partnership with Solodar.

Benjamin Bradlee of the *Washington Post* told Watergate reporters Woodward and Bernstein that they were playing in the big leagues, that "this is hard ball."

Rapee and Solodar were hard ball. Champion bridge players know who their most dangerous opponents are. There were forty pairs in this elite field, all world-class, but most of us knew, or should have, that some were more world-class than others.

The fireworks started on the first hand when Peter opened

the bidding with an offbeat weak two spades. Systematically, Peter should have a very good six-card spade suit, like A Q 10 9 5 3, but in this instance his spade suit was J 9 8 5 4 3. The bid had the effect of catapulting Rapee and Solodar into a hopeless four-heart contract that failed by two tricks.

"George," Peter said, feeling feisty, "don't you know the declaring side should have more trumps than the opponents?" Peter and I had seven trumps, Rapee and Solodar only six.

A bid such as Peter made cannot be recommended, but all great players have a certain "table presence" or "table feel"—which cannot be learned—that enables them to sense the strategic moment to deviate from a system. Peter "knew" that Rapee held the strong hand and he instinctively robbed George of two levels of bidding space. Had Peter nonchalantly passed, George and John would easily have bid to a cold three no trump.

I was delighted. Our first hand victory over Rapee and Solodar put us at least into fifth or sixth place, maybe even, I mused, first. "Nice bid, Peter," I said.

His face flushed red. I wanted to take back the compliment. What hand was that?" he asked.

"I think, number sixteen," I said.

"That's right. A hundred and one to go."

On the second hand Rapee and Solodar, defending perfectly, defeated us two tricks in a part-score contract.

The third hand was a fierce struggle between a determined declarer and an enlightened defense:

NORTH (Weichsel)
♠ 10 8 4
♥ 10 7
♦ A 10 9 5 2
♣ Q 6 4

WEST (Solodar)
♠ K 7 5 3
♥ 3
♦ K Q 6 4
♣ A K 10 2

EAST (Rapee)
♠ Q J 2
♥ A Q J 6 5
♦ J
♣ J 9 8 7

SOUTH (Sontag)
♠ A 9 6
♥ K 9 8 4 2
♦ 8 7 3
♣ 5 3

North-South vulnerable. The bidding:

WEST	NORTH	EAST	SOUTH
1 ♣	Pass	1 ♥	Pass
1 ♠	Pass	3 ♣	Pass
3 no trump	Pass	Pass	Pass

Peter led the five of diamonds, which Solodar won with dummy's jack. Solodar led a club to his king and played a spade to dummy's jack which I ducked. This, I believe, is the sort of play that wins tournaments. Most defenders in the South position would woodenly win with the ace of spades and return a diamond. That play would enable declarer to make the contract by carefully preventing North (Peter) from getting on play with the queen of clubs to run his then-established diamond suit. Declarer would take three spade tricks, two heart tricks, two diamond tricks, and two club tricks.

However, by ducking the jack of spades, I was able to

kill an entry to dummy. Solodar now had to take a club finesse which lost to Peter's queen. Peter made the expert lead of the diamond ten. If Solodar made the mistake of winning the diamond, I would be able to lead through his remaining diamond honor when I regained the lead with the ace of spades. Solodar, of course, foresaw this trap and made the fine play of letting Peter's ten hold the trick.

This hand illustrates why people love bridge and never become bored with it. There are so many ways to play and defend a hand. Three perfect plays had been made—my duck of the spade jack, Peter's lead of the diamond ten, and Solodar's refusal to win the ten—and still the issue was in doubt.

It was open cards. All the little secrets had been exposed and it was elementary for Peter to execute the fourth and killing play.

He led his heart through dummy's A Q J. This timely switch enabled us to win five tricks: the A 10 of diamonds, the Q of clubs, the K of hearts, and the A of spades.

Without Peter's heart switch, declarer would have had time to drive out my ace of spades and make the contract without risking the heart finesse, because of the fortunate 3-3 spade split.

"Ninety-nine to go," I said to Peter.

We learned we would count down from 99 through 97 against Ron Rubin and Henry Bethe. In the recent past Ron Rubin had been a frequent teammate of ours. In fact, Rubin, our teammate, accomplished the amazing feat of knocking us, his own team, out of a national championship by winning a different tournament on a different team!

It could only have happened in bridge. There are four major national championships each year—the Vanderbilt, Spingold, Reisinger, and Grand National: the first three are contested during a single tournament, but the Grand National is a grass roots ongoing event that lasts many months and is played at sites all over the country. It is a gigantic knockout event entered by some five thousand teams. A single defeat eliminates a team; thus, it is an enormously difficult tournament to win.

On the team with Peter and me in the 1977 Grand National were Mike Becker and Ron Rubin. After months of grueling competition we were one of about thirty teams out of that original 5,000 still in the running. Besides the honor of winning a national championship, each of the four teams that succeeded in capturing a national title in 1977 earned the right to qualify for the World Team Championship, which is the greatest prize in bridge.

But then a different team that Rubin and Becker were on won the prestigious Vanderbilt. Therefore, our own teammates were on a squad that already had made it to the World Team Championship in New Orleans, and our Grand National team was disqualified because we now had only two eligible players: Peter and myself.

It was our own fault. We had been advised by older and wiser heads to carry a couple of alternate team members in the Grand National (in effect to play six-handed), and our failure to do this left us without a team. The trouble with carrying extra players is you have to let them play, usually about half the time, and we felt any partnership we added from the New York area would lessen our chances: team members for the Grand National have to be from the same bridge district, of which there are twenty-five.

To make matters worse, the team Peter and I were on in the Vanderbilt was eliminated in the semifinals by the Rubin-Becker team. In effect, one defeat knocked us out of two national tournaments. Peter was hopping mad.

"Whose genius idea," he asked, "was it to carry only four players?"

"I can't remember," I said, glancing nervously at my watch to indicate I had somewhere to go.

Just then Ron Rubin walked up. "I'm really sorry about what happened," he said. He was trying to be a nice guy.

"You aren't sorry at all," Peter said. "By the way, Ron, who was the vacuum head who decided we should carry only four players?"

"I think it was—"

"I'll see you guys," I said. "I've got an important date."

"I thought it was you," Peter said.

"Peter," I pleaded. "I'll make it up to you. There are still other ways we can qualify for New Orleans."

"I ought to break your back," he said sensibly.

As a matter of fact, however, we did qualify. In July, 1977, in Chicago, we won the Life Masters Pairs and earned a berth in the qualifications for the World Team Championship and the World Pairs Championship.

In any case, we had reason to fear our Calcutta opponents, Ron Rubin and Henry Bethe. Rubin, not yet thirty, is slow, methodical, exact, and employs an extremely complicated bidding system involving a relay method whereby one partner asks questions and the other answers. Rubin is one of the very best young players in the country. He also is very skilled at backgammon. He recently finished second in a Las Vegas backgammon tournament and won $90,000!

Henry Bethe, whose father won a Nobel Prize in Physics, won the Life Masters Men's Pairs when he was only twenty-four with John Solodar as a partner. Rubin and Bethe's main problem lay in the fact that they had not played together often. A solid partnership often takes years to develop.

Taking the measure of Ron Rubin had added significance for us. Bridge players do not forget opponents who defeat them, particularly in tournaments as important as the Vanderbilt. Also, each player strives to be the best, a status that is impossible to attain if an opponent consistently defeats him.

On the first hand against Rubin-Bethe, they bid to three diamonds which we set by one trick. The second hand illustrates the potency of our system's one-diamond opening bid (covered in Chapter 2) and the strength of the one-diamond sequence (which will be discussed later).

NORTH (Weichsel)
♠ A K 6 5
♥ A 5
♦ K 9 2
♣ J 7 6 4

WEST (Bethe)
♠ Q 8 4 2
♥ Q J 7 6 2
♦ 7 6 3
♣ 2

EAST (Rubin)
♠ 7 3
♥ 9 8 3
♦ 8
♣ A K Q 10 9 8 5

SOUTH (Sontag)
♠ J 10 9
♥ K 10 4
♦ A Q J 10 5 4
♣ 3

No one vulnerable. The bidding:

WEST	NORTH	EAST	SOUTH
			1 ♦
Pass	1 ♠	2 ♣	2 ♦
Pass	2 ♥	Pass	2 ♠
Pass	3 ♦	Pass	3 ♥
Pass	5 ♦	Pass	Pass
Pass			

With some systems the South hand would not qualify for an opening bid, but with our club system it surely does. The one-diamond bid can have a wide variety of meanings but its point range is fairly narrow: usually 12 to 15 (only 11 here) but the diamond length is ambiguous. Opening bidder can have as few as one diamond. The auction on this particular hand requires some explanation.

Peter's one-spade response was natural and showed at least four spades. Over East's two clubs, my two-diamond bid confirmed a good five- or six-card diamond suit but denied more than 14 points. Peter's two-heart bid was natural and forcing. He was probing delicately for the best contract.

I next supported spades, the suit he had originally bid. Peter's bid of three diamonds guaranteed diamond support and was forcing to at least game. My three hearts showed a control in that suit (either A or K) and indicated shortness in clubs, no more than a doubleton. Peter's jump to five diamonds was a mild slam try. From the bidding I knew our diamonds were solid, we were missing the club ace (because Peter did not cue bid it), and that Peter had both major suit aces and something extra because of his slam try. It was clear that slam would depend on a spade finesse for either the queen or king.

In my opinion a 50 percent slam is not a good bet. It is a tossup, heads you win, tails you lose, and bridge should be more exact than that. Furthermore, it was likely that East, the overcaller, had the missing spade honor. I stopped at five diamonds and made six. No one else in this expert field went to six either.

Anyway, it is a fine feeling to know, when faced with a crucial bid, exactly what you are up against. Because of our bidding I knew precisely what the problem was and could make an intelligent decision. Less exact bidding might have landed a partnership in a small slam that would have been made, but over the long haul that partnership would be demolished in championship play.

The final hand against Rubin and Bethe turned into a fierce part-score battle in which we bid two hearts and would have been defeated by one trick, but the bid had the effect of pushing them to three clubs which we set two tricks.

I figured we were leading the event at this point. Later, when I was able to check the scores, I learned that at this juncture—six partnerships and eighteen hands played—we were indeed in front. But not by much.

6

A MAJOR OVER ONE CLUB

ONE CLUB—ONE OF A MAJOR SEQUENCE

THE MAJOR SUIT RESPONSE TO A ONE-CLUB OPENING IS NAT-ural and shows 9 or more high-card points and at least five cards in the suit bid. Although responder may have another suit as long as his major, it cannot be longer. If responder has 9 8 6 3 2 of hearts and A K J 9 4 of clubs, he must bid the major. Opening bidder, of course, can initiate a series of questions over responder's major suit bid.

ONE CLUB—EITHER MAJOR—
ONE NO TRUMP SEQUENCE

Opener always responds one no trump when he has a balanced hand and no long suit of his own. The bid asks responder to describe his hand in aces and kings.

OPENER	RESPONDER
1 ♣	1 ♥ or 1 ♠
1 no trump	

Responder may make one of the following bids:

1. Two Clubs. Shows 0, 1, or 2 controls (an ace equals 2 controls, a king equals 1). It is unlikely that a hand capable of making a positive response (one of a major) would not have at least 1 king. If responder held 9 points but no aces or kings, he might want to bid the negative one diamond. Over two clubs, opener can bid two diamonds to ask responder to clarify further his controls. Responder could then bid: two hearts (0 or 1 king); two spades (1 ace); two no trump (5-3-3-2 distribution and two kings); three clubs (at least four clubs and two kings); three diamonds (at least four diamonds and two kings; three of responder's major (at least six in the major, no other four-card suit, and two kings); or three of the other major (at least four cards in the suit and two kings).

2. Two Diamonds. Three controls.

3. Two Hearts. Four controls.

4. Two Spades. Five controls.

5. Two No Trump. Six or more controls. Over two no trump opener will bid three clubs to ask responder for his exact number of controls: three diamonds would show 6, three hearts would show 7, three spades would show 8, etc. Three spades would be a very rare bid. It has never come up between Peter and me.

6. Three Clubs. Natural. Shows a strong five-card club suit to go with the five- or six-card major. Because responder has deviated from showng controls, he is showing two very good suits. Generally, responder should have two of the top three honors in each of his suits. The jack and ten are also important and the possession of these cards should be considered when deciding whether to deviate from showing controls. If opener bids three diamonds over three clubs, he is asking for number of controls: three hearts would show 2 and each progressive step would show one more.

7. Three Diamonds. The same as three clubs except responder's second suit is diamonds. Over three diamonds, opener

can ask for controls by bidding three of the major that responder does not have.

8. Three Hearts. If hearts was responder's original suit, this bid shows six or seven cards in a semisolid suit. It could be headed by A K J, K Q J, or A Q J. Over three hearts, opener can bid three spades to ask for controls. If responder originally bid a spade, however, three hearts would show a strong 5-5 distribution in spades and hearts. In this case, four clubs would ask for controls. Four diamonds would then show 2 controls, four hearts would show 3, etc.

9. Three Spades. If spades was responder's original suit, the bid shows six or seven cards in a semisolid suit. Four clubs asks for controls. If spades was not the original suit, the bid shows six hearts and five spades.

After opener determines the number of controls, two no trump asks for responder's distribution. Responder bids naturally. He shows a second suit if he has one, rebids his six-card major if he doesn't, and bids three no trump if he has 5-3-3-2 distribution. Here is an example of the sequence:

OPENER	RESPONDER
1 ♣	1 ♠
1 no trump	2 ♦ (3 controls)
2 no trump	3 ♥ (at least four hearts)

Here is a second, more sophisticated, example of the sequence:

OPENER	RESPONDER
1 ♣	1 ♥
1 no trump	2 ♣ (0 to 2 controls)
2 ♦ (how many?)	2 ♠ (one ace)
2 no trump (asks distribution)	3 ♠ (at least four spades)

The system is very flexible: even if responder indicates six or more controls with the rare bid of two no trump, opener can still discover the specific number of controls *and* the distribution:

OPENER	RESPONDER
1 ♣	1 ♠
1 no trump	2 no trump (6 or more controls)
3 ♣ (how many?)	3 ♦ (six)
3 no trump (forcing, and asks distribution)	Responder now can bid a second suit, rebid spades if he has at least six and no other four-card suit, bid four no trump with 5-3-3-2 distribution, or five no trump with 5-3-3-2 distribution and extra values—queens and jacks

The W-S club system does employ a number of artificial bids, although not nearly as many as Terence Reese's "Little Major." Artificial bidding occasionally can lead to vexing situations when the opponents are beginners, do not understand a club system, and money is involved.

Peter and I stopped at the Vanderbilt Bridge Club on Long Island to visit Joel Stuart, a former teammate of ours on the Precision Team. While waiting for Joel, who manages the rubber bridge concession at the Vanderbilt, two men walked up to us and asked if we wanted to play. They were obviously father and son. The father was short and chunky and wore a suit. The son, about eighteen and dressed in jeans, was gangly and insistent. When Peter said we weren't interested, he complained that there was no one else around and volunteered to play for "high stakes." It turned out that high stakes were a half-cent a point.

"We use a club system," I said. Bridge players have an obligation to tell opponents about their bidding methods.

"Who cares what you play?" said the teenager.

We played a few hands and it was clear that the two were beginners. They knew how to follow suit but that was about all. Worse, they were down about $1.50 and complaining so much that a casual observer might have thought we had won the teenager's college education money. Then came this hand:

NORTH (Sontag)	SOUTH (Weichsel)
♠ K 6	♠ A 8 7 3 2
♥ K 4	♥ A 10 6
♦ A K Q J 9 3	♦ 8 4
♣ A K 3	♣ Q 7 2

SONTAG	WEICHSEL
1 ♣	1 ♠
1 no trump	2 ♥ (4 controls)
2 no trump (asks distribution)	3 no trump (5-3-3-2)
4 ♣ (looking for queens)	5 ♣ (queen of clubs)
7 ♦	Pass

The father made his opening lead, a trump, and I claimed the contract before the dummy went down. I knew Peter had two aces, the queen of clubs, and at least two diamonds. I could have bid seven no trump but in rubber bridge honors count.

"What is going on here?" the teenager shouted. The kid was on his feet, his face changing color. "Not once did they bid diamonds! Not once, Dad, until they bid the grand slam!"

"It does seem rather odd," the father said.

"I told you," I said, "we use a club system."

"You use a cheating system," the teenager said. "How else could you know what your partner had!"

We told them to keep the money they owed, and walked

over to the cola machine to wait for Joel. Maybe he would explain to them what had happened.

One of the key bids in the auction was the four-club queen ask. After opener asks for controls with his one no trump bid, and distribution with his two no trump bid, opener will only be interested in queens if responder shows a balanced hand by bidding three no trump. Opener will bid any suit other than responder's major at the four level to ask if responder has the queen in that suit. Responder will raise that suit if he has the queen, bid another queen if he has one at the four level, and will jump to the five level to show the queen in that suit plus the queen being asked about. Responder bids four no trump if he has no queens.

ONE CLUB—ONE OF A MAJOR— NEW SUIT SEQUENCE

When opener bids a new suit over responder's major, he is showing length in that suit and at the same time is asking responder if he has support for the suit and also whether he has 4 or more controls.

OPENER	RESPONDER
1 ♣	1 ♥ or 1 ♠
New suit	

Responder may bid as follows:

1. The lowest possible bid over the new suit. For example, if the bidding has gone one club, one heart, one spade, then one no trump would be the lowest possible bid. One no trump would show less than 4 controls and less than a queen and two others in opener's new suit. No matter what new suit opener bids, the lowest possible next bid by responder has this meaning.

2. The second lowest possible bid over the new suit. If the bidding has gone one club, one heart, one spade, then

two clubs would skip over one no trump and show: 4 or more controls and less than queen and two others, in opener's suit.

3. The third lowest possible bid over the new suit. Shows less than 4 controls and at least three of partner's suit headed by the queen, king, or ace.

4. The fourth lowest possible bid over the new suit. Shows 4 or more controls and at least three cards in the new suit headed by the queen or better.

5. The fifth lowest possible bid over the new suit. Shows 4 or more controls and four cards in the new suit headed by no more than the jack.

When responder deviates from one of these five bids, he is showing a strong two-suiter with at least 5-5 distribution. Thus, the bidding may have gone as follows:

OPENER	RESPONDER
1 ♣	1 ♠
2 ♦	3 ♥

Three hearts shows at least five spades and five hearts. Four clubs shows clubs and spades. If responder jumps in his own suit he shows a suit so strong that it normally would contain only one loser.

Bids #3, 4, and 5 show positive trump support. If opener wants to know the number of responder's controls, the asking bid is three no trump. When responder has shown less than 4 controls (Bid #3), he has four possible answers to three no trump:

1. Four Clubs. The only ambiguous response. Shows 0 controls, or one king, or one ace.

2. Four Diamonds. Shows two kings.

3. Four Hearts. Shows 3 controls, three kings or an ace and a king.

4. Four Spades. A very rare bid. Shows 3 controls, four trump, and an undisclosed singleton or void. Four no trump would then ask responder to bid his singleton or void at the

five level. If responder bids five of the trump suit, his short suit is a higher-ranking suit than the agreed trump suit.

When responder has shown 4 or more controls, the following bids over three no trump would mean: four clubs—4 controls; four diamonds—5 controls; four hearts—6 controls; and so on.

Here are two examples of the one club—one of a major— new suit sequence:

OPENER	RESPONDER
1 ♣	1 ♠
2 ♥ (natural)	3 ♦ (Bid #4, good trump and 4 or more controls)
3 no trump (asks for number of controls)	4 diamonds (5 controls)

OPENER	RESPONDER
1 ♣	1 ♠
2 ♥	2 ♠ (Bid #1, no trump support and less than 4 controls)
2 no trump (natural)	3 ♣ (shows clubs)
3 no trump (to play)	

ONE CLUB—ONE OF A MAJOR— SINGLE JUMP IN NEW SUIT SEQUENCE

Opener's jump into a new suit shows a solid suit and an unbalanced hand. If opener had a balanced hand with a strong suit of six or seven cards, he would bid one no trump over the major suit response to find out about controls. In short, with a balanced hand—perhaps 6-3-2-2—it is relatively easy for opener to assess slam potential after learning the number of responder's controls. With an unbalanced hand, however, the number of controls is not so important because there may be duplication of values: responder may have an ace opposite opening bidder's void or a king opposite opener's singleton.

There are six possible single jump sequences into a new suit following the one club—one of a major beginning: one club, one heart, two spades; one club, one heart, three clubs; one club, one heart, three diamonds; one club, one spade, three clubs; one club, one spade, three diamonds; and one club, one spade, three hearts.

When the auction begins this way, it follows a logical cue bidding pattern. No specialized conventional treatments are necessary. It is always understood that opener's jump shift suit will be the suit where the contract is played. Responder must remember that his chief responsibility is to show what values he has, as opposed to rebidding a long, poor suit.

ONE CLUB—ONE OF A MAJOR— DOUBLE JUMP IN NEW SUIT SEQUENCE

Most often the person in charge of the auction is the opening club bidder. He is the captain. He has the strong hand and it is easier for him to learn the few things he needs to know than to convey his superior values to responder. Sometimes—but rarely during a club auction—there is no captain and both players are exchanging information so the best contract can be reached. At other times, however, opening bidder wishes to pass the captaincy to his partner because he can describe his hand within a very narrow limit with a single bid. Responder can then judge in what suit and at what level the hand should be played.

There are six possible double jump sequences into a new suit following the one club—one of a major beginning: one club, one heart, three spades; one club, one heart, four clubs; one club, one heart, four diamonds; one club, one spade, four clubs; one club, one spade, four diamonds; one club, one spade, four hearts.

All six of opener's double jumps are splinter bids (they show a four- or five-card fit in responder's major and exactly one card in the suit bid). They also show 16 to 18 high-card points. The possible distributions for these double jump bids are:

1. Five trump, 4-3 either way in the other suits, and a singleton in the suit bid.

2. Four trump, 5-3 either way in the other suits, and a singleton in the suit bid. The five-card suit can contain only one of the top three honors. If opener has two honors in his five-card suit, he should bid the suit naturally to find out if responder has the remaining honor. The reason for this bid is that a strong five-card suit with a fit can be a powerful source of tricks and without the natural bid responder might not appreciate the strength of his holdings if he himself has a king and two others in the suit, or a similar hand. This bid is very specific to avoid missing slam opportunities.

3. A singleton in the suit bid and 4-4-4-1 distribution. Peter and I never have this distribution for this bid because we use an opening bid of two diamonds which shows 16 to 24 high-card points and precisely the same distribution with the singleton in any suit. The bid is mentioned here because the two diamond opening bid and its subsequent structure is relatively complicated and for players not willing to learn it, this could be a welcome option

ONE CLUB—ONE OF A MAJOR—
THREE OF THE SAME MAJOR SEQUENCE

This sequence is the same as the previous one except the point range is different (19 to 21) and the specific singleton is not yet pinpointed.

There are only two possible auctions with this sequence: one club, one heart, three hearts; and one club, one spade, three spades. Responder is obligated to learn immediately what the singleton is. The hands contain a minimum of 28 high-card points and a maximum of opener's 21 with whatever responder has (it could be 19) and slam or grand slam are definite possibilities.

OPENER	RESPONDER
1 ♣	1 ♥
3 ♥	3 ♠ (asks for singleton)

Three no trump would show a spade singleton. Four clubs or four diamonds would show a singleton in the suit bid. What if the jump raise is in spades?

OPENER	RESPONDER
1 ♣	1 ♠
3 ♠	3 no trump (asks for singleton)

Four clubs, four diamonds, or four hearts show a singleton in the suit bid.

ONE CLUB—ONE OF A MAJOR—
TWO OF THE SAME MAJOR SEQUENCE

This very specific bid is made when opener is interested in learning what responder has in his bid suit. The bid is particularly helpful in determining whether to be in slam. Two auctions exist in this sequence: one club, one heart, two hearts; and one club, one spade, two spades. Responder has six possible replies to this trump-asking bid:

1. Two Spades (over two hearts) or Two No Trump (over two spades). Show five or six cards in responder's suit but no A, K, or Q.

2. Two No Trump (over two hearts) or Three Clubs (over two spades). Show a five-card suit with one of the top three honors.

3. Three Clubs (over two hearts) or Three Diamonds (over two spades). Show a six-card suit headed by one of the top three honors.

4. Three Diamonds (over two hearts) and Three Hearts (over two spades). Show a five-card suit with two of the top three honors.

5. Three Hearts (over two hearts) and Three Spades (over two spades). Show a six-card suit with two of the top three honors.

6. Three Spades (over two hearts) and Three No Trump (over two spades). Show five or six cards and all three top honors.

Opener may want to clarify responder's trump holdings even further. This is accomplished by rebidding responder's major suit at the three level, but is possible only for the previously mentioned Bids #1 through 4. A different bid is required for Bid #5, and there is no reason to re-ask when Bid #6 is involved.

OPENER	RESPONDER
1 ♣	1 ♥ or 1 ♠
2 ♥ or 2 ♠ (trump-ask)	2 ♠ (five or six hearts and no A, K, or Q) or 2 no
3 ♥ or 3 ♠ (re-ask)	trump (five or six spades and no A, K, or Q)

Responder can now make one of four bids:

1. Three Spades (over three hearts) or Three No Trump (over three spades). Show five-card suit headed at most by the ten.

2. Three No Trump (over three hearts) or Four Clubs (over three spades). Five-card suit headed by the jack.

3. Four Clubs (over three hearts) or Four Diamonds (over three spades). Six-card suit headed at most by the ten.

4. Four Diamonds (over three hearts) or Four Hearts (over three spades). Six-card suit headed by the jack.

If responder originally has shown a five- or six-card suit with one of three top honors (Bids #2 and 3), three of a major again is the re-ask in the trump suit. Responder may bid:

1. Three spades (over three hearts) or Three No Trump (over three spades). Shows the jack. To discover which honor responder has other than the jack, opener bids three no trump (over three spades) or four clubs (over three no trump). Responder conveys this information by making the lowest possible bid to show the queen, the next lowest to show the king, and the next to show the ace.

2. Three No Trump (over three hearts) and Four Clubs (over three spades). Show the queen and four or five others, without the jack.

3. Four Clubs (over three hearts) or Four Diamonds (over three spades). The king and four or five others, without the jack.

4. Four Diamonds (over three hearts) or Four Hearts (over three spades). The ace and four or five others, without the jack.

If responder has shown a five-card suit headed by two of the top three honors (Bid #4), a rebid of the trump suit is a re-ask by opener. Responder then has four possible bids:

1. Three Spades (over three hearts) or Three No Trump (over three spades). Shows the jack. If opener wants still more information, he bids three no trump (over three spades) or four clubs (over three no trump). Responder then makes the lowest possible bid to show the K Q, the next lowest to show the A Q, and the third step to show the A K.

2. Three No Trump (over three hearts) or Four Clubs (over three spades). Show the K Q and three others, without the jack.

3. Four Clubs (over three hearts) and Four Diamonds (over three spades). The A Q and three others, without the jack.

4. Four Diamonds (over three hearts) and Four Hearts (over three spades). The A K and three others, without the jack.

If responder has shown a six-card suit headed by two of

the top three honors (Bid #5), opener can ask for further clarification of the trump suit by bidding three no trump.

OPENER	RESPONDER
1 ♣	1 ♥ or 1 ♠
2 ♥ or 2 ♠	3 ♥ or 3 ♠
3 no trump (re-asks in trump)	

Responder can make one of four bids:

1. Four Clubs. Shows the jack. Opener relays with four diamonds to learn about other honors. Four hearts would show K Q. Four spades A Q. Four no trump A K.
2. Four Diamonds. K Q and four others. No jack.
3. Four Hearts. A Q and four others. No jack.
4. Four Spades. A K and four others. No jack.

Often the opener, after asking in trump, will want information about another suit. After opener initiates a trump-asking auction in a major suit, any new suit that he bids is a special asking bid in that suit. Obviously, opener must use great care in asking these questions lest he get in a contract that is over his head. Here is an example of an auction in which opener asks information about a second suit:

OPENER	RESPONDER
1 ♣	1 ♠
2 ♠	3 ♥
4 ♦ (asks about diamonds)	

Responder can make one of six bids:

1. The Lowest Possible Bid. Shows three or four small cards in the suit being asked about.
2. The Next Lowest Possible Bid. Shows two small cards, or queen and one card, queen and two cards, or queen and three. In short, it shows third round control.

3. The Next Lowest Possible Bid. Singleton or void.

4. The Next Lowest. King and two small cards, or the ace and two small, or the king and three small, or the ace and three small.

5. The Next Lowest. The king and one, the ace and one, or the singleton king or ace.

6. The Next Lowest. Two of top three honors and any length.

With the first four responses, opener may re-ask in the suit by rebidding it:

OPENER	RESPONDER
1 ♣	1 ♠
2 ♠	3 ♥
4 ♦ (asks in diamonds)	4 ♥ (three or four small diamonds)
5 ♦ (re-asks in diamonds)	

Responder has only two bids:

1. The Lowest Possible Next Bid. Three of the suit.

2. The Next Lowest. Four of the suit.

If responder has shown a doubleton, queen and one, queen and two, or queen and three, opener rebids the suit as a re-ask. The next bid above the re-ask shows two small cards. The bid after that shows the queen with one, two, or three cards.

If responder has shown a singleton or void, the next bid above the re-ask shows a singleton and the bid just above that shows a void.

If responder has shown an ace or king with two small, or an ace or king with three small, the next bid above the re-ask shows the ace or king with two small, and the bid above that shows the ace and king with three small.

It really is important to exercise discretion when using these asking bids. I watched two young players, who incidentally were not using a club system, bid themselves right out of a promising contract by the ill-judged employment of asking bids. They held:

NORTH	SOUTH
♠ A 9 5	♠ K 7 3
♥ Q J 10 8 3	♥ A K 5 4 2
♦ K Q 9	♦ J 8
♣ A 4	♣ K 7 6

NORTH	SOUTH
1 ♥	3 ♥
4 no trump (Blackwood)	5 ♦ (1 ace)
5 no trump (Blackwood for kings)	6 ♠ (3 kings)
6 no trump	Pass

"It was unlucky," said North, after going down one, "that you had three kings. If you'd only had two kings, we could have stopped at six hearts."

This is the first time I have ever seen a player unhappy because his partner had *too many* high cards!

North, of course, was not unlucky. He did not use caution with his asking bids, and the final response hurled him into a contract he could not make.

Five no trump, asking for kings when he was already off an ace, was a nothing-to-gain, everything-to-lose gamble. Since he was going to bid a small slam anyway, he should have done so immediately after the five-diamond response. If South had three kings, the contract was cold. With two kings, six hearts might depend on a finesse.

ONE CLUB—ONE OF A MAJOR—
DELAYED TRUMP ASK SEQUENCE

Most frequently, opener will not have a hand to take charge in the bidding by immediately asking about trump. More often he will be interested in finding out about responder's controls or his support of opener's suit. With the W-S club system, opener can obtain this information first and then ask about trump. If the answer to opener's first question indicates the possibility of slam, opener can then ask in responder's major suit. For example:

OPENER	RESPONDER
1 ♣	1 ♥
1 no trump (asks for controls)	2 ♥ (4 controls)
3 ♥ (asks in hearts)	

Responder's bidding would now be the same as if the bidding had gone one club, one heart, two hearts. In this case the trump ask was merely delayed for a round.

Here is another example of the delayed trump ask:

OPENER	RESPONDER
1 ♣	1 ♠
1 no trump	2 ♣ (0 to 2 controls)
2 ♦ (clarify controls)	2 ♥ (0 or 1 king)
2 ♠ (asks in spades)	

Similarly, responder's answer to the trump ask of two spades would be the same as if the bidding had progressed one club, one spade, two spades.

A final example is needed:

OPENER	RESPONDER
1 ♣	1 ♠
2 ♦ (asks in diamonds)	2 no trump (at least the queen and two small diamonds, less than 4 controls)
3 ♠ (asks in spades)	

Again, responder bids as if the auction had proceeded one club, one spade, two spades.

This chapter has covered the entire one club—one of a major structure. The structure is equipped with many valuable special asking bid sequences: trump asking, delayed trump asking, control asking, special suit asking, support asking, and distribution asking.

Most partnerships in the United States play only one asking bid auction, Blackwood, which is geared to slams. This simply is not enough. More science is needed if the correct contract is to be reached regularly. The special asking bid sequences provide a partnership with an important edge, an edge that can make the difference between winning and losing.

CHAPTER

7

END OF THE FIRST QUARTER

Our seventh opponents of the session were Bobby Levin and Jack Blair, and what I knew before we started this tournament was confirmed: there would be no letup at all.

Bobby Levin is a nineteen-year-old phenom who became, in 1973, the youngest Life Master in history. Bobby shows frightening promise at bridge. He has ambition, dedication, and brains. All he lacks is experience.

Jack Blair has plenty of that. He is forty-four, several times a national champion. He is tough, gritty, and uncompromising at the bridge table, a successful Tulsa, Oklahoma, business-man who drinks whiskey straight and makes big bets on football games. I first met Jack in 1972 during the Spring Nationals in the finals of the Vanderbilt in Cincinnati. The Precision Team I was on beat Blair's team, but it was a desperate battle that left everyone drained of energy.

On the first hand Levin and Blair misjudged a competitive auction and allowed Peter and me to steal a cheap part-score in hearts when they could easily have made three no trump. Bobby Levin seemed crestfallen. Jack Blair was angry.

Next came a hand that had me congratulating myself for having the good sense to have Peter as a partner:

NORTH (Sontag)
♠ Q 2
♥ K 2
♦ K 7 5
♣ 10 9 7 4 3 2

WEST (Blair)
♠ K J 7 4 3
♥ Q 10 3
♦ J 8
♣ A K Q

EAST (Levin)
♠ 10 5
♥ A J 9 8 5 4
♦ Q 10 4 2
♣ 6

SOUTH (Weichsel)
♠ A 9 8 6
♥ 7 6
♦ A 9 6 3
♣ J 8 5

East-West vulnerable. The bidding:

WEST	NORTH	EAST	SOUTH
	Pass	2 ♥	Pass
4 ♥	Pass	Pass	Pass

I enjoy asking people, if you were Peter Weichsel, sitting South, what would you lead? The question assumes added importance because the results of bridge tournaments are often close and in this case the answer could mean more than $50,000.

The opening lead by a defender frequently determines whether a contract is defeated. All textbooks advise against underleading an ace, but there are exceptions. On the diagrammed hand, Peter felt an attacking lead was necessary. He reasoned that if he led a club or trump, declarer would be able to draw trump and discard his losers on dummy's club suit. This was pure conjecture, but it turned out Peter was right.

Peter led a low spade, a brilliant stroke. Declarer, Bobby Levin, could not believe Peter had led away from an ace, so Levin played the jack of spades from dummy losing to my queen. We quickly cashed the ace and king of diamonds and the ace of spades to set the contract. At almost every other table declarer got an opening club lead and easily made *five* hearts.

It was humid, crowded, and smoky in the big Cavendish card room, but at that moment it seemed the best place on earth to be.

The third hand against Levin and Blair was passed out, an anticlimax.

Things were about to speed up, to our chagrin.

My friends Peter Nagy and Eric Kokish from Canada sat down to play. "I'm still pulling for the best partnership to win," I said.

"Fairweather," said Eric Kokish.

In 1969 Kokish was already a friend and a good player, but not nearly as good as he would become. That year I watched him and his partner being manhandled by two veteran New York players. The New Yorkers were obviously the superior pair (although not any more), and it became clear that I was cheering for them. Kokish angrily confronted me after the match.

"What's this business," he said, "of rooting against me?"

It was then I told him I wanted the best partnership to win, always.

"Some fairweather friend you are," he said.

And I'm still the only person I have heard of who is known as "Fairweather."

Eric Kokish, from Montreal, makes his living playing bridge. He teaches the game and is an excellent writer. Eric and his attractive wife, Sharyn, who also teaches bridge, make up the best mixed pair in Canada.

Peter Nagy, from Toronto, moved to New York a few years ago to try his luck at being a bridge professional. He was fairly successful, but not as much as he would have liked—very few experts make much money from the game —and he returned to Montreal, where now he and Eric Kokish form the most powerful partnership in Canada.

It seems during a tournament that when bridge appears to be the simplest, when the bidding is just right and the card play is faultless, when you are sure you are in the lead and can only pull further ahead—that is when the game, like a great, sly, treacherous monster, rises up and tries to squeeze the life out of you. The truth is that bridge is so complex and has so many variations that no partnership ever will completely master it.

Kokish and Nagy fairly beat us to death. Part of it was inspired play on their part; the remainder was a horrendous blunder we made.

Kokish and Nagy bid and made three no trump on the first hand through skillful bidding and play and fortunate distribution in the spade suit. On the second hand we made that terrible error, humiliating under any circumstances but so much worse in this tournament where the stakes were so high. Here was the hand:

NORTH (Nagy)
- ♠ 10 6 5 3
- ♥ Q 9 7 6
- ♦ J
- ♣ Q 10 9 4

WEST (Sontag)
- ♠ A 9
- ♥ A
- ♦ A K Q 6 2
- ♣ A K 7 5 2

EAST (Weichsel)
- ♠ J 8 7 4 2
- ♥ 10 8 5 3
- ♦ 9 5
- ♣ J 8

SOUTH (Kokish)
- ♠ K Q
- ♥ K J 4 2
- ♦ 10 8 7 4 3
- ♣ 6 3

Both vulnerable. The bidding:

WEST	NORTH	EAST	SOUTH
			Pass
1 ♣	Pass	1 ♦	Pass
3 ♦	Pass	3 ♠	Pass
4 ♣	Pass	4 ♦	Pass
4 ♥	Pass	4 ♠	Pass
5 ♥	Pass	5 ♠	Pass
5 no trump	Pass	6 ♠	Pass
7 ♠	Pass	Pass	Pass

Beginners should not bid this way. The proper contract was three no trump, which if played expertly can be made. But seven spades? Seven rounds of razzle-dazzle bidding to look like blithering idiots? Houdini, even if he were cheating, could not make this contract. How could such bidding be possible?

Peter made the most costly mistake, I made the second error, but even Kokish, sitting South and passing eight straight times, suffered an eclipse of reason. Only Nagy with his seven straight passes was guiltless.

There is no excuse for such bidding, but there are reasons. Here is what we did and what we thought we were doing:

SONTAG

1 ♣—means at least 16 high-card points and is forcing for one round.

3 ♦—forces to game and shows strong diamond suit.

4 ♣—my second suit. I have mistaken impression of Peter's hand.

4 ♥—shows the ace.

5 ♥—grand slam try showing absolute control in hearts.

5 no trump—trying for seven spades. I have a *great* hand and cannot know about his mistake.

7 ♠—My mistake. A totally incongruous and off-the-wall bid.

WEICHSEL

1 ♦—our only negative bid, showing 0 to 8 high-card points.

3 ♠—one of the worst errors Peter has ever made. He just was not paying attention. Three spades shows 5 to 8 points and at least 5 spades. Peter should have bid 3 hearts, which is artificial and shows 0 to 4 points.

4 ♦—shows a preference to my first suit.

4 ♠—Peter realizes his mistake and desperately wants me to pass.

5 ♠—Peter has panicked. Won't Alan *please* pass?

6 ♠—I hope Alan has the decency not to write about this auction.

We went down five!
Peter smiled at me.

I stared at Kokish and with my eyes dared him to say something about "pulling for the best partnership to win." But Eric said nothing. He was too busy avoiding Nagy's angry gaze. Eric, of course, should have doubled seven spades. He had the K Q trump combination, which guaranteed a trick. He had been so spellbound by our madness that he had overlooked the obvious.

A partnership with a precise bidding system such as ours had better be certain they do not make a mistake. The result can be catastrophic. Players using a less sophisticated system can sometimes recover from a bidding error. Between Peter and me, however, recovery is virtually impossible because all our bids are very specific. Also, we have confidence in each other, and we have worked so long on our system that we do not expect mistakes to be made and therefore are unprepared for them. It is true that learning such a system requires effort, but the results make it worthwhile.

I believed this hand might have cost us the tournament, no matter how well we played from here on. I thought about Mike Becker saying he wouldn't give a nickel for our chances of repeating as champions. Suddenly it was very hot in the room, the smoke burned my eyes.

"Look up," Peter said. "You'll see a rain cloud over your head." He was still smiling, which told me how badly he felt.

Screw you, I wanted to say. This was your fault and look what you've done. We work and work and you don't pay attention and now everything was for nothing.

But we had gone over such a contingency in every pre-tournament session we had ever had and agreed the best thing we could do was avoid screaming or sulking and try to regain our normal rhythm. That was fine as strategy *away* from the table, but maybe humans simply cannot operate that way.

Kokish and Nagy ate us up on the third hand too. In a highly competitive auction they did an excellent job of assessing their values and arrived at a cold six spades with a combined high-card point total of just 22. Only about one-third of the field reached this contract.

It was our turn to move to another table and I almost upended my chair getting away from Nagy and Kokish. They were an aberration, I decided, a jinx, a hex. They were friends and I hated them.

Our next opponents, David Berah and Dr. Francis Vernon from Venezuela, did more to lift our spirits than any pretournament strategy session ever could. Berah, a former World War II RAF pilot, always reminds me of a daredevil, yet he is one of the friendliest and most agreeable men in bridge: also one of the richest. A Caracas industrialist, he somehow has combined a successful business career with the difficult years of work necessary to become perhaps the best-known bridge player in Latin America. This is an accomplishment I find difficult to comprehend. Peter and I do nothing but play bridge. We agree that any outside interest would detract from and diminish our game. Trying to be best at bridge, a mere card game, may not be a high ambition, but it takes effort and undiminished attention. Except, it seems, for people like David Berah.

Anyway, I was not even in my chair when Berah bounced out of his with a wide grin and outstretched hand. "Alan," he said. "So good to see you again. I hope you'll be able to come to my tournament in Caracas."

It was easy to like him. He was fifty-six, dressed in an elegant custom-made gray suit, immaculate white silk shirt, subtly striped blue and green tie, supple black leather shoes, and his breast pocket contained a handkerchief that matched his tie. Now he was striding around the table to pump Peter's hand. "I'll be in New York for a week," he said. "Perhaps you and Alan would join me for dinner?"

"Only if Alan dissolves that rain cloud," Peter said.

"Things aren't going well?" He seemed genuinely concerned.

"They're okay. But partner gets discouraged."

"You'll do fine," Berah said to me.

David Berah was champion of South America three times and a member of the winning squad in Venezuela's National Open Teams a phenomenal eleven times.

Berah's partner, Dr. Francis Vernon, was a successful forty-three-year-old Caracas engineer who was twice champion of South America and represented Venezuela in the World Team Olympiad in 1968. Dr. Vernon was slim, shy, balding. He had delicate features and a small-boned face. Except for his fastidious dress, he could not have been more unlike his gregarious partner.

It was David Berah who pulled me out of my depression. He was cheerful and entertaining. The debacle against Kokish and Nagy seemed not to be such an earthshaking event. When Berah said, "Shall we pick up our hands?" it seemed the most normal thing in the world to do.

The first hand was tame, a dull part-score—Peter was declarer at one no trump—but he made the most of it by scoring an overtrick. Almost every other partnership, a study of the record revealed, also bid one no trump, but few scored the overtrick.

Peter opened the bidding on the second hand with a vulnerable preempt and we arrived at a cold four-heart contract. Some experts did not open the bidding with three hearts and did not reach the unbeatable four hearts; in fact, once again we scored an overtrick.

"You have no problems," Berah said. "It looks just like last year."

"Let's look at the third hand," Peter said.

NORTH (Berah)
♠ Void
♥ A J 10
♦ K 9 7 5 3 2
♣ Q 8 7 4

WEST (Sontag)
♠ 3
♥ 7 6 5 4 2
♦ 8 6 4
♣ A J 10 2

EAST (Weichsel)
♠ K 9 8 7 6 2
♥ K 9 8 3
♦ J
♣ 9 6

SOUTH (Dr. Vernon)
♠ A Q J 10 5 4
♥ Q
♦ A Q 10
♣ K 5 3

No one vulnerable. The bidding:

WEST	NORTH	EAST	SOUTH
			2 ♠
Pass	3 ♦	Pass	4 ♣
Pass	6 ♦	Pass	Pass
Pass			

David Berah, instead of being prudent and carefully investigating his slam possibilities, bashed into a contract that had less than a 50 percent chance of success. Although Berah got a very favorable opening lead—the heart three—he still went down one. After the opening lead, he should have made the contract.

Berah mistakenly drew two rounds of trump and that was his undoing. The play should have gone as follows: after the heart queen won the first trick in dummy, Berah should have discarded his jack of hearts on his winning ace of spades; he then should have led dummy's spade queen to try to establish the suit but my discard of a heart would spell the end of that strategy; Berah should ruff the queen with the two of diamonds, cash the ace of hearts (discarding a small club from dummy) and play a club to the king which loses to my ace; I would return a club, won by declarer's queen, and Berah would then ruff a club with dummy's diamond ten; Berah should cash the ace of diamonds, dropping Peter's jack, ruff another spade in his hand, a club with dummy's last trump, and safely enter his hand by ruffing another spade; Berah's K 9 of trump would take the last two tricks because of the lucky placement of the singleton diamond jack in Peter's hand.

The play of the hand requires no fancy end plays, squeezes, or smother plays. After the fortuitous opening lead, a workmanlike declarer should have made the contract. But everyone has lapses.

In any case, the slam should not have been bid. Had Peter's opening lead been a trump, Berah would have been finished before he ever played a card. Peter could not be faulted, however. Most experts believe in aggressive leads against small slams.

But there is still the question of Berah's over-enthusiastic bidding. If Peter and I had held the Berah-Vernon cards, this is how we would have bid the hand:

SOUTH (Weichsel)

1 ♣ (strong, forcing opening)

2 ♠ (natural)

3 ♠ (strong and long spades)

4 ♦ (good diamond support)

4 ♠ (shows the ace)

5 ♦ (the *key* bid. Peter knows I have the heart ace, the diamond king, a small honor in clubs, and at most a singleton spade. Although there is a play for slam, taking twelve tricks would be difficult because the most important suits—spades and diamonds—would have to be have most favorably, an unlikely event.)

NORTH (Sontag)

2 ♦ (positive, 9 or more points, five or more diamonds)

2 no trump (artificial, no spade support and less than 4 controls)

3 no trump (natural, shows stoppers in unbid suits)

4 ♥ (shows the ace)

4 no trumps (mild slam try in diamonds)

Pass (the final decision has been made by Peter)

David Berah is an incomparably better player than this hand indicates. It was interesting to observe his reaction: he closed his eyes and groaned.

We moved on to play our tenth and last opponents of the first session. Whenever I go to another table, my anticipation and curiosity turn into excitement. It is an excitement never experienced by football, baseball, and tennis players. Who else goes into a sports event not knowing the identity of the next opponent? A bridge player leaves a table and until he arrives at the next, has no idea who he is up against.

The suspense in the Cavendish is less than in other events, where you might breeze over to a table and find yourself gaping at Benito Garozzo and Giorgio Belladonna; or you might grin as you spot two novices who came in off the street because it was raining.

The Cavendish provides less suspense because the next opponents are certain to be a strong pair. But the suspense is still there because you don't know *which* strong pair it will be.

It was Amos Kaminsky and Jeff Westheimer, two of the most colorful and volatile players in bridge. Westheimer, forty-three, a floor trader on the silver exchange in New York, is known as "The Pipe" because he smokes one. Westheimer bids and plays a bridge hand with the speed usually associated with jet planes and Mario Andretti. He plays backgammon, at which he is also expert, so fast that his checkers seem to move by themselves. Jeff is not impatient; it is just that his mind works at a highly accelerated pace. Also, at backgammon, he believes the faster he plays, the more games he can get in and the more money he can win. Westheimer does not look like a speed demon, however. He usually dresses in a conservative suit and tie.

This was the third Cavendish Calcutta. Westheimer had won the first with Jim Jacoby as his partner. He did not compete in the second Calcutta, which Peter and I won. In that sense, three of the four players at the table were defending champions.

Amos Kaminsky, a Wall Street investment manager, would frighten his conservative clientele if they watched him play bridge. Kaminsky is daring and imaginative, a gambler. He loves to make psychic bids, dangerous preempts, redoubles, doubles, light opening bids, risky slams, and is fond of sandbagging and even passing suits with as many as nine cards in them, hoping when he bids the suit later he will be doubled. He especially enjoys these machinations in high-stake games against world-class players, which proves he is not insane. Against less skilled opponents, he can play safe and generally be confident of victory. Kaminsky is also a very fast player, but not in the same league with the rocket-like Westheimer.

We were faced with two immediate problems against Kaminsky and Westheimer. First, because of Kaminsky's unorthodox bidding, it would be difficult to understand and assess their auctions. Second, Westheimer would use his quick mind and rapid play to try to rush us off the table. This was more easily countered: we would slow our own play down and refuse to be hurried.

Peter and I had prepared this strategy in advance. No serious player of any game fails to analyze his opponent. I read football player Jerry Kramer's book, *Instant Replay*, and was impressed by the thoroughness with which he studied each defensive lineman he was going to face.

The first hand against Kaminsky-Westheimer produced no fireworks at all. They bid one no trump and made two easy overtricks. Since the partnership at most other tables did the same, it was a push.

The second hand featured an excellent double, not by Kaminsky but by Peter:

NORTH (Weichsel)
♠ A 3 2
♥ A 10 7 3
♦ 10 9 7 4
♣ 4 2

WEST (Kaminsky)
♠ 10 9 6 5
♥ J 5 2
♦ K J 8 6 5
♣ J

EAST (Westheimer)
♠ Q 7
♥ Q 9 4
♦ 3 2
♣ A K Q 10 8 5

SOUTH (Sontag)
♠ K J 8 4
♥ K 8 6
♦ A Q
♣ 9 7 6 3

Both vulnerable. The bidding:

WEST	NORTH	EAST	SOUTH
	Pass	1 ♣	Pass
1 ♦	Pass	2 ♣	Pass
Pass	Double	3 ♣	Pass
Pass	Pass		

Peter's unusual double was beautifully reasoned. Kaminsky and Westheimer, aggressive bidders, were stopping at only two clubs. What kind of hands could they have? I had not bid, but Peter sensed there must be a reason: I had length in the club suit. His double asked me to bid two of a major, which he felt we might make. Of course, Westheimer bid three clubs. In fact, we might have made two of a major.

No way existed, however, for Westheimer to make three clubs. We cashed our top five tricks, for plus 100, worth about 70 IMPs. If Peter had permitted them to play two clubs, we would have lost 30 IMPs.

On the final hand Kaminsky got revenge. He held the following cards:

WEST (Kaminsky)
♠ A J 8 3
♥ A Q 4
♦ J 9 2
♣ Q 7 6

Amos opened the bidding in third chair with one diamond! This bid had the effect of keeping Peter and me out of the auction in a suit in which we could easily have taken ten tricks—diamonds. What made it more painful was that Kaminsky had a normal one-club opening bid, and his devious diamond stole the pot. Ultimately they bid and made four spades. Had we been in the auction, we would have taken an inexpensive save at five diamonds and gone down one. Or, perhaps, they would have gone to five spades, which we would have set.

The first session—ten opponents, thirty hands—was over. I wanted to keep going. I was not the least tired, and thought it was a terrible time for us to break. We had regained our rhythm after the nightmare against Kokish and Nagy. It was only 5 P.M. and the second session would not start until 8, plenty of time for us to lose that rhythm.

The results of the first session would not be posted until 7:30 and Peter and I decided not to torment ourselves by waiting for them. We would find out soon enough when we returned for the 8 P.M. session. It was impossible, however, not to replay each hand in our heads and try to guess what our standing would be.

We had slightly the best of Cayne and Eisenberg; we trounced Lebovic and McPhail; we did very well against Mittelman-Goldberg; we had the worst of it against the Cappellettis; we edged out Rubin and Bethe; we clearly defeated Rapee and Solodar; we crushed Blair and Levin; Nagy and Kokish humiliated us; we beat Berah and Vernon; and lost some ground against Kaminsky and Westheimer.

When we were out on the street I started to cough. My head was stuffy and lights were popping. I was afraid I was going to throw up on the sidewalk. The change from the fetid air of the Cavendish, even to New York City's air, was shocking. That, and the temporary release from pressure, much of it heaped on by myself, from saying over and over we had to win, had caught up with me. But part of my brain was still up in that card room.

"I figure about tenth place," I said to Peter between laughs

"Let's go," he said. "And don't worry. It could be better than we think."

It was. These were the leading five partnerships at the end of the first session:

POSITION	PARTNERSHIP	COUNTRY	IMPS
1.	Sharif-Yallouze	Egypt-France	634
2.	Bethe-Rubin	U.S.A.	591
3.	Wolff-Hooker	U.S.A.	559
4.	Weichsel-Sontag	U.S.A.	514
5.	Blau-Ginsberg	U.S.A.	457

Sharif and Yallouze won $3,000 for finishing first in the session. Rubin and Bethe received $2,000. Both Wolff-Hooker and Peter and I received $1,000 per partnership for finishing third and fourth.

We were higher than I had dared to hope. I was delighted, but not nearly so delighted as the French television producers who had come primarily to film Sharif and found him and his French partner, Yallouze, leading the pack. It had to be good for the ratings.

I did not know it at the time, but we would soon be playing Sharif and Yallouze under those bright white lights.

SESSION II

8

STARTING FRESH

BETWEEN THE FIRST AND SECOND SESSIONS PETER AND I walked from the Cavendish Club to my apartment on East 70th Street. After my coughing spell subsided, I decided I wanted to talk, make plans, whip ourselves into a high state of excitement so we would be up for the second session. At this time I did not believe we were as high in the standings as it turned out.

We bought hot dogs, potato salad, and Coke at a deli and took them up to the apartment. I launched into a pep talk about a new convention we might adopt for the second session. Peter rolled over and fell asleep. He had been listening, however.

"If we have to adopt new conventions in the middle of the Cavendish," he said the instant he woke up, "then we shouldn't be playing."

He was right. I remember reading about a boxer—I think he was fighting Joe Louis—who explained his loss by saying he had not trained hard enough. If we were not prepared for this event, the richest in bridge history, we would never be prepared to play in anything worthwhile.

We caught a cab back to the Cavendish, arriving about

7:45, were pleasantly astonished by our fourth place standing, and collected the guide card with our number on it that directed us to our seating assignments for the second session.

The Cavendish, more smoky than ever, was much more crowded for the night session than for the one that afternoon. It was Saturday night in New York and the publicity of Omar and the attraction of the world's finest players competing for big money made this a spectacle not to be missed. You could tell the stargazers from the connoisseurs by what tables they crowded around. Around Omar's table it was SRO, bright lights, smoke, noise, autograph hunters, but hardly a face an expert bridge player would recognize. The aficionados drew close to tables where the partnerships were Cayne-Eisenberg, Rubin-Hamilton, Hamman-Larsen. It was not that Omar lacked the skills of a great player (he was, after all, leading the event), but because the knowledgeable spectators wanted the hassle-free enjoyment of studying champions fighting it out.

The Cavendish was hot, sticky. We had to dodge clusters of people to reach our table. Waiting for us were two of the best players in bridge: the great Ira Rubin and his partner Fred Hamilton.

"Oh, *no*," said Peter.

"Just behave yourself," I said.

"That's not possible."

Peter and Ira Rubin do not like each other.

"That Ira Rubin is one of the most ill-mannered players in the game," Peter once told me.

"Your partner Weichsel," Rubin once confided, "doesn't know the meaning of manners at a bridge table."

I admit to a certain prejudice, but still have to side with Peter. In the bridge world Ira Rubin is called "The Beast." He even bears a slight resemblance to Frankenstein's monster. He is 6 feet 2, has dark, receding hair combed back, and dark eyes. He earned his nickname because of a volcanic temper and the abuse he portions out to partner and opponents alike. He rankles Peter, and vice versa, and they seem to take turns inviting each other outside to fight. Away from the table, each will admit the other is one of the best players in the world.

When things go poorly for Ira, he pounds the table and shouts. When things go well, he often converses with himself in baby talk. "Goony babooney," he will say, or "nixt noitchka," or he will squeal with delight, like a just-fed infant, and make faces. All this drives Peter crazy which, when I think about it, might be why Ira does it.

Ira Rubin is a *great* player. Usually he does not need luck, but he would be the last person to discount the role it can play. In 1974 in San Antonio he was playing in the fourth and last semifinal session of the Reisinger Board-o-Match National Team Championship. Only eleven teams would qualify for the finals. Going into the very last hand, Ira and Fred Hamilton had to win the board to qualify. They bid to six spades, missing the Q J 10 2 of trump. The rest of the hand was solid. One of their opponents made a poorly judged double and during the play Ira realized the only reason for the double was that their opponent held all four trump. This knowledge enabled Ira to make the contract. Without the double, Rubin and Hamilton would have gone down in six spades and would not have qualified for the finals.

Rubin and Hamilton won the Reisinger the next day and qualified for the National Team trials to select the United States representative for the Bermuda Bowl, the World Championship. They won the trials and played for the World Championship—which they also won—in Monte Carlo, defeating the great Italian Blue Team in the finals. None of it would have happened without that ill-conceived double in San Antonio.

Ira Rubin, forty-seven, has won just about everything there is in bridge: the Reisinger three times, the Vanderbilt twice, the Spingold three times, the Life Masters Pairs, the Blue Ribbon Pairs, the Open Pairs, and, of course, the World Championship.

Fred Hamilton, Rubin's partner, is called "Fast Freddie,"

and to meet him is to understand why. He has a mustache and goatee, is thin, sharp-featured, and wears dark glasses and a black leather jacket reminiscent of Marlon Brando and motorcycles and switchblades. In short, he is the ideal partner for the tumultuous Rubin.

Fred Hamilton loves to win, which also endears him to Rubin, and has an impressive list of accomplishments: second in the Vanderbilt in 1972, second in the Grand National in 1974, first in the Reisinger in 1974 and 1975, and that World Championship with Ira Rubin.

I felt something out of the ordinary would happen against Rubin and Hamilton, and it did on the very first hand:

NORTH (Rubin)
- ♠ 10 6
- ♥ J 10 8 2
- ♦ Q J 7 3
- ♣ K 10 8

WEST (Sontag)
- ♠ Q 7 5 3
- ♥ Q 7 4 3
- ♦ 8 6 2
- ♣ 5 3

EAST (Weichsel)
- ♠ J 9 4
- ♥ K 9 6 5
- ♦ 10 9
- ♣ J 9 6 4

SOUTH (Hamilton)
- ♠ A K 8 2
- ♥ A
- ♦ A K 5 4
- ♣ A Q 7 2

No one vulnerable. The bidding:

WEST	NORTH	EAST	SOUTH
	Pass	Pass	2 ♦
Pass	2 ♥	Pass	4 ♣
Pass	4 ♦	Pass	4 ♥
Pass	5 ♥	Pass	5 ♠
Pass	6 ♥	Pass	7 ♣
Pass	Pass	Pass	

South's opening bid was one of Ira's own inventions. He calls it a three-way two-bid and it can mean one of three things: a strong two-bid in the suit mentioned; a weak two-bid in the next highest suit; or an unspecified intermediate two-bid. Fred's second bid, of four clubs, confirmed an extremely strong 4-4-4-1 hand with an unspecified singleton ace.

After Fred's opening two-bid, Rubin had said "Alert!" which means the bid does not have its natural meaning, and the player calling "Alert!" will explain if the opponents desire.

"I don't want an explanation," I told Rubin.

He was disappointed. He is very proud of his three-way two-bid and was itching to explain it. I already knew what it meant, but that was not my reason for refusing an explanation. Rubin's invention is complicated and I did not want him *explaining it to Hamilton.* Perhaps they would have a misunderstanding.

And that is what happened. They arrived at a ludicrous seven-club contract that had virtually no chance. Fred's four-heart bid was intended to show the singleton ace, but Ira thought it showed a four-card suit. Fred's seven clubs was intended to leave the choice of the final contract to Ira, but Ira passed because he had no idea what Fred's bidding meant.

We took two trump tricks to defeat the contract for 100 points. This was the top score for the board and won us about 190 IMPs.

The best contract for Rubin and Hamilton would have been six diamonds, which is difficult to reach without a system such as Peter and I employ. This is the way we would have bid the hand:

NORTH (Sontag)

Pass

2 ♥—semi-automatic response

3 ♥—asks number of controls

4 no trump—asks for queens

5 ♥—any more queens?

6 ♦—ends auction

SOUTH (Weichsel)

2 ♦—either a weak two-bid in hearts or a strong 4-4-4-1 distribution with any singleton and 16 to 24 high-cards points

3 ♦—*exactly* 4-1-4-4 distribution and 20 or more points

4 ♥—10 controls

5 ♣—club queen

5 no trump—no

Pass

Plus 920!

Either way we would have scored a lot of IMPs on this hand. We could do it defending, or playing.

Peter and I did not know which to enjoy more: the big score we had made or the fight that was raging between Rubin and Hamilton.

"You numbskull," Rubin was saying. "How can you forget this convention?"

Fast Freddie was turning red and tugging on his goatee.

"You airhead," Rubin continued, "I gave you the notes to study."

Fast Freddie was gritting his teeth.

"Tell me, Fred, how can you be so stupid?"

"Just *shut up*, Ira," Hamilton hissed through clenched teeth.

"Lovely partnership," Peter said. He couldn't resist.

Rubin jerked his head toward Peter and started to come out of his chair. This scene had played before.

"Tell me it isn't true," Peter said. "You're not *the* Ira

Rubin and *the* Fred Hamilton, current World Champs?"

"Let's play the next hand," I said.

Somehow it was calmed down and we went on to the second hand. It had been a very untypical display; usually Peter is affable. Ira Rubin gets on his nerves.

The second hand was tranquil. We bid two spades and went down a trick, which is what happened to most partnerships playing in the same direction.

I could not believe what happened on the third hand. Ira's three-way two-bid struck again. Unfortunately, it once again struck him. He and Hamilton ended in a four-heart contract when they easily could have made six. It was another big score for us.

"You blundering dolt," Rubin began, but I steered Peter away before we could hear more.

Bridge is a strange game. Only three hands were played against Rubin and Hamilton in this supposedly sedate and civilized pastime, yet the competition and the interplay of personalities had been as intense as any Super Bowl or Stanley Cup playoff.

The personality of a bridge player is very important. I do not think a high-strung person could possibly succeed. Even if he could, his partner could not. With all their surface differences, Peter and Ira Rubin are probably very much alike. They can focus every cell of their working brains on the solution of a single problem to the exclusion of everything else. They can *concentrate*.

I think Ira Rubin, especially when he is complaining, does not hear himself. He is saying one thing and thinking another. I know for a fact such is the case with the great bridge teacher and theorist Al Roth, who has apologized to offended partners for remarks he has made during the heat of competition that he later cannot even remember. And Rubin's complaints serve a purpose, perhaps unintentionally: they often upset, distract, and infuriate opponents. Rubin himself remains unruffled because he is thinking about the next hand, not about what he is saying. The disadvantage is that his partner can become rattled, but this is usually not the case because Rubin's partners know how to live with him.

It was nice to get back to the normal world. We sat down to play Estee Griffin, one of the best women players in the United States, and Sergio Barbosa, who was on the winning Brazilian team in the 1976 Olympiad.

Peter likes Estee Griffin, almost everyone does, and he has frequently been her partner. Estee is a goodwill ambassador for bridge. As a representative of *The Bridge World* magazine she has reported on countless national and international championships. Often she has invited hungry bridge players (me and Peter included) to her apartment for a delicious home-cooked meal.

Sergio Barbosa is a Brazilian civil servant in the Ministry of Education. This was a combination business-pleasure trip for Barbosa. A few days earlier he had spoken before the Guatemalan Congress, and then had flown to New York for the Calcutta.

Peter and I did not know Barbosa so Estee introduced us. We did know he was a dangerous opponent. His victory in the 1976 Olympiad was achieved against teams from more than forty countries. The most important match of this Olympiad—between Brazil and Italy—was never consummated because of a seating foul-up: during the match, both Brazilian partnerships were sitting North-South. This will never happen again because of a suggestion made by Alan Truscott, bridge editor of *The New York Times.* In subsequent team matches, after half of the hands are played at one table, and before they are passed to the next table, a small card is filled out listing the name and direction of each player.

On the first hand Estee and Barbosa underestimated their values and played what would have been an ice-cold four-spade contract at two spades. Most other partnerships bid and made the four spades.

We used our Precision Diamond opening bid on the second hand:

NORTH (Weichsel)
- ♠ A K 6 4
- ♥ K
- ♦ J 10 3 2
- ♣ A 5 4 3

WEST (Barbosa)
- ♠ Q 10 9 2
- ♥ Q 10 6 4
- ♦ K 6 5
- ♣ Q 6

EAST (Griffin)
- ♠ 8 7 5
- ♥ J 9 5 3 2
- ♦ A 9 7
- ♣ J 2

SOUTH (Sontag)
- ♠ J 3
- ♥ A 8 7
- ♦ Q 8 4
- ♣ K 10 9 8 7

North-South vulnerable. The bidding:

WEST	NORTH	EAST	SOUTH
	1 ♦	Pass	1 no trump
Pass	2 ♣	Pass	2 ♥
Pass	3 no trump	Pass	Pass
Pass			

Peter's one-diamond opening bid was our catchall bid, and diamonds could be virtually any length, from one to many. My one no trump response showed 6 to 10 points and denied a four-card major. Peter bid two clubs because he knew from my response that I had a minimum of seven minor suit cards and therefore at least a four-card minor. My two-heart response indicated I had a strong fit with one of his minors, probably clubs, a maximum in high-card points, and something in hearts. He had the king so he knew I had the ace. His three no trump was well judged. He had spades controlled, we had two top winners in hearts, and he hoped our minor suit fit would produce sufficient tricks for game.

When Barbosa led the two of spades, we were able to take ten tricks: five clubs, two hearts, and three spades.

We had won almost 300 IMPs on the first two hands against Griffin and Barbosa. We had been lucky on the first hand when they made an error, but the second hand was successful because of solid bidding.

On the final hand we bid two hearts and went down a trick. Still, it had been a successful round.

Estee and Barbosa moved to another table. I leaned back to stretch and yawn and suddenly was jolted by a stampede of people and a psychedelic show. I went blind for a moment and almost panicked. Coming at us were white lights and half of New York.

"Omar," Peter said.

"Can't they tone down the lights?"

"You're going to be on television."

Out of the lights and the crowd came Omar, smoking a cigarette and smiling, and his partner Leon Yallouze, who seemed equally at ease amid the confusion. Hurrying technicians situated equipment all around the table, bathing it in light and raising the temperature twenty degrees. It would be like playing bridge in an operating room.

Omar was every inch the movie star. He wore a navy-blue suit, white shirt, and tie. I wondered how he managed to look so cool. What I wondered most was how he managed to grab the first session lead with so many people bustling around him and those television lights scorching his brain.

Omar Sharif is a bridge player of the first rank. He captained the Egyptian team in the 1968 Olympiad, was Egyptian National Champion in 1960, 1962, 1963, 1964, and won the International Bridge Press Association Sportsman of the Year award in 1974, an award I was voted in 1975.

Omar's greatest love is bridge. He cannot get enough of the game. When he is not playing it, he is writing about it. He is coauthor with Charles Goren of a nationally syndicated column.

Omar was smiling, friendly with everyone. I knew he loved the high stakes of the tournament, but that he had to wish

for some breathing space. "A cutthroat lot," Raymond Soko-
lov had called world-class bridge players, in *The New York
Times*, and those competing in the Calcutta had to appreciate
the added pressure the crowd and cameras put on Sharif.

The Albarran Club in Paris, one of the best and smartest
in Europe, is perhaps where Omar most likes to play. The
money stakes are high and the competition top caliber.

Whenever I am scheduled to play against Omar Sharif I
find myself the object of sudden bursts of popularity. People
I might not recognize on the street become good friends and
want to be introduced to Sharif. Even my family, which is
still not sure what I do for a living, claim to be bridge fans
when they hear I am going to play against Sharif. The night
before I had talked with my sister-in-law.

"Would you ask him to autograph a picture for me?" she
said.

"No, I won't," I said.

"Would you ask him for a trinket?"

"No."

"A lock of hair?"

"Look, Libby, this is madness."

"If you won't do it for me, won't you do it for the children?"

Sharif's partner, Leon Yallouze, is one of the great players
of Europe. He was a past winner of the *London Sunday Times*
tournament and a member of the famous Bridge Circus that
toured North America and Europe. The Bridge Circus played
an incredible 840-deal match against the Dallas Aces in 1970.
The Aces won, 1,793 IMPs to 1,692.

Yallouze, like Sharif, exhibited a remarkable composure
and was impeccably dressed.

It was hot and getting hotter, but Peter loved it. A camera-
man was right over his shoulder. Other people were snapping
pictures. I tried to ignore the commotion—it would only last
for three hands—and reminded myself that at last count this
partnership had been ahead of us.

Sharif and Yallouze use a club system patterned after one employed by the great Blue Team. It is quite different from what Peter and I use.

On the first hand Sharif and Yallouze bid an excellent three-club contract and made it. Nonetheless, we won a few IMPs on this hand because some aggressive South players bid spades once too often, were doubled, and went down a few tricks.

The second hand illustrated the effectiveness of our two-club opening bid:

NORTH (Weichsel)
♠ J 7
♥ K J 8
♦ 10 8
♣ A K J 8 7 5

WEST (Yallouze)
♠ K 10 3
♥ A 10
♦ 6 3 2
♣ 9 6 4 3 2

EAST (Sharif)
♠ Q 9 8 4
♥ Q 9 7 5 4 2
♦ Q 9 5
♣ Void

SOUTH (Sontag)
♠ A 6 5 2
♥ 6 3
♦ A K J 7 4
♣ Q 10

No one vulnerable. The bidding:

WEST	NORTH	EAST	SOUTH
Pass	2 ♣	Pass	2 ♦
Pass	2 ♠	Pass	3 ♦
Pass	3 ♥	Pass	3 no trump
Pass	Pass	Pass	

Peter's opening bid of two clubs showed at least a six-card club suit with 12 to 16 points. My two diamonds asked if he had a major suit and, if not, what other strength he possessed. His two-spade response revealed a minimum two-club bid with no four-card major and, 95 percent of the time, a stopper in only one suit other than clubs. My three diamonds asked him what the suit was. His three hearts told me. I now confidently bid three no trump.

We took eleven tricks and tied for top score with a number of other partnerships.

Once we actually started to play cards against Sharif and Yallouze, I did not even feel the heat from the television lights. I have read of many people during war, just before a major battle, who have completely lost themselves in a bridge game. Whatever worries an individual has can usually be forgotten over a good game of bridge.

On the final hand Sharif and Yallouze bid four hearts and made five. This seemed a normal result at the time, but when the hands were later analyzed we were in for a surprise. Several pairs had bid a very bad small slam in hearts that depended upon the king and one heart being in front of the ace. Since there were four hearts to the K 10 9 outstanding, the contract had only a 20 percent chance of success. Sharif and Yallouze won about 100 IMPs on this hand and had the best of us for the round.

It was our turn to switch tables. Everyone else, except for Peter's loyal parents, stayed to watch Omar and Leon.

We had finished the round early—Sharif and Yallouze are fast players—so there was time to visit the washroom and splash cold water on my face. I picked up some ice coffee in the kitchen and joined Peter at the next table.

Our next opponents were already there. Their combined ages were more than double Peter's and mine and, I realized ruefully, those extra years had been spent playing bridge and winning championships.

CHAPTER

ONE NO TRUMP OVER ONE CLUB

ONE CLUB—ONE NO TRUMP SEQUENCE

RESPONDER SHOULD BID ONE NO TRUMP OVER OPENER'S ONE club when he has a balanced hand and 9 to 14 high-card points. His hand pattern can be one of only three types: 4-3-3-3 distribution with the four cards in any suit; 4-4-3-2 with the long suits being unknown; and 5-3-3-2 with the five-card suit being a minor and headed at most by a jack. Opener will need more information.

ONE CLUB—ONE NO TRUMP— TWO CLUBS SEQUENCE

Opener's two clubs asks about distribution and point count.

OPENER	RESPONDER
1 ♣	1 no trump
2 ♣ (asks responder to define)	

Responder has nine possible bids:

1. Two Diamonds. Four hearts and 9 to a poor 12 high-card points.
2. Two Hearts. Four spades, denies four hearts, 9 to a poor 12 high-card points.
3. Two Spades. No four-card major and 9 to a poor 12 high-card points.
4. Two No Trump. Good 12 to 14 high-card points and exactly 4-3-3-3 distribution with any four-card suit.
5. Three Clubs. Good 12 to 14 high-card points, four clubs and 4-4-3-2 distribution, but second four-card suit is unknown.
6. Three Diamonds. Good 12 to 14 high-card points, four diamonds and four hearts.
7. Three Hearts. Good 12 to 14, four hearts and four spades.
8. Three Spades. Good 12 to 14, four diamonds and four spades.
9. Three No Trump. Good 12 to 14, 5-3-3-2 distribution, plus the long suit is a minor.

Some of these responses are more revealing than others. Opener may need additional information (he knows responder had to have at least one king for the original positive response in no trump), such as a more precise picture of distribution, number of controls, and number of honors in one or both of responder's suit.

OPENER	RESPONDER
1 ♣	1 no trump
2 ♣	2 ♦ (9 to a poor 12
2 ♥ (asks in hearts)	and four hearts)

Responder now has six choices:

1. Two Spades. No A, K, or Q in hearts.
2. Two No Trump. One of top three honors in hearts.
3. Three Clubs. One of top three honors in hearts plus the

jack. The jack, especially on 4-4 fits, could be a key card. If opener has K 8 3 2 in hearts and responder has Q 7 5 4 there is small likelihood of this suit playing for one loser. For this to happen, an opponent must have the ace doubleton and declarer still must guess which hand has it. If, however, responder has Q J 5 4, all declarer needs to keep the losses to one is a 3-2 break in hearts, almost a 68 percent probability.

4. Three Diamonds. Two of top three honors.
5. Three Hearts. Two of top three honors plus the jack.
6. Three Spades. All three top honors.

After opener has asked in hearts, he may still want to learn the number of responder's controls. He garners this information by making the next highest *suit* bid over responder's reply.

OPENER	RESPONDER
1 ♣	1 no trump
2 ♣	2 ♦
2 ♥	2 no trump (one high
3 ♣ (asks for controls)	heart honor)

Responder has five possible bids: the next highest response over opener's bid shows one king or one ace; the next highest shows two kings; next, three kings, or an ace and a king; next, four kings, or two aces, or an ace and two kings; and finally, two aces and a king.

The bidding has gone in this fashion:

OPENER	RESPONDER
1 ♣	1 no trump
2 ♣	2 ♦ (four hearts)
2 ♥ (asks hearts)	2 ♠ (no A, K, Q in hearts)
2 no trump (asks for another four-card suit) or three clubs (asks controls)	

Opener can only use the two no trump bid over the two-spade response to the heart ask. If opener at his third turn had wanted to find out if responder had a second four-card suit, he could have bid two no trump over the diamond response. Responder would then bid the other four-card suit if he has one, bid three no trump if he does not, and there is one exception: if responder rebids his four-card major he is showing three of the top four honors plus 4-3-3-3 distribution.

Frequently, when responder shows a second suit over the two no trump ask, opener will want more information about the suit. He obtains it by raising responder's second suit to the four level.

OPENER	RESPONDER
1 ♣	1 no trump
2 ♣	2 ♦
2 no trump (asks for second suit)	3 ♦ (four diamonds)
4 ♦ (asks in diamonds)	

Responder now replies in the same way (with six possible choices) as with the original trump ask in hearts.

There is only one other auction that regularly occurs after the one club, one no trump, two clubs, two diamonds sequence:

OPENER	RESPONDER
1 ♣	1 no trump
2 ♣	2 ♦
2 ♠ (a balanced hand, 19 or more high-card points, five spades)	

Responder should bid naturally. He raises with three spades, bids four spades with good trump, bids two no trump with a minimum and two spades, three no trump with a maximum and two spades and spread-out values, and three of a suit with concentrated values such as K Q and one, K Q and two, A Q and one, etc., in that suit. The remainder of this auction should be natural.

ONE CLUB—ONE NO TRUMP—TWO
CLUBS—TWO HEARTS SEQUENCE

Responder's two hearts shows 9 to a poor 12 points, denies four hearts, but shows four spades.

OPENER	RESPONDER
1 ♣	1 no trump
2 ♣	2 ♥
2 ♠ (asks in spades) or 2 no trump (asks distribution) or 3 hearts (shows five hearts, at least 19 points, and balanced hand)	

This sequence helped Peter and me to one of our greatest and most important victories. It helped qualify us, in one stroke, to play in New Orleans in 1978 for the World Championship in both the Open Pairs and the Open Teams. This was the hand:

NORTH (Weichsel)
♠ Void
♥ A K Q J 6
♦ A K 6 4
♣ A K 10 5

WEST
♠ 10 7 3
♥ 10 5 4 2
♦ J 9 8 2
♣ Q 9

EAST
♠ J 9 8 6 5 4
♥ 8 7
♦ Q
♣ J 4 3 2

SOUTH (Sontag)
♠ A K Q 2
♥ 9 3
♦ 10 7 5 3
♣ 8 7 6

Neither vulnerable. The bidding:

WEST	NORTH	EAST	SOUTH
	1 ♣	Pass	1 no trump
Pass	2 ♣	Pass	2 ♥
Pass	2 no trump	Pass	3 ♦
Pass	4 ♦	Pass	4 ♥
Pass	6 no trump	Pass	Pass
Pass			

Many pairs bid seven hearts with this hand, a grand slam that requires the queen and jack of diamonds to fall under the ace and king, a very unlikely occurrence. We would have easily bid the grand slam if I had possessed the diamond queen instead of the spade queen. This was one of the strongest hands Peter has ever picked up, and when I made a positive response to his one-club opening bid a grand slam did indeed seem likely.

Peter's two clubs asked for my distribution and high cards. My two hearts showed four spades and 9 to 12 high-card points. Peter bid two no trump to ask if I had another four-card suit and I named it by bidding diamonds. Peter's raise of diamonds asked about the suit. My four hearts denied the A, K, and Q. Peter unhappily settled for six no trump

He was happy several days later, however, when bridge experts were finished analyzing our performance in the tournament and on this hand. Alan Truscott wrote in *The Times* that "The New York partnership of Peter Weichsel and Alan Sontag added another title to its collection here last night by winning the life-masters-pair championship, thus strengthening their claim to be regarded as America's strongest pair."

Columnist Dick Kaplan, writing about the diagrammed hand, said almost the same thing: "The young, expert partnership of Alan Sontag and Peter Weichsel strengthened their claim as America's strongest pair by adding the coveted Life Masters Pairs crown to their many titles of the past few years at the American Contract Bridge League's recent Summer National Championships in Chicago."

There were other pairs who bid six no trump, but not all of them made it. Despite the overwhelming *appearance* of our two hands, six no trump was a difficult contract to make. The problem was getting to my hand to cash the spade tricks.

I won the opening heart lead in dummy with the ace and immediately cashed the ace of diamonds. When East played the queen I decided it was an honest card. Therefore, I reasoned, the diamond distribution was 4-1. I cashed three more heart tricks in dummy, discarding the two of spades and six of clubs from my hand. Next I cashed the A K of clubs and then led a low diamond from dummy which I ducked around to West. Whatever he now played I could win in my hand. A spade lead would be into my A K Q and a diamond would ride around to the protected ten.

The one club, one no trump, two clubs, two hearts auction is very similar to the one club, one no trump, two clubs, two diamonds sequence previously discussed. Over two spades, responder clarifies his spade holdings as follows:

1. Two No Trump. No A, K, or Q in spades.
2. Three Clubs. One of top three honors in spades.
3. Three Diamonds. One of top three honors plus the jack.
4. Three Hearts. Two of top three honors.
5. Three Spades. Two of top three honors plus the jack.
6. Three No Trump. All three top honors.

Opener now bids the next highest suit over responder's to ask responder to define his controls. Responder's next highest bid over opener's shows one king or one ace; the next highest, two kings; next, three kings, or an ace and a king; next, four kings, or two aces, or an ace and two kings; finally, two aces and a king.

When opener's bid in this auction is two no trump (asking for distribution), responder must bid another four-card suit if he has one, three no trump with no other four-card suit, or three spades with three of the top four honors and no other four-card suit.

Opener may ask for information about the second four-card suit (if responder has one) by raising it. Responder then shows honors in the suit by making the cheapest bid with no A, K, or Q; the next cheapest if he has one of the top three honors; next, one plus the jack; next, two of top three; next, two plus the jack; finally, the A K Q.

When opener's third bid in the auction is three hearts (showing five hearts, at least 19 points, and a balanced hand), responder bids naturally: three spades with good spades; three no trump with the doubleton heart; four hearts with three hearts; and four clubs or four diamonds with A or K Q in the suit and three hearts to an honor.

ONE CLUB—ONE NO TRUMP—TWO CLUBS—TWO SPADES SEQUENCE

Two spades shows 9 to a poor 12 points and no four-card major.

OPENER	RESPONDER
1 ♣	1 no trump
2 ♣	2 ♠
2 no trump (asks distribution)	

Responder has five possible bids:

1. Three Clubs. Shows 4-4 in the minors and 9 to 11 points. Over three clubs opener can bid three diamonds (an ask in diamonds), three hearts (asks major suit distribution), three spades (asks for controls), or four clubs (an ask in clubs). In answer to three diamonds or four clubs, responder shows honors as previously described. Opener can then ask for controls by bidding the next suit over the response. In answer to three hearts, responder bids three spades to show three of them, and three no trump to show three hearts. Opener can

now ask in either minor by bidding at the four level. Finally, in answer to three spades, responder uses the established method to show controls (cheapest possible bid to show one king or one ace, etc.). Incidentally, any time *opener* bids three no trump during auctions described in this chapter, responder must pass, and the same is true whenever opener raises responder's three-card major to game.

2. Three Diamonds. 4-3-3-3 distribution and the four-card suit is a minor. Opener bids three hearts to learn the minor suit with the length: responder's three spades shows clubs, and three no trump shows diamonds. If opener bids four of the minor responder has shown, he is asking in that suit. If he bids four of the other minor, he is asking for controls. If opener asks in the four-card minor, the next suit bid over responder's reply asks for controls. Four no trump by opener in any of these auctions must be passed.

3. Three Hearts. Shows exactly 2-3-4-4 distribution with 11 or 12 points and two small spades. Opener asks for controls by bidding three spades, four clubs or four diamonds are asks in those suits, and four hearts is to play.

4. Three Spades. 3-2-4-4 distribution with 11 or 12 points and a weak doubleton in hearts. Opener bids four clubs or four diamonds to ask in those suits, four hearts to ask about controls, and four spades to play.

5. Three No Trump. Shows a five-card minor headed by at most the jack and the remaining distribution is 3-3-2 with the doubleton unknown. Opener bids four clubs to learn which minor contains the five cards (four diamonds shows clubs, four hearts shows diamonds). When opener knows responder's suit, he can ask for controls by bidding four hearts (over four diamonds) or four spades (over four hearts).

ONE CLUB—ONE NO TRUMP—TWO CLUBS—TWO NO TRUMP SEQUENCE

Two no trump shows a good 12 to 14 points and exactly 4-3-3-3 distribution but the four-card suit is unknown.

OPENER	RESPONDER
1 ♣	1 no trump
2 ♣	2 no trump
3 ♣ (asks what four-card suit is)	

Responder bids diamonds to show diamonds, hearts to show hearts, spades to show spades, and no trump to show clubs.

If opener bids the next highest suit over responder's reply, he is asking for controls. If opener wants to ask for honors in responder's four-card suit, he skips over one suit.

OPENER	RESPONDER
1 ♣	1 no trump
2 ♣	2 no trump
3 ♣	3 ♥ (shows four hearts)
3 ♠ (asks for controls) or	
4 ♣ (asks in hearts)	

ONE CLUB—ONE NO TRUMP—TWO CLUBS—THREE CLUBS SEQUENCE

Three clubs shows a good 12 to 14 points, four clubs, 3-2-4-4 distribution and the second four-card suit is unknown.

OPENER	RESPONDER
1 ♣	1 no trump
2 ♣	3 ♣
3 ♦ (asks for second suit) or	
4 ♣ (asks in clubs)	

Over three diamonds, responder reveals his second four-card suit by bidding three hearts to show hearts, three spades to show spades, and three no trump to show diamonds.

Once responder's other four-card suit is known, opener can bid as follows:

OPENER	RESPONDER
1 ♣	1 no trump
2 ♣	3 ♣
3 ♦ (asks for second suit)	3 ♥ (hearts)
3 ♠ (asks controls) or 4 ♣ (asks in clubs) or 4 ♦ (asks in hearts) or 4 ♥ (to play)	

OPENER	RESPONDER
1 ♣	1 no trump
2 ♣	3 ♣
3 ♦	3 ♠ (spades)
4 ♣ (asks in clubs) or 4 ♦ (asks controls) or 4 ♥ (asks in spades) or 4 ♠ (to play)	

OPENER	RESPONDER
1 ♣	1 no trump
2 ♣	3 ♣
3 ♦	3 no trump (diamonds)
4 ♣ (asks in clubs) or 4 ♦ (asks in diamonds) or 4 ♥ (asks controls)	

ONE CLUB—ONE NO TRUMP—TWO CLUBS—THREE DIAMONDS SEQUENCE

Three diamonds shows a good 12 to 14 points, four diamonds and four hearts.

OPENER	RESPONDER
1 ♣	1 no trump
2 ♣	3 ♦
3 ♥ (asks in hearts) or	
3 ♠ (asks for controls) or	
4 ♦ (asks in diamonds)	

If opener asks in one of responder's suits, and then bids the next highest suit (excluding no trump or responder's major), he is asking for controls.

ONE CLUB—ONE NO TRUMP—TWO CLUBS—THREE HEARTS SEQUENCE

Three hearts shows a good 12 to 14 points, four hearts and four spades.

OPENER	RESPONDER
1 ♣	1 no trump
2 ♣	3 ♥
3 ♠ (asks in spades) or	
4 ♣ (asks for controls) or	
4 ♦ (asks in hearts)	

If opener first asks in spades, his next bid at the four level (except four of a major, which is to play) is a control ask. Then, after asking for controls, the cheapest minor suit bid at the five level asks in hearts.

If opener first asks in hearts, his next new suit bid other than four of a major is also a control ask. After this sequence, too much room would probably have been used to ask in the other suit. When opener wants to ask responder several questions, he should choose the most economical sequence available. Planning the auction is as important as remembering the asking bids and their responses.

If opener first asks for controls (by bidding four clubs), his next bid of four of a major is to play. In this sequence, opener can no longer ask in responder's suits after a control ask.

ONE CLUB—ONE NO TRUMP—TWO CLUBS—THREE SPADES SEQUENCE

Three spades shows a good 12 to 14 points, four spades and four diamonds.

OPENER	RESPONDER
1 ♣	1 no trump
2 ♣	3 ♠
4 ♣ (asks for controls) or	
4 ♦ (asks in diamonds) or	
4 ♥ (asks in spades)	

When opener first asks for controls and then bids four spades, four no trump, or five diamonds, they are to play. However, five clubs would ask in diamonds and five hearts in spades. Again, extreme caution must be used. The bidding is at the five level and questions are still being asked.

When opener first asks in diamonds, the first suit bid other than spades or diamonds by opener would ask for controls. If there is any room, the next suit bid other than spades or diamonds would ask in spades.

If opener first asks in spades, the next suit bid other than spades or diamonds is a control ask. There is probably no room left after this to ask in the second suit. Whenever opener bids either of responder's suits at the game level, or three or four no trump, he wants responder to pass except for one unusual auction: if opener has asked in one of responder's suits and for controls, asking in the second suit might drive the hand prematurely to the slam level—in this case, opener would sign off in responder's second suit at the five level, and responder would have to judge whether to go on to slam. Here is an example:

OPENER	RESPONDER
♠ K 9 8 6	♠ Q J 7 5
♥ A 5	♥ K 9
♦ A K J	♦ Q 10 8 6
♣ K Q 4 2	♣ A J 10

OPENER	RESPONDER
1 ♣	1 no trump
2 ♣	3 ♠
4 ♣ (asks controls)	4 ♠ (3 controls)
5 ♣ (asks in diamonds)	5 ♥ (one honor)
5 ♠ ("Signs off")	6 ♠

Six spades in this instance was well judged by responder. His Q J of spades is very strong opposite either honor in opener's hand. There should be no more than one loser in the trump suit. The jack of spades is the key card.

ONE CLUB—ONE NO TRUMP—TWO CLUBS—THREE NO TRUMP SEQUENCE

Three no trump shows a good 12 to 14 points, 5-3-3-2 distribution, and the long suit is a minor.

OPENER	RESPONDER
1 ♣	1 no trump
2 ♣	3 no trump
4 ♣ (asks what minor suit is)	

Responder bids four diamonds to show five diamonds headed by at most the jack, or four hearts to show five clubs headed by at most the jack. After opener knows responder's suit, he can ask for controls by bidding the next free suit over the response.

This completely covers the one club, one no trump, two clubs sequence, an extremely important sequence because of the frequency with which it arises. The sequence is especially helpful in reaching intelligent slams, because of the detailed information opener can elicit from responder. Most important, it is a *scientific* sequence, and science is increasingly what the game is all about. But science does not preclude art, and great bridge bidding is art.

In the 1950s and 1960s, Al Roth and Tobias Stone were probably the most scientific partnership in America. They pioneered a system that was miles ahead of everything else and it took the bridge world by storm. Players using the Roth-Stone system, especially Roth and Stone, were unstoppable at major tournaments.

But bridge evolves. In 1970 Roth and Stone were still using

their system when in the semifinals of the Spingold they ran up against an unknown group of young players employing a new and obscure system called Precision Club. Here is a hand played in that semifinal match by Roth and Stone in one room and by Peter Weichsel and Tom Smith in another:

NORTH	SOUTH
♠ A K 6 2	♠ J 10 9 7 3
♥ A 5	♥ Q 9 2
♦ Void	♦ A Q 7
♣ K Q 8 7 5 4 2	♣ 10 3

ROTH	STONE
1 ♣	1 ♠
2 ♥	3 no trump
4 ♠	5 ♦
6 ♠	Pass

WEICHSEL	SMITH
1 ♣	1 ♠
2 ♠	2 no trump
3 ♣	3 ♥
4 ♠	Pass

Both partnerships took exactly ten tricks. Although the clubs broke 2-2, the spade queen was protected in the East hand. After a heart lead, declarer could not get to his hand to discard his losing heart on the ace of diamonds. Although it was unlucky to take only ten tricks, slam was an extremely bad proposition.

Weichsel and Smith reached the optimum contract because of a scientific investigation of the partnership's assets. Weichsel's two spades asked in spades and Smith's two no trump showed a five-card suit without the A, K, or Q. Three clubs by Peter asked in clubs and the reply showed a queen or a doubleton; obviously, Peter knew it was a doubleton. Peter knew they were missing the ace of clubs and the queen of spades and therefore that slam was a poor proposition.

When this auction occurred, the no trump response over

the two spades ask showed a five-card suit with no A, K, or Q. Peter and I now play that such a response could show five or six cards with no A, K, or Q.

Roth and Stone's auction never uncovered the really important information: the ace of clubs and the queen of spades. They used up a lot of room without accomplishing much. On the other hand, when the bidding was at only three hearts Peter knew he was not going to slam.

The Precision Team defeated the Roth-Stone Team and went on to capture the Spingold.

There are several other one club, one no trump sequences that need to be discussed.

ONE CLUB—ONE NO TRUMP—TWO OF A NEW SUIT SEQUENCE

This sequence occurs less frequently (about 20 percent of the time) than one club, one no trump, two clubs.

OPENER	RESPONDER
1 ♣	1 no trump
2 ♦, 2 ♥, 2 ♠, or 2 no trump	

When opener has a balanced hand (with two exceptions) he will bid two clubs over one no trump to begin the process of learning about responder's hand. The first exception is when opener has a 4-3-3-3 hand and 18 to 20 high-card points. With this hand he will bid three no trump because his balanced distribution makes slam an unlikely possibility. Of course, with 13 or 14 points responder may keep the bidding alive. The second exception is when opener has a minimum one-club bid (16 to 18 points, a balanced hand with a five-card major). Slam is extremely unlikely so opener's responsibility is to look for the best game, either four of a major or three no trump. Thus, he would bid his five-card major at the two level and responder would clarify his controls and his support for the major.

However, when the bidding goes one club—one no trump and opener has an unbalanced hand, he should bid his suit at the two level: two diamonds would show diamonds, two hearts would show hearts, two spades would show spades, and two no trump would show clubs. Responder has only five possible answers to these new suit bids:

1. The cheapest bid (including no trump) over opener's new suit bid shows less than 4 controls and less than queen and two others in opener's long suit.

2. The next cheapest bid shows 4 or more controls and less than queen and two others in opener's long suit.

3. The next cheapest bid shows at least queen and two others in opener's long suit and less than 4 controls.

4. The next cheapest bid shows 4 or more controls and at least the queen and two others in opener's long suit.

5. The next cheapest bid shows 4 or more controls and four-card support to at most the jack in opener's long suit.

When opener makes Bids #3, 4, or 5, three no trump by opener asks for the number of controls.

OPENER	RESPONDER
1 ♣	1 no trump
2 ♥ (five or more hearts)	3 ♣ (at least the queen and two other hearts and less than 4 controls)
3 no trump (asks for controls)	4 ♣ (one king or one ace) or 4 ♦ (two kings) or 4 ♥ (3 controls)

When responder makes Bids #4 or 5, four clubs over opener's control ask would show 4 controls and each bid above four clubs would show an additional control.

If, instead of bidding three no trump, opener bids a new suit or rebids his long suit, it is a natural bid and the auction should proceed naturally.

ONE CLUB—ONE NO TRUMP—THREE OF A NEW SUIT SEQUENCE

Three of a new suit by opener shows six or seven cards to the A K Q and a singleton or void. This suit will be trump!

OPENER	RESPONDER
1 ♣	1 no trump
3 ♣, 3 ♦, 3 ♥, 3 ♠	

Responder should bid where his high cards are, not necessarily his four-card suit or suits. Three no trump by responder would deny any aces and show honors in each of the three unbid suits.

Any new suit bid by opener after his jump is a cue bid showing first or second round control and invites responder to cue bid in return.

OPENER	RESPONDER
1 ♣	1 no trump
3 ♦ (six or seven cards to the A K Q and a singleton or void)	3 ♥ (A or K)
3 ♠ (A or K, invites cue bid)	

ONE CLUB—TWO NO TRUMP SEQUENCE

Two no trump shows 15 or more high-card points, a balanced hand, and no five-card suit.

OPENER	RESPONDER
1 ♣	2 no trump

Opener has six possible bids:

1. Three Clubs. Asks responder to name cheapest four-

card suit. Three diamonds by responder shows four diamonds and perhaps any other four-card suit. Three hearts shows four hearts and perhaps four spades or clubs, but not diamonds. Three spades shows four spades and perhaps four clubs but denies four diamonds or four hearts. Three no trump shows four clubs and no other four-card suit. When a fit has been found, that is, when opener or responder has raised partner's suit, the next highest bid by responder or opener asks for controls. The cheapest response after this shows 3 controls, and it goes up one control for each higher bid. It is extremely rare for the bidding to start one club, two no trump, and not reach a slam. This sequence forces to at least five of a suit or five no trump. After the fit has been found, opener may only be interested in learning about aces. He should bid Blackwood.

2. Three Diamonds. Natural, five or six diamonds, asks responder to define controls and support for diamonds. Responder has five possible bids, the cheapest (three hearts) showing less than 4 controls and less than queen and two others in diamonds, the next cheapest (three spades) showing 4 or more controls and less than queen and two others in diamonds, the next cheapest, less than 4 controls and good support, the next 4 or more controls and good support, and finally the last which shows 4 or more controls and 4 diamonds to at most the jack.

3. Three Hearts. Shows hearts and bidding proceeds the same as if the bid had been three diamonds.

4. Three Spades. Shows spades and again bidding is the same as with three diamonds.

5. Three No Trump. Shows 4-3-3-3 distribution and 18 or 19 high-card points. Responder bids four clubs to learn opener's four-card suit. With exactly the same distribution, but 20 to 21 points, opener would bid four no trump instead of three no trump, and responder would bid five clubs to ask for the four-card suit.

6. Four Clubs. Shows clubs and bidding is the same as with three diamonds.

ONE CLUB—UNUSUAL POSITIVE
RESPONSE SEQUENCE

The unusual positive response shows 4-4-4-1 distribution, 9 or more high-card points, at least one king, and the singleton in the suit just above the one bid.

OPENER	RESPONDER
1 ♣	2 ♥ (1-4-4-4 distribution)
	or 2 ♠ (4-4-4-1) or 3 ♣
	(4-4-1-4) or 3 ♦ (4-1-4-4)

Opener, when he has a 4-4 fit with responder, would usually bid responder's singleton to ask for controls. The cheapest bid responder could then make would show one king or one ace, the next cheapest would show two kings, the next cheapest would show 3 controls, etc.

OPENER	RESPONDER
1 ♣	2 ♠
3 ♣ (asks for controls)	3 ♠ (3 controls)
4 ♣ (asks for queens)	

A further cue bid by opener after the control ask is a queen ask. Responder bids no trump with no queens. Responder raises the asking bid with three queens (the queen in the singleton does not count). With one or two queens, responder bids the suit that contains the lowest queen. If opener wants to learn if there are two queens, a further cue bid or the cheapest no trump is a second queen ask. Responder shows the other queen by bidding the suit it is in, or denies the queen by bidding the lowest possible no trump or the singleton.

Responder should never include a singleton king in the replies to a control ask.

There is one exception when opener uses four no trump

as the queen ask instead of responder's singleton, and it occurs when responder shows 5 or more controls:

OPENER	RESPONDER
1 ♣	3 ♣ (4-4-1-4)
3 ♦ (asks for controls)	4 ♦ (5 controls)
4 no trump (queen ask)	

Responder shows no queens by bidding five diamonds. After the control ask and the queen ask, opener should be able to place the final contract with complete confidence.

ONE CLUB—SOLID SUIT TRANSFER RESPONSE SEQUENCE

The solid suit transfer is used when responder has an excellent suit of his own over opener's one club.

OPENER	RESPONDER
1 ♣	3 ♥, 3 ♠, 3 no trump, or 4 ♣

Responder's bids have the following meanings:

1. Three Hearts. Any six-card suit headed by the A K Q J. There may be additional strength.

2. Three Spades. Any seven-card suit headed by the A K Q with no outside A or K.

3. Three No Trump. Any seven-card suit headed by the A K Q with at least one outside A or K.

4. Four Clubs. Any eight-card suit headed by the A K Q and the outside strength is unknown to opener.

Three no trump by opener over three hearts or three spades is to play. Over one club, three hearts, responder will cue bid an outside A or K over three no trump. Over one club, three spades, responder will cue bid any outside void or singleton at the four level over opener's three no trump.

Opener almost always knows immediately what responder's strong suit is. Over three hearts, three spades, or three no trump, a bid of four clubs by opener shows he knows the suit and asks responder to cue bid an A or K if he has one. If responder bid three spades over one club (showing no outside A or K), opener's four clubs would ask responder to show a singleton or void. Responder could deny a void or singleton by bidding his original suit.

OPENER	RESPONDER
1 ♣	3 ♥ (six-card suit headed by A K Q J and possible additional strength)
4 ♣ (asks for outside A or K)	4 ♠ (responder's strong suit, denies A or K) or 4 ♦ or 4 ♥ or 5 ♣ (shows A or K in suit)

If responder has shown an ace or king, four no trump by opener asks which it is: five clubs shows the king, five diamonds shows the ace. If responder has shown a singleton or void, four no trump asks which it is: five clubs shows a singleton, five diamonds shows a void.

When responder has denied an outside ace or king, a new suit bid by opener (except for responder's solid suit) is an asking bid in that suit.

OPENER	RESPONDER
1 ♣	3 ♥
4 ♣	4 ♥ (the solid suit, no
4 ♠ (asks in spades)	outside A or K)

Responder may make one of three bids: the cheapest, including no trump, shows no first or second round control; the next cheapest shows a singleton; the next cheapest shows a void.

On rare occasions opener will not know responder's solid suit. Over the three hearts, three spades, and three no trump responses, four diamonds by opener asks for the solid suit and responder should bid it.

Four hearts by opener over responder's four clubs tells responder that his solid suit is unknown.

When four clubs is bid over opener's one club, opener bids four diamonds to show he knows responder's solid suit and also asks responder to bid an ace or a king.

Four of a major over three hearts, three spades, or three no trump is a natural bid by opener and asks responder to pass.

Except for the one club, two of a minor sequence (to be covered in the next instruction chapter), readers have a complete picture of the entire Weichsel-Sontag one-club structure, the essence and lifeblood of the system.

CHAPTER

10

BLAZING ALONG

HOWARD SCHENKEN WAS ONCE CONSIDERED THE BEST BRIDGE player in the world. Certainly he is one of the best four or five who ever played. He set records which perhaps never will be beaten: he won the Vanderbilt ten times, the Spingold ten times, the Life Masters Pairs five times (all of these are records), and he was on the team that captured the first official World Championship in 1935.

Schenken could very easily have won the Vanderbilt *eleven* times. In 1951 in Chicago he decided to miss the preliminary rounds of the tournament and leave their success in the hands of his teammates: John Crawford, B. Jay Becker, George Rapee, and Sam Stayman. Schenken intended to compete in the semifinals but when they rolled around all other top teams were eliminated and his presence was not needed. He was not listed, therefore, as a member of the championship team.

In 1933 Schenken was on this country's first truly great team, the Four Aces: others were Oswald Jacoby, David Burnstine, and Richard Frey.

Late in 1935 Schenken was on a team that faced a group of French players who had won the European Championship.

The finals were promoted by Mike Jacobs and held at Madison Square Garden. It was quite an extravaganza. For the benefit of spectators, 52 men stood on a stage, each holding a six-foot playing card. When a trick was played, the four men holding the appropriate cards would step forward, place their cards facedown on the floor, and leave the stage. It was similar to playing chess with real people.

Being an expert in bridge gives a player one major advantage possessed by competitors in very few other sports. Unlike football, baseball, tennis, and golf players, a bridge expert is not washed up when he reaches age thirty-five or forty. Howard Schenken is seventy-four and still competes successfully at the very highest level of the game. He and his wife, Bee, have made a standing offer that they will accept a challenge match against any married couple in the country.

Schenken and his partner Peter Leventritt were our fourth opponents of the second session and our fourteenth of the Calcutta. When we had finished playing them we would have completed 42 of the 117 hands of the Calcutta.

"Who's this?" I joked to Schenken, nodding toward Peter Leventritt. "You've come down in the world. Won't good players be your partner any more?" The year before Howard had played in the Calcutta with his wife, Bee.

"Haven't you met Mr. Leventritt?" Schenken said. "He's just taken up the game." Actually Leventritt, sixty-one, one of the country's top players, had competed in the World Championship when I was in second grade.

Bridge is wonderful for older players like Howard Schenken who remain perpetually young by consistently trouncing new generations of upstarts, but it is even better for the young. What baseball star today can say he played against Ty Cobb, or Babe Ruth, or even Joe DiMaggio? Yet Howard Schenken, Oswald Jacoby, and Baron Waldemar von Zedtwitz, who date from the inception of contract bridge, are the Cobbs and Ruths and DiMaggios of the game. And still going strong.

Schenken is over 6 feet tall and has twinkling blue eyes. He wears reading glasses that fall down on his nose, giving an absentminded professor impression. Schenken is never critical of his partner or his opponents.

Peter Leventritt is also over 6 feet, but huskier. He is an outstanding bridge teacher and lecturer, a past president of the ACBL, and a co-founder of the prestigious New York Card School. Leventritt chain-smokes cigarettes, one of several nervous mannerisms he displays at the table. He is a witty raconteur and one of Howard Schenken's favorite partners for many years.

The first hand against Schenken and Leventritt increased my confidence that we would be in the running for top money from start to finish:

NORTH (Weichsel)
♠ Q J 5 3 2
♥ A 7 6
♦ 9 8 3
♣ 9 2

WEST (Leventritt)
♠ 10 6 4
♥ J 8 5
♦ Q 6 2
♣ A 8 7 6

EAST (Schenken)
♠ A K 8
♥ Q 10 4 2
♦ A K 7 4
♣ Q 10

SOUTH (Sontag)
♠ 9 7
♥ K 9 3
♦ J 10 5
♣ K J 5 4 3

Both sides vulnerable. The bidding:

WEST	NORTH	EAST	SOUTH
		1 no trump	Pass
Pass	Pass		

I made the normal lead of the fourth best club and Howard had no trouble taking ten tricks. It was a victory for us because they had contracted for only seven tricks.

Most experts agree that 25 high-card points are sufficient for a three no trump contract. Leventritt and Schenken were playing 16 to 18 high-card points as necessary for an opening no trump bid. Leventritt did not think his 7 points would produce a game, unless Howard had the absolute maximum, and he was unwilling to risk the slight chance of this possibility existing. It was much more likely, he felt, that they would arrive at two no trump and go down. That was why he passed and he did nothing wrong.

On this hand, had we held their cards, we would have reached the three no trump game. Peter, with Schenken's cards, would have opened one club; I would have responded one diamond; Peter's one no trump rebid would show 18 or 19 high-card points; and I would automatically bid three no trump with my 7 points.

Schenken and Leventritt failed to bid a borderline small slam in hearts on the second hand that had a 52½ percent chance. A few pairs did bid the slam and made it, so we picked up a few more IMPs.

On the last hand Howard opened the bidding with one heart in third seat and I held the following cards:

SOUTH (Sontag)

♠ 8 2

♥ A Q 9 8

♦ A K Q J 9 7 2

♣ Void

I overcalled five diamonds and made six. Peter had the K Q of spades and, incredibly, the J 10 3 of hearts, I can think of no sensible way of arriving at the slam contract, and no partnership bid it.

Schenken and Leventritt moved on to another table. Following the guide instructions, we switched from the North-South seats to East-West. I drummed my fingers against the table. I was eager to play, to keep going. In fact, I was making a mistake Howard Schenken himself had once written against:

"Bridge is a highly emotional game. It is also a game that should be played completely devoid of emotion."

Irving Rose of London, England, came bubbling over to the table, accompanied by his English partner, Maurice Esterson. "Gas Meter!" he greeted Peter, because Rose is Cockney and the two words rhyme. I suppose it makes sense.

"And Gallon!" He flashed a big toothy grin. "A Gallon of Gas!"

If he expected us to applaud he was wrong.

"How are you, Irving?" I asked.

"Not well, old chap. Maurice and I can't seem to get untracked."

"That's tough," I said.

"Worse than bloody tough. I bet on myself."

During the auction Rose and Esterson had sold for the considerable sum of $6,500. In the previous year's Calcutta Rose and his partner had been in first place going into the final session, before ultimately finishing eighth. That had been his first visit to the United States, and many people believed he would do much better this year.

Rose, thirty-nine, is a delightful rascal, one of the most colorful characters in the game. He manages a London bridge club called The Eccentric. I was playing against him in a 1974 backgammon tournament in Brussels at the Sheraton Hotel and I was leading the event when the lights went out. "I guess that cancels out what went before," Rose said. "We'll have to start the whole tournament over tomorrow."

He started to get up to leave.

"Hold on," I said. I lit a match and held it over the board. "Let's finish the game."

"Love to. You know that. But I just can't see."

Actually, he could see just fine. I was about to gammon him and he knew it.

"Have a heart," I said. "I'll get some candles."

"What's your American phrase? Game canceled because of darkness?"

"That's only in baseball."

"Seems pretty apt here."

"I told you. I'll get candles. Just sit tight."

"I'm allergic to candles. I think I inherited the allergy from—"

"I don't want to hear it, Irving. Be a good sport and play out the game."

Irving had no intention of adopting my idea of sportsmanship. He was on his way out of the room when the lights came back on. "Bloody bad luck!" he grumped.

Irving is impish, street smart, looks like Howdy Doody. He is an excellent gambler, popular with women, and very dangerous at bridge because he is unpredictable and follows his hunches, which are usually right. One of his bold bids almost cost me the 1973 *London Sunday Times* championship.

Maurice Esterson, Irving's partner, looks like the accountant he is. He is short and balding, wears glasses, and was well-dressed in a conservative, tailored blue suit. He is a man who would take pride in precise bidding.

Often Irving's bold style works. Other times, such as the first hand we played against him and Esterson in the Calcutta, it does not:

NORTH (Rose)
- ♠ K 8 5 4
- ♥ K Q 10 8
- ♦ K 7 5
- ♣ J 8

WEST (Sontag)
- ♠ Q J 7
- ♥ 7 4 2
- ♦ J 10 8 6 2
- ♣ Q 3

EAST (Weichsel)
- ♠ A 9 6
- ♥ J 9 6 5 3
- ♦ Void
- ♣ 10 9 7 6 2

SOUTH (Esterson)
- ♠ 10 3 2
- ♥ A
- ♦ A Q 9 4 3
- ♣ A K 5 4

Both sides vulnerable. The bidding:

WEST	NORTH	EAST	SOUTH
	1 ♥	Pass	2 ♦
Pass	2 no trump	Pass	3 ♣
Pass	3 no trump	Pass	4 no trump
Pass	Pass	Pass	

Irving's optimistic one-heart opening bid has little to recommend it. Peter and I often open the bidding light, but not with an aceless 12 high-card points and a balanced hand vulnerable. As it was, Rose caught his partner with a very good hand and the bidding took on a life of its own. Irving's two and three no trump bids were meant to discourage but Esterson, with 17 high-card points and three aces, was not easily deterred. He went to four no trump in a final slam try. Because of the unlucky diamond distribution, four no trump was one level too high.

There are four contracts all bridge players should try to avoid: four no trump, five no trump, five hearts, and five spades. One player, Jeff Westheimer, used to warn his partners that if they ever played five no trump and went down, he would fine them $100.

Peter and I won about 150 IMPs on the first hand against Rose and Esterson. It was difficult not to feel good. This had been a hand we could not have lost, no matter which direction we were sitting. Had we held the Rose-Esterson cards, we would have bid as follows:

NORTH (Weichsel)
Pass—the key to the auction. Peter has less than an opening bid.

SOUTH (Sontag)
1 ♣

1 no trump—9 to 12 high-card points, no good five-card suit.

2 ♣—asks Peter to define his hand in terms of points and distribution.

3 ♥—shows 4 ♠, 4 ♥, and 12 points.

3 no trump—this is where I want to play the hand. Since Peter's length and strength is in the majors, it is unlikely we have a minor suit slam.

On the second hand we bid a simple one no trump and made it. Rose and Esterson bid a vulnerable game in hearts on the third hand and took an overtrick.

We had scored well, but Rose was in good spirits. "What do you say, Gas and Gal," he asked, "how about showing me New York tonight?"

"Tomorrow night," Peter said.

"I don't blame you," he said, showing an infrequent serious side. "It would be jolly something if you won again."

Kit Woolsey and Steve Robinson, "The Little People," were our sixteenth opponents of the Calcutta. Robinson is about 5 feet 2; Woolsey perhaps 5 feet 5. But bridge is a game where size matters not a whit. Brains do.

We had reason to respect this partnership. Together they had won the Blue Ribbon Pairs in 1973 and 1975. Robinson was a former Reisinger champion and had won the World Olympiad Mixed Team-of-Four in 1974. In 1977 Robinson and Woolsey had the heartbreaking experience of losing in the finals of the Grand National by one IMP.

It is always desirable to be cordial with a partner, but Woolsey and Robinson may have carried the notion too far. Woolsey and his wife were divorced, and Robinson married the former Mrs. Woolsey. In addition, Robinson often plays on a team with a woman who has been married five times. Usually two of her ex-husbands are on the team with her and Robinson.

Steve Robinson, thirty-six, is from Alexandria, Virginia, and Kit Woolsey, thirty-four, is from Arlington. Like many bridge players, they work in the computer industry.

Al Roth thinks a great deal of Woolsey and Robinson as a partnership. He bet me ten dollars on the side, before the Calcutta began, that they would finish ahead of Peter and me.

Everyone admires Roth's judgment, so this had to be a blow to the ego.

"I want to finish ahead of these guys," I told Peter, "more than I want to win the tournament."

"Win the tournament," he said reasonably, "and you're sure to finish ahead of them."

Woolsey and Robinson wisely stayed away from an iffy slam contract on the first hand, contracting for four hearts and making five.

They were less enlightened on the second hand. Because of fierce competitive bidding on our part, they missed a lay-down grand slam in hearts that would have been easy to reach if we had stayed out of the auction.

Although only a part-score, the third hand was the most interesting of the round:

NORTH (Weichsel)
- ♠ K 5 3
- ♥ A 8 7 2
- ♦ Q 8 5
- ♣ K 9 7

WEST (Woolsey)
- ♠ A 10 9 7 4 2
- ♥ K 3
- ♦ 9 7
- ♣ Q 10 5

EAST (Robinson)
- ♠ Q J 8 6
- ♥ Q 9 6 4
- ♦ A J 10
- ♣ 8 3

SOUTH (Sontag)
- ♠ Void
- ♥ J 10 5
- ♦ K 6 4 3 2
- ♣ A J 6 4 2

North-South vulnerable. The bidding:

WEST	NORTH	EAST	SOUTH
		Pass	Pass
2 ♠	Pass	Pass	2 no trump
Pass	3 ♣	3 ♠	Pass
Pass	Pass		

My void in spades made it attractive to reopen the bidding. The choice was between doubling or going to two no trump. If I had not been a passed hand, I would have been forced to double because two no trump would have shown a strong hand with a stopper in spades. I elected to bid two no trump for two reasons: first, I was not eager to defend two spades doubled; second, I wanted Peter to bid one of my five-card suits. Two no trump asked Peter to bid a minor. In addition, when Robinson passed the two-spade opening bid, he "hitched," meaning that he hesitated. This indicated to me he had a spade fit and would not allow us to buy the hand at the three level.

We would have made three clubs. They could not make three spades. We scored about 80 IMPs on this hand.

I felt we had to be ahead in the standings. But we had been ahead before and blown it against Kokish and Nagy. Walking to the next table I thought about how losing was more painful than winning was fun, and about how long Peter and I had worked at this game. Others had worked longer, I knew, but that realization could not drive out what was hammering at my brain: if you make a stupid play and lose this tournament, you are *pathetic*.

CHAPTER

11

TWO OF A MINOR OVER
ONE CLUB

ONE CLUB—TWO OF A MINOR SEQUENCE

RESPONDER SHOULD BID TWO CLUBS OVER THE ONE-CLUB
opening when he has five or more clubs, 9 or more points,
and clubs is his longest suit.

OPENER	RESPONDER
1 ♣	2 ♣

Because of the many possible distributions and high-card
point totals responder could have, it is important for opener
to find out what he has. In original Precision Club systems,
garnering this information was a hit-and-miss affair charac-
terized by misunderstandings and poor contracts. Along came
the great Italian players, Garozzo and Belladonna, and they

developed a system called Super-Precision which solved most of the problems in the minor suit positive sequence over the one-club opening. Peter and I have been able slightly to refine and improve what Belladonna and Garozzo developed.

OPENER	RESPONDER
1 ♣	2 ♣
2 ♦ (asks clarification)	

Responder may make one of the following bids:

1. Two Hearts. Four or more hearts and five or more clubs.

2. Two Spades. Four or more spades, five or more clubs.

3. Two No Trump. Four or more diamonds, five or more clubs. With any of these first three responses, if the second suit is five cards in length, then the club suit must be at least six cards long.

4. Three Clubs. Six or seven clubs and no other four-card suit.

5. Three Diamonds. Six or seven clubs and four diamonds.

6. Three Hearts. Exactly five clubs and 5-3-3-2 distribution with any doubleton. Also shows 0 to 2 controls.

7. Three Spades. The same as three hearts except there are 3 controls and fewer than 13 high-card points.

8. Three No Trump. Also the same as three hearts except there are 4 to 6 controls and less than 13 high-card points.

9. Four Clubs. Same as three hearts except there are 3 controls and 13 or more high-card points.

10. Four Diamonds. Same as three hearts except there are 4 controls and 13 or more high-card points.

11. Four Hearts. Same as three hearts except there are 5 controls and 13 or more high-card points.

12. Four Spades. Same as three hearts except there are 6 controls and 13 or more high-card points.

13. Four No Trump. Same as three hearts except there are 7 controls and 15 or more high-card points.

ONE CLUB—TWO CLUBS—TWO DIAMONDS— TWO HEARTS SEQUENCE

Two hearts shows four or more hearts, five or more clubs.

OPENER	RESPONDER
1 ♣	2 ♣
2 ♦	2 ♥
2 ♠ (asks clarification of distribution)	

Responder has one of eight possible bids.

1. Two No Trump. Shows four spades, four hearts, and five clubs.
2. Three Clubs. Six or seven clubs and four hearts.
3. Three Diamonds. Five clubs, four hearts, three diamonds, and one spade.
4. Three Hearts. Five clubs, four hearts, two diamonds, and two spades, and less than a good 12 high-card points.
5. Three Spades. Five clubs, four hearts, three spades, and one diamond.
6. Three No Trump. Five clubs, four hearts, two spades, two diamonds, and a good 12 or more high-card points.
7. Four Clubs. Six clubs, five hearts, and any distribution in remaining suits.
8. Four Diamonds. Five clubs, four hearts, four diamonds.

After opener has learned responder's distribution, he can ask for controls and make a trump-asking bid in one or both of responder's suits. If opener wants to ask in clubs, he bids the cheapest number of clubs over responder's last bid.

OPENER	RESPONDER
1 ♣	2 ♣
2 ♦	2 ♥
2 ♠	3 ♦ (1-4-3-5)
4 ♣ (asks in clubs)	

A trump ask in clubs can be made in two other ways.

OPENER	RESPONDER
1 ♣	2 ♣
3 ♣ (asks in clubs)	

OPENER	RESPONDER
1 ♣	2 ♣
2 ♦	2 ♥
3 ♣ (asks in clubs)	

Opener may want to ask in hearts.

OPENER	RESPONDER
1 ♣	2 ♣
2 ♦	2 ♥
3 ♥ (asks in hearts)	

OPENER	RESPONDER
1 ♣	2 ♣
2 ♦	2 ♥
2 ♠	3 ♥
4 ♦ (asks in hearts)	

OPENER	RESPONDER
1 ♣	2 ♣
2 ♦	2 ♥
2 ♠	3 ♣
3 ♥ (asks in hearts)	

If opener is able to bid three hearts, that is the heart ask. Otherwise, he must use one of the free suits (in this case spades and diamonds) as the heart ask. The cheapest of these two available bids asks for controls. The more expensive asks for hearts. Usually responder will ask for controls before asking in either of responder's suits, because it is more economical.

Opener may ask for controls after one or two distributional asks by bidding the cheapest suit responder does not have.

OPENER		RESPONDER
1 ♣		2 ♣
2 ♦		2 ♥
3 ♦ (asks for controls)		

OPENER		RESPONDER
1 ♣		2 ♣
2 ♦		2 ♥
2 ♠		3 ♣
3 ♦ (asks for controls)		

The cheapest bid by responder after a control ask shows 0 to 2 controls; the next cheapest shows 3 controls; next, 4 controls, etc.

When opener asks in one or both of responder's suits during a minor suit positive auction, responder's bids depend upon whether the exact length of the suit being questioned is known. If opener knows only that responder has five or more clubs (and this would be the case if the bidding had gone one club, two clubs, two diamonds, two hearts; or one club, two clubs, two diamonds, two spades, or one club, two clubs, two diamonds, two no trump), opener bids three clubs or four clubs to ask in clubs. Responder replies as follows: the next cheapest bid over three clubs or four clubs shows five or six clubs with no A, K, or Q; the next bid shows five clubs with one of top three honors; the next shows six clubs with one of top three honors; next, five clubs and two of top three honors; next, six clubs and two of top three honors; finally, five or six clubs and the three top honors.

When opener knows the trump length in the minor suit, he bids the suit (usually four clubs) to ask about it. Responder replies as follows: cheapest bid possible shows no A, K, or Q; next, one of top three honors; next, one of top three plus the jack; next, two of top three; next, two of top three plus the jack; finally, all three top honors.

The same set of responses is used when opener is asking in responder's second suit. The second suit will always be four cards in length unless responder has shown 6-5 distribution. The asking bid is, once again, three of the suit being asked, or the more expensive of the free suits. Responder replies as outlined in the preceding paragraph. In fact, whenever the length of responder's suit or suits is known in a minor suit positive auction, his bids will be the same as just described.

After opener has made two distributional asking bids, three no trump or four of responder's major suit are sign-offs and urge responder to pass. The exception is when responder has many more high cards than opener could reasonably expect.

ONE CLUB—TWO CLUBS—TWO DIAMONDS— TWO SPADES SEQUENCE

Two spades shows four or more spades, five or more clubs.

OPENER	RESPONDER
1 ♣	2 ♣
2 ♦	2 ♠
2 no trump (second distributional ask)	

The responses are:

1. Three Clubs. Six or seven clubs and four spades.

2. Three Diamonds. Five clubs, four spades, three diamonds, and one heart.

3. Three Hearts. Five clubs, four spades, three hearts, and one diamond.

4. Three Spades. Five clubs, four spades, two hearts, two diamonds, and up to a poor 12 points.

5. Three No Trump. Five clubs, four spades, two hearts, two diamonds, and a good 12 or more high-card points.

6. Four Clubs. Six clubs, five spades, and other distribution is unknown.

7. Four Diamonds. Five clubs, four spades, four diamonds.

Over any of these responses, the next free suit by opener asks for controls. The cheapest bid by responder over this control ask would show 0 to 2 controls, etc.

Here are two examples of how opener asks for controls and how asks are made in clubs and spades:

OPENER	RESPONDER
1 ♣	2 ♣
2 ♦	2 ♠
2 no trump (asks further distribution)	3 ♦ (4-1-3-5)
3 ♥ (cheapest free suit bid available—asks controls)	3 no trump (3 controls)
4 ♣ (club ask)	4 ♠ (five clubs headed by one of top three honors plus the jack)

OPENER	RESPONDER
1 ♣	2 ♣
2 ♦	2 ♠
2 no trump	3 ♣ (six or seven clubs and four spades)
3 ♦ (asks for controls)	3 no trump (4 controls)
4 ♦ (asks in spades)	

Since opener has already asked for controls in the second diagrammed auction, the next free suit bid (four diamonds) is not needed to ask for controls so it becomes a spade ask.

Peter and I were in a money rubber bridge match in Pasadena in March, 1977, just before the Vanderbilt. A hand came up that not only allowed us to use our one club, two clubs auction, but to test an old bridge "superstition" as well. We were playing for ten cents a point per partnership, so about $150 was riding on the hand.

NORTH (Weichsel)
♠ K 10 7 5 2
♥ A
♦ K Q 6
♣ A Q 7 3

SOUTH (Sontag)
♠ A J 4
♥ K Q 8
♦ 7 5
♣ K J 10 8 2

Weichsel	Sontag
1 ♣	2 ♣
3 ♣ (trump ask)	3 ♥ (five clubs with one of three top honors)
3 ♠ (ask in spades)	4 ♥ (A or K with two or three others)
4 ♠ (re-ask in spades)	4 no trump (A or K and two others)
5 ♦ (ask in diamonds)	5 ♠ (doubleton, or the queen with any length)
6 ♣ (signs off)	Pass

Peter took control of the bidding after my positive response to one club by using several asking bids. If my response to his diamond ask had shown the singleton or doubleton ace, he would have bid the grand slam in clubs.

The opening lead was a heart. If the ace of diamonds is in the West hand in front of Peter's K Q, or if it had been the opening lead, the small slam would have made without the need to resort to a spade finesse. But East had the ace of diamonds and did not lead it.

After all the suits except spades had been played, the queen of spades still had to be picked up. But which hand was it in? Peter had no clue at all. Both opponents had followed to two rounds of clubs and had shown in with three hearts and three diamonds. He did, of course, have the option of taking the finesse either way.

Peter crossed his fingers and played West for the queen of spades. He led low to the ace and then low to the ten. It worked.

"Never a doubt," Peter said.

"I had plenty of doubts," I said.

"The queen over the jack. It works every time."

Then how come, I thought, did you cross your fingers?

Peter, of course, was joking, but there was a reason for his play, even if it was of doubtful validity. Bridge "superstition" or speculation holds that in rubber bridge the queen will be behind the jack more than 50 percent of the time. The reason is that the queen may have taken the jack in the previous deal and because of an inadequate shuffle the two cards might not have been separated.

The Official Encyclopedia of Bridge credits this discovery to someone named Clagett Bowie, but I have reason to believe the theory was invented by a well-known player named George Kennedy in 1929. In fact, Kennedy told me he was the inventor. Whatever, making that slam in Pasadena made me grateful to whoever came up with this dubious assumption.

ONE CLUB—TWO CLUBS—TWO DIAMONDS— TWO NO TRUMP SEQUENCE

Two no trump shows four or more diamonds and five or more clubs.

OPENER	RESPONDER
1 ♣	2 ♣
2 ♦	2 no trump
3 ♣ (asks further distribution)	

Responder may bid as follows:

1. Three Diamonds. 2-2-4-5 and less than 13 high-card points.

2. Three Hearts. 1-3-4-5.

3. Three Spades. 3-1-4-5.

4. Three No Trump. 2-2-4-5 and 13 or more high-card points.

5. Four Clubs. ?-?-5-6.

The next free suit by opener over these responses asks for controls.

OPENER	RESPONDER
1 ♣	2 ♣
2 ♦	2 no trump
3 ♣	3 ♠ (3-1-4-5)
4 ♥ (asks controls)	

Opener asks in clubs or diamonds by bidding the suit.

OPENER	RESPONDER
1 ♣	2 ♣
2 ♦	2 no trump
3 ♦ (asks in diamonds)	
or 4 ♣ (asks in clubs)	

OPENER	RESPONDER
1 ♣	2 ♣
2 ♦	2 no trump
3 ♣ (further distri-bution ask)	3 ♠ (3-1-4-5)
4 ♣ (asks in clubs)	4 ♥ (one of top three honors without jack)
4 ♠ (control ask)	

The second of these auctions needs explanation. Although it is usually preferable to ask for controls before asking in a suit, in this case if opener had first asked for controls he would have had to bid four hearts over responder's three spades. By first asking in clubs, he only bid four of them and thus saved very valuable bidding space. Opener must constantly remind himself to ask questions in the proper order.

Opener's three no trump bid over responder's two no trump always ends the auction unless responder has great additional values.

ONE CLUB—TWO CLUBS—TWO DIAMONDS— THREE CLUBS SEQUENCE

Three clubs shows six or seven clubs and no other four-card suit.

OPENER	RESPONDER
1 ♣	2 ♣
2 ♦	3 ♣

Opener has five possible bids over three clubs.

1. Three Diamonds. A control ask. Responder bids cheapest suit to show 0 to 2 controls, etc.

2. Three Hearts. Natural bid showing four or five hearts and looking for best game. Responder may raise hearts with three to a top honor, rebid his club suit, bid three spades with a high honor in spades and bad diamonds, or three no trump with something in spades and diamonds.

3. Three Spades. Natural bid showing four or five spades. Responder may bid three no trump if he has stoppers in hearts and diamonds, raise spades with a high honor and two others, or bid four clubs.

4. Three No Trump. Signs off.

5. Four Clubs. Asks in clubs. Responder bids as if his length is known. Four diamonds shows no A, K, or Q; four hearts, one of top three honors; four spades, one of top three plus jack; four no trump, two of top three; five clubs, two of top three plus jack; and five diamonds, all three top honors.

OPENER	RESPONDER
1 ♣	2 ♣
2 ♦	3 ♣
3 ♦ (control ask)	3 no trump (4 controls)
4 ♣ (asks in clubs)	

When the response to the control ask has been four clubs or higher, opener's next cheapest bid is a club ask.

ONE CLUB—TWO CLUBS—TWO DIAMONDS— THREE DIAMONDS SEQUENCE

Three diamonds shows six or seven clubs and four diamonds.

OPENER	RESPONDER
1 ♣	2 ♣
2 ♦	3 ♦

Opener can make the following bids over three diamonds:

1. Three Hearts. A control ask. Responder bids cheapest suit to show 0 to 2 controls, etc.
2. Three Spades. Shows some strength in spades but little in hearts. Responder should bid three no trump with a protected heart honor; otherwise, he should make a descriptive bid.
3. Three No Trump. Signs off.
4. Four Clubs. Asks in clubs.
5. Four Diamonds. Asks in diamonds. Responder's reply is the same as to four clubs: the cheapest suit shows none of the top three honors, the next cheapest shows one of the top three, without the jack, etc.

If opener asks for controls and the response takes him past the minor suit he wants to ask about, opener's next highest bid over the response asks in clubs and the highest after that asks in diamonds.

OPENER	RESPONDER
1 ♣	2 ♣
2 ♦	3 ♦
3 ♥ (control ask)	4 ♦ (5 controls)
4 ♥ (club ask) or	
4 ♠ (diamond ask)	

ONE CLUB—TWO CLUBS—TWO DIAMONDS—THREE HEARTS SEQUENCE

Three hearts shows exactly five clubs, 0 to 2 controls, 5-3-3-2 distribution, and any doubleton.

OPENER	RESPONDER
1 ♣	2 ♣
2 ♦	3 ♥

Opener may bid as follows:

1. Three Spades. A further control ask. Three no trump by responder would show 0 to 1 control, four clubs would show 2 controls. Opener could then ask in clubs by bidding four clubs over three no trump and four diamonds over four clubs.
2. Three No Trump. Signs off.
3. Four Clubs. Asks in clubs.

OPENER	RESPONDER
1 ♣	2 ♣
2 ♦	3 ♥
3 ♠ (further control ask)	4 ♣ (2 controls)
4 ♦ asks in clubs)	5 ♣ (two of top three honors without the jack)

ONE CLUB—TWO CLUBS—TWO DIAMONDS—THREE SPADES SEQUENCE

Three spades shows exactly five clubs, 3 controls, fewer than 13 high-card points, 5-3-3-2 distribution, and any doubleton.

OPENER	RESPONDER
1 ♣	2 ♣
2 ♦	3 ♠

Opener has two possible bids:

1. Three No Trump. Signs off.
2. Four Clubs. Asks in clubs.

ONE CLUB—TWO CLUBS—TWO DIAMONDS— THREE NO TRUMP SEQUENCE

Three no trump shows exactly five clubs, 4 to 6 controls, less than 13 high-card points, 5-3-3-2 distribution, and any doubleton.

OPENER	RESPONDER
1 ♣	2 ♣
2 ♦	3 no trump

Opener has three possible bids:

1. Pass.
2. Four Clubs. Asks in clubs.
3. Four Diamonds. A further control ask. Responder bids four hearts with 4 controls, four spades with 5 controls, and four no trump if he has three aces.

OPENER	RESPONDER
1 ♣	2 ♣
2 ♦	3 no trump
4 ♣ (asks in clubs)	4 no trump (two honors without the jack)
5 ♦ (asks for controls)	5 spades (5 controls)

In the preceding auction, it is clear that when responder bids four no trump he is showing at least the A or K of clubs. When opener then re-asks for controls, responder again shows this card when he bids his total number of controls. If opener bids Blackwood after responder has cue bid an ace, this ace is included in responder's reply.

ONE CLUB—TWO CLUBS—TWO DIAMONDS—
FOUR OF A SUIT SEQUENCE

Four of a suit shows at least an opening bid, 5-3-3-2 distribution with any doubleton, and, in order of the suits, 3, 4, 5, and 6 controls.

OPENER	RESPONDER
1 ♣	2 ♣
2 ♦	4 ♣, 4 ♦
	4 ♥, or 4 ♠

Since the controls are already known, the only information opener needs at first concerns responder's club suit. The cheapest bid over responder's reply asks in clubs.

OPENER	RESPONDER
1 ♣	2 ♣
2 ♦	4 ♠ (6 controls)
4 no trump (asks in clubs)	

ONE CLUB—TWO CLUBS—TWO DIAMONDS
FOUR NO TRUMP SEQUENCE

Four no trump shows exactly five clubs, 7 controls, at least 15 high-card points, 5-3-3-2 distribution, and any doubleton.

OPENER	RESPONDER
1 ♣	2 ♣
2 ♦	4 no trump

Opener bids five clubs over four no trump to ask in clubs. It is virtually inconceivable that opener and responder are missing even one control. Over the response to the club ask, opener bids a new suit to ask for third round control (a doubleton or queen) in that suit. Responder bids a grand slam in clubs if he has this holding, and he signs off at six clubs or six no trump, whichever is cheaper, if he does not.

OPENER	RESPONDER
1 ♣	2 ♣
2 ♦	4 no trump
5 ♣ (club ask)	5 ♠ (one honor plus the jack)
6 ♥ (asks third round control)	6 no trump (no third round control) or 7 ♣ (has third round control)

There are three occasions when opener might not bid two diamonds over the one club, two clubs sequence. The first is:

ONE CLUB—TWO CLUBS—TWO HEARTS SEQUENCE

Two hearts shows at least five hearts.

OPENER	RESPONDER
1 ♣	2 ♣
2 ♥	

Responder has one of eight replies:

1. Two Spades. Less than 4 controls and less than queen and two others in hearts.

2. Two No Trump. Four or more controls and less than queen and two others in hearts.

3. Three Clubs. Less than 4 controls and at least queen and two others in hearts.

4. Three Diamonds. Four or more controls and at least queen and two others in hearts.

5. Three Hearts. Four or more controls and exactly four hearts headed by at most the jack.

If after one of these five responses opener bids clubs, it is a club ask. Because the length is not known, responder will bid the same as if opener had immediately raised his suit. If after Responses #3, 4, or 5 opener wants to learn about controls, he bids three no trump: for Response #3, over three no trump, responder bids four clubs to show 0 controls or one king or one ace, four diamonds to show two kings, and four hearts to show 3 controls; for Responses #4 and 5, over three no trump, responder bids four clubs to show 4 cotnrols, four diamonds to show 5 controls, etc. Over Responses #1 and 2, three no trump ends the auction. Any other bid by opener over these five responses is natural and responder should also bid naturally.

6. Three Spades. Five spades and six clubs. A specific number of controls is not required for this bid, but the two suits should be strong.

7. Four Clubs. A semisolid suit with six or seven cards and 4 or more controls.

8. Four Diamonds. Five diamonds and six clubs. The suits should be strong.

The second exception when opener might not bid two diamonds over the one club, two clubs sequence is.

ONE CLUB—TWO CLUBS— TWO SPADES SEQUENCE

Two spades shows at least five spades.

OPENER	RESPONDER
1 ♣	2 ♣
2 ♠	

Responder should define his hand in exactly the same fashion as the preceding one club, two clubs, two hearts auction except the first five responses would be one notch higher. Responses #7 and 8 are also the same. Response #6 would be four hearts instead of three spades.

The third and final exception when opener might not bid two diamonds over the one club, two clubs sequence is:

ONE CLUB—TWO CLUBS—
TWO NO TRUMP SEQUENCE

Two no trump shows at least five diamonds.

OPENER	RESPONDER
1 ♣	2 ♣
2 no trump	

Responses #1 through 5 are the same except they are again one notch higher. However, if responder makes the fifth reply (three no trump over two no trump to show 4 or more controls and four diamonds headed by at most the jack), opener's four-club bid would still ask in clubs but four diamonds would ask for the exact number of controls. With the one club, two clubs, two no trump auction, Responses #6 through 8 would mean:

1. Four Clubs. A semisolid suit with six or seven clubs and 4 or more controls.
2. Four Hearts. Six clubs and five hearts.
3. Four Spades. Six clubs and five spades.

This concludes the one club, two clubs sequence. All that remains to complete the discussion of the enormously powerful one-club opening bid and its subsequent structure is the one club, two diamonds auction.

ONE CLUB—TWO DIAMONDS SEQUENCE

Two diamonds by responder shows five or more diamonds and 9 or more points, and diamonds will be the longest suit with one exception: when clubs are the same length.

OPENER	RESPONDER
1 ♣	2 ♦

Opener will usually bid two hearts over the one club, two diamonds auction.

ONE CLUB—TWO DIAMONDS—TWO HEARTS SEQUENCE

Two hearts asks for clarification of responder's hand.

OPENER	RESPONDER
1 ♣	2 ♦
2 ♥	

Responder may make one of the following bids:

1. Two Spades. Four or more spades and five or more diamonds.
2. Two No Trump. Four or more hearts and five or more diamonds.
3. Three Clubs. Four or more clubs and five or more diamonds.
4. Three Diamonds. Six or seven diamonds and no other four-card suit.
5. Three Hearts. Six or seven diamonds and four hearts.
6. Three Spades. 5-3-3-2 distribution with any doubleton, 0 to 3 controls, and up to a poor 12 high-card points.
7. Three No Trump. 5-3-3-2 distribution with any doubleton, 4 to 6 controls, and up to a poor 12 high-card points.
8. Four Clubs. 5-3-3-2 distribution with any doubleton, exactly 3 controls, and 12 or more high-card points.
9. Four Diamonds. Same as four clubs except 4 controls.
10. Four Hearts. Same as four clubs except 5 controls.
11. Four Spades. Same as four clubs except 6 controls.
12. Four No trump. Same as four clubs except 7 or more controls.

ONE CLUB—TWO DIAMONDS—TWO HEARTS—TWO SPADES SEQUENCE

Two spades shows four or more spades and five or more diamonds.

OPENER	RESPONDER
1 ♣	2 ♦
2 ♥	2 ♠
2 no trump (asks further distribution)	

Responder may bid as follows:

1. Three Clubs. 4-1-5-3 distribution.
2. Three Diamonds. Six or seven diamonds and four spades.
3. Three Hearts. 4-3-5-1.
4. Three Spades. 4-2-5-2 and up to a poor 12 high-card points.
5. Three No trump. 4-2-5-2 and a good 12 or more high-card points.
6. Four Clubs. 4-0-5-4.
7. Four Diamonds. Six diamonds and five spades and any other distribution.
8. Four Hearts. 4-4-5-0.

After opener has learned responder's distribution, he can ask for controls and make a trump-asking bid in one or more of responder's suits. If opener wants to ask in diamonds, he can raise the suit immediately after the positive response, or he can bid the cheapest amount of diamonds after one or two distributional asking bids.

After any of the previous eight responses, opener bids the most economical free suit (one not shown by responder) to ask for controls: responder would show 0 to 2 controls by bidding as cheaply as possible, 3 controls would be shown by the next cheapest bid, etc.

If opener wants to ask in spades, he bids three spades if there is room, and the more expensive free suit if there is no room.

OPENER	RESPONDER
1 ♣	2 ♦
2 ♥	2 ♠
2 no trump (second distributional ask)	3 ♠ (4-2-5-2 and 12 or fewer points)
4 ♣ (asks for controls) or	
4 ♦ (asks in diamonds) or	
4 ♥ (asks in spades)	

If opener bids three no trump, four of responder's major, or five of his minor, he is signing off.

When opener knows responder's length in the minor suit and asks about it, the responses are: cheapest possible bid, no A, K, or Q; next cheapest, one of three top honors; next, one of top three plus the jack, etc.

The same set of responses applies when opener asks in responder's second suit.

If opener knows only that responder has five or more diamonds, responder bids as follows: cheapest bid shows five or six cards with no A, K, or Q; next, five-card suit with one of three top honors; next, six-card suit with one top honor; next, five-card suit with two top honors; next, six-card suit with two top honors; finally, all three top honors with any length.

The one club, two diamonds, two hearts auction is, except for the rank of suits, analogous to the one club, two clubs, two diamonds auction. Because of the similarities in distributional-asking bids, trump-asking bids, second-suit-asking bids, control-asking bids, the concept of the free suits, and generally the development of the entire auction, it is not necessary to go into exhaustive detail on the follow-up to the one club, two diamonds auction.

Good bidding is far more important than inspired card play in the making of a top bridge player. An enlightened card playing whiz, expert at every conceivable obscure maneuver, would have virtually no chance at bridge against a competent technician with superior bidding methods. Nevertheless, in May, 1975, I learned a lesson that long before should have been obvious: always play a hand out.

It was the zonal stage of an important match in the Grand Nationals and during the play of a three no trump contract it became obvious I would go down one. I conceded the point but our suspicious opponent insisted we continue to play, no doubt believing the contract could be set by several tricks. But he made a mistake and we made the contract, proving that nothing should be conceded at bridge, and then came a gigantic hassle.

"Down one," he said.

"Nonsense," I said. "You messed up and I made the contract."

"You conceded."

The fellow had nerve. There had been the subtle suggestion when he refused the concession that I was cheating, and now that his refusal to accept had turned sour he was trying to save face.

Alan Truscott wrote about what happened: "The director, Maury Braunstein, ruled that the contract had succeeded, and the Weichsel team gained 6 points when they were about to lose 5. The ruling on the point of law was upheld after reference to higher authority, a National Laws Commission member, Edgar Kaplan of New York."

I never claim or concede contracts any more, except in non-tournament matches with students or beginners. In these situations during routine hands, to save time, I will speed up the play with a quick claim or concession.

ONE CLUB—TWO DIAMONDS—TWO HEARTS—TWO NO TRUMP SEQUENCE

Two no trump shows five or more diamonds and four or more hearts.

OPENER	RESPONDER
1 ♣	2 ♦
2 ♥	2 no trump
3 ♣ (asks further distribution)	

Responder may bid as follows:

1. Three Diamonds. 1-4-5-3.
2. Three Hearts. 2-4-5-2, and 9 to 12 high-card points.
3. Three Spades. 3-4-5-1.
4. Three No Trump. 2-4-5-2, and 13 or more high-card points.
5. Four Clubs. 0-4-5-4.
6. Four Diamonds. Six diamonds and five hearts and any other distribution.

The next free suit over these responses is a control ask.

OPENER	RESPONDER
1 ♣	2 ♦
2 ♥	2 no trump
3 ♣	3 ♦ (1-4-5-3)
3 ♠ (control ask)	

Whenever, over two no trump, opener bids three diamonds or three hearts, it is an asking bid in that suit.

OPENER	RESPONDER
1 ♣	2 ♦
2 ♥	2 no trump
3 ♦ (asks in diamonds) or	
3 ♥ (asks in hearts)	

If opener in the preceding auction bids three spades over two no trump, it is a control ask. Three no trump would ask responder to pass unless he had great additional values.

After two distributional asking bids have been made, opener can ask in diamonds by bidding four diamonds (if there is room) or by bidding the more expensive of the free suits if there is not.

OPENER	RESPONDER
1 ♣	2 ♦
2 ♥	2 no trump
3 ♣	3 no trump
4 ♦ (asks in diamonds)	4 no trump (one of top three honors plus the jack)
5 ♣ (control ask)	

ONE CLUB—TWO DIAMONDS—TWO HEARTS—THREE CLUBS SEQUENCE

Three clubs shows five or more diamonds and four or more clubs.

OPENER	RESPONDER
1 ♣	2 ♦
2 ♥	3 ♣
3 ♦ (asks further distribution)	

Responder may bid as follows:

1. Three Hearts. 1-3-5-4.
2. Three Spades. 3-1-5-4.
3. Three No Trump. 2-2-5-4, and 9 to a poor 13 high-card points.
4. Four Clubs. Five diamonds and five clubs and any other distribution.
5. Four Diamonds. Six diamonds and four clubs and any other distribution.

6. Four Hearts. 2-2-5-4, 3 controls, and 13 or more high-card points.

7. Four Spades. 2-2-5-4, 4 controls, and 13 or more high-card points.

8. Four No Trump. 2-2-5-4, 5 or more controls, and 13 or more high-card points.

9. Five Clubs. Six diamonds and five clubs and up to 10 high-card points in the minors.

10. Five Diamonds. Six diamonds and five clubs and 11 or more high-card points in the minors.

The next free suit over the first five responses is a control ask. The next free suit over Responses #6 through 8 asks in diamonds. Over Responses #9 and 10, five hearts asks in clubs and five spades asks in diamonds.

Three hearts by opener over three clubs is a control ask. Three spades by opener would show good spades and poor hearts. Three no trump would be to play. Four clubs would ask in clubs and four diamonds in diamonds.

Opener may ask in one of responder's suits after a control ask by bidding four of either minor to ask in that suit, and if these bids are unavailable the cheapest free suit asks in diamonds and the other asks in clubs.

ONE CLUB—TWO DIAMONDS—TWO HEARTS—THREE DIAMONDS SEQUENCE

Three diamonds shows six or seven diamonds and no other four-card suit.

OPENER	RESPONDER
1 ♣	2 ♦
2 ♥	3 ♦

Opener may bid as follows:

1. Three Hearts. Asks for controls.
2. Three Spades. Natural, shows good spades and weak

hearts. Responder should bid three no trump if he has a heart stopper.

3. Three No Trump. Signs off.

4. Four Diamonds. Asks in diamonds.

ONE CLUB—TWO DIAMONDS—TWO HEARTS—THREE HEARTS SEQUENCE

Three hearts shows six or seven diamonds and four hearts.

OPENER	RESPONDER
1 ♣	2 ♦
2 ♥	3 ♥

Opener may bid as follows:

1. Three Spades. A control ask. Responder bids three no trump to show 0 to 2 controls, four clubs to show 3 controls, etc.

2. Three No Trump. Signs off.

3. Four Clubs. Asks in hearts. Responses to the heart ask include the jack.

4. Four Diamonds. Asks in diamonds. Responses include the jack.

Opener can still ask in responder's suits after asking for controls. If there is room, four diamonds would ask in diamonds and four spades would ask in hearts. If there is no room, the cheapest free suit asks in diamonds and the more expensive free suit asks in hearts.

OPENER	RESPONDER
1 ♣	2 ♦
2 ♥	3 ♥
3 ♠ (asks for control) then	4 ♦ (4 controls)
4 ♥ (to play) or 4 ♠ (asks in diamonds) or 4 no trump (to play) or 5 ♣ (asks in hearts) or 5 ♦ (to play)	

ONE CLUB—TWO DIAMONDS—TWO HEARTS—THREE SPADES SEQUENCE

Three spades shows 5-3-3-2 distribution with any doubleton, 0 to 3 controls, and up to a poor 12 high-card points.

OPENER	RESPONDER
1 ♣	2 ♦
2 ♥	3 ♠

Opener may bid as follows:

1. Three No Trump. Signs off.
2. Four Clubs. Further control ask. Responder bids four diamonds to show zero or one king or one ace, four hearts to show two kings, or four spades to show 3 controls.
3. Four Diamonds. Asks in diamonds. Responses include the jack.

After asking for controls or in diamonds, the cheapest free suit asks for the other. Four no trump or five diamonds by opener in a sign off.

ONE CLUB—TWO DIAMONDS—TWO HEARTS—THREE NO TRUMP SEQUENCE

Three no trump shows 5-3-3-2 with any doubleton, 4 to 6 controls, and up to a poor 12 high-card points.

OPENER	RESPONDER
1 ♣	2 ♦
2 ♥	3 no trump

Opener may bid as follows:

1. Four Clubs. Further control ask. Responder bids four diamonds to show 4 controls, four hearts to show 5 controls, and four spades to show 6 controls.

2. Four Diamonds. Asks in diamonds. Responses include the jack.

After asking for controls or diamonds, the cheapest free suit again asks for the other. Four no trump by opener is a sign-off.

ONE CLUB—TWO DIAMONDS—TWO
HEARTS—ANY FOUR-LEVEL SEQUENCE

Any bid by responder at the four level over two hearts shows a specific number of controls, 5-3-3-2 distribution with any doubleton, and an opening bid in high cards.

OPENER	RESPONDER
1 ♣	2 ♦
2 ♥	4 ♣ (3 controls) or
	4 ♦ (4 controls) or
	4 ♥ (5 controls) or
	4 ♠ (6 controls) or
	4 no trump (7 or more controls)

The next free suit by opener over any of these responses asks in diamonds. Responses include the jack. After asking in diamonds, a new suit by opener asks for third round control (queen or a doubleton) in the suit bid. Responder makes the cheapest bid without this control, and bids seven diamonds if he has the control.

The four no trumps response shows 7 or more controls. In the unlikely event opener wants clarification, he bids five hearts. Responder bids five spades to show 7 controls and five no trump to show 8.

Over every one club, two of a minor auction, after opener has made two distributional asking bids and a control ask, the cheapest free suit asks in responder's minor. The next free suit over that response asks in the second suit.

OPENER	RESPONDER
1 ♣	2 ♦
2 ♥	2 no trump
3 ♣ (second distributional ask)	3 ♠ (3-4-5-1)
4 ♣ (control ask)	4 ♥ (3 controls)
4 ♠ (asks in diamonds)	4 no trump (no A, K, or Q)
5 ♣ (asks in hearts)	

There are three occasions when opener might not bid two hearts over the one club, two diamonds sequence. These occur when opener has a long suit of his own and wants to find out immediately if responder has support for the suit. Obviously, opener's strong suit is not headed by the A K Q.

OPENER	RESPONDER
1 ♣	2 ♦
2 ♠ (shows at least five spades) or 2 no trump (at least five hearts) or 3 ♣ (at least five clubs)	

The responses to these natural suit bids are very similar to the already described exceptions to the one club, two clubs, two diamonds sequence. The subsequent bidding is also very similar.

The responses to these auctions are identical:

OPENER	RESPONDER
1 ♣	2 ♣
2 ♠ (at least five spades)	

OPENER	RESPONDER
1 ♣	2 ♦
2 ♠ (at least five spades)	

The responses to these auctions would be slightly different:

OPENER	RESPONDER
1 ♣	2 ♣
2 ♥ (at least five hearts)	

OPENER	RESPONDER
1 ♣	2 ♦
2 no trump (at least five hearts)	

The difference between the first and second auction is that the cheapest bid over two hearts is two spades, while three clubs is the cheapest bid over two no trump.

The responses to these auctions would also be slightly different:

OPENER	RESPONDER
1 ♣	2 ♣
2 no trump (at least five diamonds)	

OPENER	RESPONDER
1 ♣	2 ♦
3 ♣ (at least five clubs)	

The differences between these auctions, of course, are that different suits are being shown by opener, and also the cheapest response over two no trump is three clubs and over three clubs it is three diamonds.

This concludes the entire one-club structure. A club system is infinitely superior to Standard bidding methods, and the W-S one-club structure is the most accurate and exact in the world.

12

THE END OF A LONG DAY

FOUR PARTNERSHIPS REMAINED BEFORE WE BROKE FOR THE day. It was time to be extra serious. A good night's rest, and more, was at stake.

I thought if we did well against the four remaining partnerships we would have the lead at the halfway point and leading, despite what come-from-behinders say, is the best position in a bridge tournament. I *know* if we were behind we would spend a sleepless night worrying, agonizing, analyzing what went wrong.

We sat down to play Jacqui Mitchell and John Roberts. Jacqui, forty-one, one of the great women players in the world, looks much younger. She is small and shy and tough. She has dark blonde hair, blue eyes, dresses like a tomboy, wears her hair in a ponytail, and was the recipient of a tremendous honor: in 1958, in only her second year of tournament play, she won the New York Player of the Year Award.

Jacqui is married to Vic Mitchell, a bridge great. Interestingly, Jacqui's partner in the Calcutta was John Roberts, while Vic's partner was John's brother, Bill.

One of the most important and popular events in the early days of bridge was the Masters Individual. Only the very best players were invited to participate. In February, 1977, a new event, patterned after the Masters Individual, was inaugurated in New York and called the Blue Ribbon Individual. An Individual consists of each participant—at one time or another—having for a partner every other player in the field.

Jacqui won the Blue Ribbon Individual in 1977. Peter and I were in this tournament, as were such bridge stars as Al Roth, Sam Stayman, Mike Becker, the late Harold Ogust, Alan Truscott, Dorothy Truscott, Harold Lilie, and Roger Stern.

John Roberts, thirty-two, Jacqui's partner, is also an interesting character. John owns a music recording studio and was one of the original promoters of the famous Woodstock Festival. Roberts' initial idea was to open a recording studio in Woodstock. A group of musicians advised him to throw a press party to coincide with the opening of the studio, but the press party mushroomed into something so elaborate that it sounded to Roberts like it should be a concert. In the end, with others helping, John promoted the biggest and most publicized concert in history.

John Roberts, a fine bridge player, would be even better if a day was not limited to twenty-four hours. Besides his recording studio, he has coauthored a popular book on Woodstock which may become a movie, plays squash and tennis regularly, and enjoys numerous other interests. John has two children and his wife understandably does not want him spending what little free time he has at bridge tournaments.

The first two hands against Jacqui and John were indecisive. On the first we bid and made one no trump. On the second they bid and made one no trump. This was hardly high drama and I wondered about the computer that pre-dealt the hands by random shuffling. Surely the results of these hands had been duplicated at practically every other table. I looked at Peter and he shrugged.

The aggravating part was that we were going well and wanted challenging hands. That way we could test ourselves against all the others and rise or fall on merit. I am sure that is what Jacqui and John wanted too.

There seems to be no solution to the problem, however: if all boring hands were thrown out, the game would no longer resemble bridge as it is really played and experts would so specialize in the unusual that the commonplace would become foreign to them.

I later listened to other players complain about these two "wasted" hands. I was sympathetic, but there really was nothing that could be done about it.

The computer does not always deal unexciting hands—how could it when its function is to simulate real bridge?—and the third deal was tense and testing:

NORTH (Jacqui Mitchell)
- ♠ A 6 5 4
- ♥ K J 9
- ♦ K J 6 2
- ♣ K 8

WEST (Sontag)
- ♠ Q J
- ♥ 10 8 6 4
- ♦ Q 10 9 7
- ♣ 7 6 5

EAST (Weichsel)
- ♠ 8 2
- ♥ A 7 5 3
- ♦ A 5 4 3
- ♣ A Q 3

SOUTH (John Roberts)
- ♠ K 10 9 7 3
- ♥ Q 2
- ♦ 8
- ♣ J 10 9 4 2

North-South vulnerable. The bidding:

WEST	NORTH	EAST	SOUTH
	1 no trump	Pass	2 ♠
Pass	3 ♦	Pass	3 ♠
Pass	3 no trump	Pass	Pass
Pass			

Jacqui and John were in the wrong contract. They should have played a part-score in spades but there was a mix-up in their bidding. Jacqui's one no trump showed 15 to 17 points.

John's two spades was intended to mean that is where he wanted to play the contract, but he forgot they were using Jacoby Transfers over no trump. Jacqui thought his bid meant he had the minor suits and she bid three diamonds. John bid spades again but this time, systematically, the bid showed one or no spades. Jacqui bid three no trump and John had to pass.

Peter's opening lead was a heart and we set the contract two tricks. It was worth almost 140 IMPs because most partnerships played the hand in a spade part-score. Here is how we would have bid the hand:

NORTH (Weichsel)

1 no trump—15 to 17 high-card points.

SOUTH (Sontag)

2 ♥—Jacoby Transfer to spades.

2 ♠—accepts the transfer and denies both maximum high cards and a fit. He may have one but not both.

3 ♣—natural and non-forcing. Shows five spades, four or five clubs, and 5 to 7 high-card points.

3 ♠—the final decision. Realizes the average hand I would have for this bidding yields a poor play for game. If, instead of the K J in either red suit, he held the A, he would bid four spades.

Pass.

After the third hand against Jacqui and John I felt a sense of well-being, of healthy confidence. I did not say so to Peter, but I was sure we would win this tournament.

Our next opponents were Matt Granovetter and Sam Stayman. Stayman's name, like Charles Goren's, is practically synonymous with bridge. He is the inventor of one of the two most widely used conventions in the world (the other is Blackwood). Stayman has written a number of books, has made a fortune in the stock market and, most important, was World Champion three times (1950, 1951, 1953).

In the early 1960s Sam Stayman, his wife, and his wife's sister, Rita Gore (now Rita Rand), went to Europe on a combined business and pleasure trip. The two women stopped at a bridge club where they were introduced as Mrs. Stayman and Mrs. *Goren.* Of course, these were the two most famous names in bridge, and dozens of people crowded around their table to watch them play. At the time the women hardly knew what a finesse was.

Matt Granovetter, twenty-six, is a frequent teammate of ours. Matt started playing bridge when he was twelve and at age thirteen a system he invented was written up in the New York *Herald Tribune.* Granovetter composes music, plays the piano, and enjoys analyzing the psychological aspect of bridge. He even has a theory about sex as it applies to the game. He believes it is a good idea to have sex before Team-of-Four bridge events, because it is relaxing; he believes it is a bad idea before pair games because extra alertness is required. The partnership is always shooting for the highest score in pair games, while in Team-of-Four bridge overtricks are usually not of great importance.

Perhaps the most heartbreaking thing that can happen to bridge players is to finish second in a national tournament, since only first place permits a team to go to the qualifications that lead to the World Championship. Sam and Matt were on the team that finished second in the Reisinger in both 1976 and 1977. Granovetter later wrote in *The Bridge World,* "It's better to be 100th than second. It's better to lose by nine boards than by half a matchpoint."

We scored heavily right from the start against Stayman and Granovetter. Sam, in third chair, held the following cards:

♠ A J 2
♥ J 8 7 5 4
♦ A 10
♣ Q 10 5

Sam was vulnerable and there were two passes in front of him. He passed, which turned out poorly for his side, and the hand was passed out. Upon inspection of Matt's hand, it was discovered that four hearts depended on little more than a successful club finesse. Although only a few partnerships bid and made the game, no one passed it out, and we scored 100 IMPs on the hand. Sam should have opened the bidding with one heart.

Many partners would have exploded. That is not Matt Granovetter's style, however. Of course, even Ira Rubin would think twice before berating the venerable Stayman.

Sam and Matt bid one no trump on the second hand and made an overtrick. On the final hand we bid four spades which failed by one. We lost perhaps 40 IMPs on this hand, but for the round we were in the plus column.

It was warm and stuffy in the Cavendish. The fluorescent lights on the ceiling were blurred and ghostly. It was late in the second session of a long day and even Peter seemed out of focus. Still, it would be easy to concentrate. Only six more hands.

The first three were played against Mike Becker and Alan Greenberg. Becker, a good friend of mine, is a member of the most prolific bridge family in the world. Certainly the Jacobys—Oswald, James, Oswald's wife, Mary Zita, and James' wife, Judy—are in contention for the honor, but there are "only" four of them. Mike Becker's dad is the great B. Jay Becker, Mike's brother Steve is a top player, so is Mike's uncle, Simon, and Simon has two sons, Bob and Murray, who are Life Masters.

Mike occasionally carries our friendship too far. I was dating a pretty schoolteacher he also found attractive. He called me on the phone.

"Alan, you wouldn't mind if I asked Joan out, would you?"

"Of course I would."

"Think of all the things I've done for you."

"What were they?"

"I wouldn't object if the situation were reversed."

"I don't believe you."

"Well, if that's how you feel, I'm sorry I was nice enough to ask. I'll just call her on my own. By the way, what's her phone number?"

Mike Becker is the most orderly and conscientious player I know. He has a bridge bookkeeping system that would put a CPA to shame. He keeps records of *every* session he plays, analyzes them, calculates how he could have done better. He studies which partner he had the most success with, which system produced the best results, which opponents displayed weaknesses that might later be exploited. Mike's records must fill a medium-sized room.

B. Jay Becker taught Mike how to play bridge, and B. Jay believes in completely natural bidding, nothing artificial. For a time B. Jay would not even use Stayman.

When I first played with Mike as my partner it was impossible to get him to agree to any conventions whatever. He was his father's son. But a generation gap gradually developed. Exposed to high-powered modern bidding methods, Mike could not avoid breaking with his traditionalist father. And when the break came it was total. Mike now employs perhaps the most complicated and artificial bidding system played anywhere in the world.

Alan Greenberg, Mike Becker's partner, is fifty years old and excels at everything he does: he is the senior partner of an important brokerage house; he is an expert magician; he trains champion dogs; he is a crack archer; and, of course, he is a top bridge player.

Greenberg would probably be a winner at anything he tried. He learned to play bridge only a few years ago with Jimmy Cayne as his teacher. Greenberg won the *first* national championship he ever entered, the 1977 Reisinger, and at the same time became a Life Master. Another team Greenberg was on—which included Peter and me—won the Spero

Award for the best performance in team events in New York City during 1977. That year I won the individual award as New York Player of the Year.

Becker and Greenberg were friends and we played on teams together, which guaranteed that the round would be contested with high intensity. No player wants to be outperformed in head-to-head competition by a teammate. Each member of a team tends to think of himself as the indispensable ingredient.

The round against Mike and Alan was one of the most exciting of the Calcutta. On the very first hand our strong club opening bid was tested by expert interference from Becker and Greenberg:

NORTH (Becker)
♠ Q 5
♥ K 5 3 2
♦ Q 10 8 6 3
♣ K 2

WEST (Sontag)
♠ 9 6 3
♥ Q J 10 8 7 4
♦ 4
♣ J 9 5

EAST (Weichsel)
♠ A K J 8 7 4
♥ A
♦ 7 2
♣ A 8 6 3

SOUTH (Greenberg)
♠ 10 2
♥ 9 6
♦ A K J 9 5
♣ Q 10 7 4

East-West vulnerable. The bidding:

WEST	NORTH	EAST	SOUTH
		1 ♣	2 no trump
Pass	4 ♦	Pass	Pass
4 ♥	Pass	4 ♠	5 ♦
Pass	Pass	Double	Pass
Pass	Pass		

Becker and Greenberg accurately judged that we could make four spades and took an intelligent sacrifice at five diamonds. We defeated the contract by only two tricks. It seemed like a poor result for us, but later we learned that half the field, holding our cards, did not bid four spades. After a one-spade opening bid by East, many players sitting West did not think their hand was good enough to bid and the contract was played at one spade. I was able to bid at the four level because I knew Peter had a strong hand.

On the second hand we won a staggering 220 IMPs! It resulted from a calculated risk I took based on the vulnerability factor. With most forms of scoring a partnership should take extra chances and be more aggressive when they are vulnerable because there is more to gain than to lose. I held the following cards: A 6 5 of spades, Q 8 7 5 of hearts, 9 of diamonds, and 10 9 8 5 3 of clubs.

Peter opened the bidding with one no trump showing 15 to 17 high-card points and the next hand passed. Almost every West player with my cards passed. I elected to bid Stayman (two clubs) hoping Peter would have a major. In fact, he had both majors, and our system calls for bidding the lower one first. I raised to three hearts, he bid four hearts, and we made five hearts!

Becker and Greenberg were horrified when they saw the dummy and they felt worse when the hand was over. It was clear to them that few if any other pairs would be in this contract.

Peter and I bid and made an overtrick on the third hand in a routine four-spade contract.

One more opponent and the first day—and more than half the tournament—would be over. I was not even tired. I knew that was because we were going well. Exhaustion usually occurs only when players are off their game and scoring poorly.

Ken Cohen and Walk Walvick, our final opponents of the second session, were not among the leaders, but Cohen in particular did not seem the least bit weary. Cohen, from

Philadelphia, is a skilled gambler and gamesman and accustomed to long, pressure-packed marathon sessions at pinochle, poker, backgammon, gin, and craps as well as bridge. The baby-faced, fast-talking, thirty-year-old Cohen is cheerful, likable, and unlike almost every other successful gambler I know. He does not search for soft touches when choosing a gambling opponent.

Ken Cohen has played backgammon for high stakes against Paul Magriel, the backgammon columnist for *The New York Times* and perhaps the best in the world at the game (Magriel and Broadway Billy Eisenberg were recently featured on CBS's "Sixty Minutes"). Cohen has played pinochle for money against Bobby Jordan, one of the best in the world at that game. He even has played scrabble for high stakes against perhaps the world's best, Mike Senkiewicz. All of these people, in my opinion, are to be avoided where cash and gambling are concerned, but Cohen seems to do all right.

The money in the Calcutta, Cohen told me, was not for him the primary allure of the event. He enjoyed instead the challenge of competing against a strong field in an important tournament.

Walt Walvick, Cohen's partner, is a Washington, D. C., lawyer, a big, husky, lazy-looking bear of a man who smokes a pipe and is either smiling or frowning. Walvick's stories are funny and usually detail a disaster that has befallen him at the bridge table. A chance listener might think he is the unluckiest player on earth: his stories depict some wildly unlikely slam his opponents have bid and miraculously made, or some exquisitely reasoned move on his part that is checkmated by once-in-a-light-year distribution.

No one should be taken in by Walvick's misery-laden stories. He has won numerous championships, including the 1975 Life Masters Men's Pairs.

Cohen and Walvick set us by one trick in each of the three hands we played. All of them could have been made if we had gotten distributional or positional breaks, but fortunately the defeats were tempered because we were in a strong field and most other partnerships sitting in the same direction bid the same as we did.

I usually do not stay around after a bridge session to learn the results. My being there won't change them and talking to anxious competitors is guaranteed to fray the nerves.

But this was different. It was billed as the "most important pairs event on the continent" and it carried the richest prize. I wanted to find out where we stood before trying to get some sleep,

Peter and I reviewed the second session: we routed Rubin-Hamilton; we did the same to Griffin-Barbosa; Sharif and Yallouze had slightly the best of us; we did well against Schenken-Leventritt; we defeated Rose-Esterson; we had the best of Woolsey-Robinson; we had the advantage over Jacqui Mitchell and John Roberts; the same was true with Stayman-Granovetter; we had excellent results against Becker-Greenberg; and we had the worst of it against Cohen and Walvick.

The ninety-minute wait for the results was worthwhile, but it would not be honest to say we were surprised. There had been an occasionally enlightened hand—such as the game contract against Becker and Greenberg—but generally we had been simply consistent and professional.

POSITION	PARTNERSHIP	COUNTRY	IMPS
1.	Weichsel-Sontag	U.S.A.	1467
2.	Blair-Levin	U.S.A.	1296
3.	Sharif-Yallouze	Egypt-France	1180
4.	Blau-Ginsberg	U.S.A.	1167
5.	Kokish-Nagy	Canada	941

Dr. Sam Marsh and Lou Blum won $3,000 for finishing first in the session. Peter and I won $2,000 (to go with the $1,000 we had won in the first session) for finishing second. Blair-Levin and Kokish-Nagy each won $1,000 for third and fourth place finishes in the session.

The rest of the event, I figured, would be a breeze.

"Don't be cocky," was the last thing Peter said to me before heading home for Queens.

But we were playing and bidding well, and luck was with us, and I decided Peter was just an alarmist. I went back to my apartment and had a wonderful night's sleep.

SESSION III

CHAPTER

13

THE SECOND DAY

THE PHONE RANG AT 10 A.M. IT WAS MY FRIEND MARTY
Reisman, the former table tennis champion, and he wanted
to tell me a story. Reisman is one of the most colorful characters who inhabit New York City's wonderful world of
games. He can defeat almost anyone at table tennis using a
Coca-Cola bottle or a shoe or a chess piece as a racquet.

"I made a hundred dollars the other day," he said.

"That's good," I said. It was also good to hear from Marty.
I did not want to start worrying about the Calcutta at 10 A.M.

"I was walking down the street," he said, "and spotted
some furniture in front of this apartment building. I stopped
to look it over."

I imagined I knew what was coming next but told him to
go ahead anyway.

"I asked the guy who carried it down if I could have it.
He said sure. Then another guy popped over and asked if the
furniture was mine. I said yes. He asked what I wanted for it.

I said a hundred and ten dollars. He offered ninety. We compromised at a hundred."

"Something about this seems a little disreputable," I said.

"What?" Marty asked. "Do you think I sold it too cheap?"

I could see through the window that it was a beautiful spring day, perfect for walking in the park. I tried to get back to sleep but the phone rang again.

"Alan, it's Alan," the voice of Alan Marlowe bubbled over the phone. Alan Marlowe is a very talented man, but available acting jobs are such that at present he is best known for appearing in porno films. He had a major part in *Oriental Blue* and the starring role in *The Private Afternoons of Pamela Mann*. I met him at a bridge tournament years before.

"I've got a great thing for you to do this afternoon," he said.

"I'm playing bridge this afternoon."

"Raise your sights. What I'm talking about is your movie debut."

"Movie debut?"

"Right. A male cast member in my latest film is sick and you'd be a great replacement."

"You think so?"

"Definitely. Be ready in ten minutes. I'll pick you up and we're going to Van Cortlandt Park."

A movie debut. Beautiful women. I wondered what Peter would say when I told him I was quitting in the middle of the Calcutta. I decided it didn't matter what he would say. It was what he would do. He would come out to Van Cortlandt Park and kill me.

"I can't do it," I said.

"Do you want to be a bridge player all your life?"

I thought it over.

"Yes," I said.

The phone rang a few more times—I have a wacky collection of friends—and then I took a peaceful Sunday morning stroll the dozen blocks to the Cavendish. Peter was not yet there. I had a cup of coffee and sat on a sofa and stared at the first day's results.

Estee Griffin walked up. She told me she was writing a column for a major newspaper and that she would want a hand from us if we won the event.

Peter bustled in. He was smiling, happy, exuding confidence. He remembered as well as I did the day in 1972 when at the two-thirds point we were leading the Life Masters Pairs in Denver. Al Roth came over and put his arms around our shoulders. "You kids aren't nervous, are you?" he said.

Roth won the event and we finished second.

"I passed up a movie career for you," I said to Peter.

"You shouldn't have done that," he said.

"Let's win by a hundred miles," I said.

Standing in the way of that dream were James Jacoby and Dave Berkowitz, our first opponents of the second day. I didn't know it at the time, but Jim Jacoby would soon do me a great favor. Along with his father, Oswald, he was a syndicated columnist for Newspaper Enterprise Association (NEA) with a column that appears in more than 300 newspapers nationwide. Jim Jacoby decided to curtail some of his bridge activity to go into business and recommended that I work with his father on the column. It was a marvelous opportunity. Whatever city I now go to I can usually count on seeing my name next to Oswald's in the local paper, although readers should know that he does the lion's share of the writing.

Jim Jacoby is a big man, 6 feet 3 and 225 pounds, and I have never heard anyone say a nasty word against him, an enormous compliment to his character considering the countless jealousies and petty insecurities that infect the upper strata of America's bridge culture.

Jim Jacoby had won the first Cavendish Calcutta. He won consecutive World Championships in 1970 and 1971, and was a charter member of the Dallas Aces, one of the greatest bridge teams ever assembled. He was, in other words, a player of the caliber of Billy Eisenberg, against whom we had started this tournament. I thought it was a good omen. We had started well against Billy, and if we did okay against Jacoby I thought it impossible, inconceivable, that we would blow the event.

Dave Berkowitz, Jacoby's partner, later endured endless bad-taste Son of Sam jokes when his name-alike was arrested for the killings that made national headlines and terrorized much of New York City. But Berkowitz is a good bridge player, confident enough in his own skills and worth not to be derailed by silly and frivolous references.

Unfortunately, Berkowitz bears a remarkable resemblance to Son of Sam. Peter held himself back as best he could, but at a later tournament, in December, 1977, he could no longer resist.

"Shot any teenage girls lately?" Peter asked Berkowitz.

"Show some sensitivity," I said.

"What do you mean? This guy may be a murderer. The wrong person is probably in jail."

"He does *look* like Son of Sam," I said.

"Let's report him," Peter said.

"It's our duty," I said.

"By the way, Berkowitz," Peter said, "don't you think the death penalty is deserved in your case?"

"I may," said Berkowitz, "impose the death penalty on a couple of sick bridge players by cracking their skulls together."

Berkowitz is 6 feet 2 and weighs 240 pounds. We quickly assured him that we were speaking hypothetically.

But that was in the future. In the present we raced off to a big lead:

NORTH (Berkowitz)
♠ Q 6
♥ J 5
♦ Q 10 7 3 2
♣ 10 9 5 3

WEST (Sontag)
♠ J 10 2
♥ K 4 3
♦ J 9 8 6 5 4
♣ 4

EAST (Weichsel)
♠ 9 8 7 5 4 3
♥ 9 7 6 2
♦ K
♣ K 8

SOUTH (Jacoby)
♠ A K
♥ A Q 10 8
♦ A
♣ A Q J 7 6 2

North-South vulnerable. The bidding:

WEST	NORTH	EAST	SOUTH
		Pass	2 ♣
3 ♦	Double	Pass	4 ♣
Pass	5 ♣	Pass	6 ♣
Pass	Pass	Pass	

Many partnerships, when they get the lead in a tournament, tend to sit on it. Occasionally this strategy works, but more often the momentum built up is dissipated. Tournaments are not won by playing scared, and it is folly to relax. Also, it is true that more mistakes are made at the beginning of a session than in the middle of it. For all of these reasons and more Peter and I agree we should play each hand with utmost concentration and intensity. Bridge is our livelihood, it is all we do, yet at most only 10 percent of our time is spent actually playing: we believe that 10 percent should be used to the fullest.

On the diagrammed hand my three-diamond preempt might seem wild and unfounded, but I was trying to deny them bidding space over their artificial, game-forcing, strong two-club opening bid. I might have gone down six tricks doubled, but Peter's original pass and their vulnerability gave me a measure of protection. As it turned out Jim Jacoby was not willing to sacrifice a slam possibility for what he thought would be a meager penalty. In addition, Jim knew we were leading the event and he did not believe I would risk an audacious, rash preempt on the very first hand.

It has always seemed strange to me that conventional bridge wisdom dictates that players should interfere at all costs over the strong, artificial one-club opening with nonsense like IDAK (Instant Destroyer and Killer), CRASH (Color, Rank, Shape), Exclusion Overcalls, Two Suit Overcalls, and Transfer Overcalls, yet these same players cannot see the logic of interfering against the far more dangerous and vulnerable strong two-bid.

The contract Jacoby and Berkowitz arrived at was not a bad one. Jim took the best percentage play—cashing the ace of clubs and hoping the singleton king would fall—but it didn't work out and he later entered dummy with the ten of clubs to take a heart finesse which lost.

Down one was worth about 140 IMPs to us because many pairs missed this slam, and others who bid it made the contract through a fortunate opening lead (I led a neutral diamond) or an inferior line of play (taking the club finesse).

Peter's hands were straight out in front of him gripping the table tightly. He was staring straight at me but not seeing. Pain showed in his eyes. They were glassy, one hand had drained the mental energy he had so carefully conserved (how hard he had rooted for Jacoby to lose that slam!), and he was trying to recapture the resources that had helped get us to the lead and were needed to keep us there.

We lost a few IMPs on the next two hands against Jacoby and Berkowitz but there was an unspoken recognition between Peter and me that the tournament was ours.

"Do you think I should have made that slam?" Jacoby asked.

"No," I said. "You played it right."

"I guess so. But sometimes everything you do crumbles."

It was true. I genuinely hoped they did well (like second to Peter and me) and as a matter of fact they would score highest in this session and win $3,000.

Next came Ron Blau and Marty Ginsberg, a partnership that had sold at auction for the deceptively low price of $3,900. They had been a regular partnership and friends for as long as I could remember. A partnership a cut below the best will invariably bury the two finest individual players in the world if it is a true partnership. That is why, I believe, the College All-Stars, an excellent collection of individual talent, almost always lost to the NFL champion. It is also why I would make almost any concession to Peter to keep him as a partner, and I believe he would do the same for me. We have too many years invested to let anything come between us.

Blau and Ginsberg were that way. They were not flashy, but they were a *partnership*. There would be a lot of red faces among the so-called bridge handicappers when the money was divided after the Calcutta.

Ron Blau is both a CPA and a lawyer, and he once did me an important favor. I won a Lancia automobile in 1975 from the Fiat Corporation, which was so confident that members of Italy's famous Blue Team (plus Omar Sharif) were invincible that it offered five new cars to any team that could defeat them. Ron Rubin, Matt Granovetter, Peter, and I won the cars.

I sold mine (the four of us sold the fifth car and divided the proceeds). The dealer I sold my car to withheld 8 percent of the price we agreed on to cover the sales tax he said I owed.

"That's crazy," Blau said when I told him about the transaction. He called the dealer and that same day I had a check for almost $500.

Only a connoisseur would have appreciated our dry round against Blau and Ginsberg. There was none of Ira Rubin's theatrics, or Omar Sharif's glamour, or Amos Kaminsky's bravado, just good, solid bridge. The round was a virtual standoff, although they did score a few IMPs against us.

In a sense it was good that we had not blitzed Jim Jacoby and Dave Berkowitz on the last two hands, or Blau and Ginsberg on any hand. Bidding and then beating that first hand against Jacoby and Berkowitz had given us additional breathing space, but it had squeezed us emotionally and we were lucky to keep our losses to a minimum. It was time, I hoped, for someone to suffer for our letdown.

"Look who's next," Peter said.

"I see," I said.

Peter knew that I was twisted when it came to Vic Mitchell. Unintentionally, he had grounded me in the basics of bridge and taught me how to play. Now, whenever I'm against him, I feel I have something to prove.

I am not sure the way I learned the game would work for anyone else. I learned by watching, not playing, and the person I watched most was Vic Mitchell. He was an expert bridge bidder and nonpareil cardplayer, and he always made me feel less than stupid by answering whatever questions I asked.

Vic Mitchell is an insomniac. At tournaments around the country, even at 4 or 5 A.M., I can always roam through the hotel lobby and find Vic. But there is more that is peculiar about Vic Mitchell. He often brings his Siberian Husky, Little IMP, to watch him play. He has three other Siberian Huskies —Big IMP, Tagalong, Sasha—but Little IMP, who looks like a white wolf, is often the kibitzer.

Playing against Vic Mitchell's partner, Bill Roberts, has often been an unpleasant experience for me. I seem to bring out the best in Roberts.

Whenever Peter and I play against Vic Mitchell and Bill Roberts, and it has happened more than two dozen times, I start believing a dentist's chair would be more enjoyable.

A month before, Peter and I defeated Vic and Bill Roberts by the razor-thin margin of 5 IMPs in a desperately close war in a 64-board match of the semifinals of the Grand Nationals in New York City; two weeks later they edged us out in the

Swiss Teams championship in Miami Beach; earlier one hand had decided the Von Zedtwitz Double Knockout in our favor.

I wanted this to be different. We were leading the Calcutta, they were trying to catch up, but we would not let them.

We bid three hearts and made it: plus 30 IMPs. We bid two spades and made three: plus 42 IMPs. They bid four clubs when they should have bid five: plus 90 IMPs.

We seemed to be ahead by half a hundred miles.

"Play harder," Peter said.

CHAPTER

14

TWO-LEVEL OPENING BIDS

TWO-LEVEL OPENING BID SEQUENCES

TWO CLUBS BY OPENER SHOWS 11 TO 16 HIGH-CARD POINTS and six or more clubs. Opener may also have another four- or five-card suit.

OPENER	RESPONDER
2 ♣	2 ♦ (artificial, asks for further description)

Opener may make the following bids:

1. Two Hearts. Shows a four-card major. Responder bids two spades to learn which major. Two no trump by opener shows four hearts, three clubs shows four spades. If responder has a fit with opener's major, he bids four of the major to play, three of the major as an invitation to game, or three diamonds as a slam invitation in opener's major. If opener and responder have not found a major suit fit, responder may elect to bid three no trump to play, two no trump over two hearts as a natural invitation to game (shows 10 or 11 points

and no four-card major), three clubs to show a club fit, 9 to 11 points, four clubs as a slam try in clubs, or three of either major to show a fair six-card suit in the suit bid with at least game values. In the latter instance, opener needs only a doubleton to raise.

2. Two Spades. Shows minimum bid, 12 to 14 high-card points and no four-card major. Responder bids two no trump to invite to game in no trump; three clubs is to play; three diamonds asks opener what suit he has stopped besides clubs —opener bids three hearts to show a stopper in hearts, three spades shows a spade stopper, and three no trump shows a diamond stopper; three of either major shows six cards in the major and asks opener to raise with two- or three-card support, bid three no trump with a singleton or void in the major, or bid four clubs with seven or more clubs and an unsuitable no trump hand; three no trump is to play; and, finally, four clubs is a slam try in clubs.

3. Two No Trump. Shows stoppers in two other suits besides clubs and 14 to 16 points. Responder bids three clubs to invite game in clubs or no trump; three diamonds asks which suits opener has stopped—three hearts by opener shows hearts and diamonds stopped, three spades to show spades and diamonds stopped, and three no trump to show hearts and spades stopped (if responder discovers that a suit is not stopped, he will retire to four clubs which is usually passed unless opener likes his hand and has a singleton in the unstopped suit); three of a major shows a six-card suit in the suit bid and asks opener to raise to game with a two- or three-card fit, cue bid a new suit to show a maximum raise to game in responder's major and control in the suit bid; three no trump to play; or four clubs as a slam try in clubs.

4. Three Clubs. Shows a good six- or seven-card club suit, a stopper in one other suit, and no other four-card suit. Responder bids three diamonds to learn the stopper—three hearts shows hearts, three spades shows spades, three no trump shows diamonds; three of a major shows the same as the previous auction; three no trump is to play; four clubs invites to

game in clubs; and four diamonds is an artificial slam try in clubs—opener would bid four of a major to cue bid, four no trump to cue bid in diamonds, and five clubs to sign off.

5. Three Diamonds. Shows a good four- or five-card diamond suit, at least six clubs, and more than a minimum two-club opening bid—with a *minimum* two-club opening and four diamonds, opener would bid two spades. Over three diamonds, responder bids three of a major to show six cards in the suit bid; three no trump to play; four of a minor as a slam try in that suit; and four hearts is Blackwood (four spades would show 0 or 3 aces, four no trump 1 or 4 aces, and five clubs would show 2 aces).

6. Three Hearts. Shows six clubs and five hearts. Responder bids three no trump to play; four clubs invites game in clubs; four diamonds is a slam try in hearts; four hearts is to play; and four spades is Blackwood (Roman).

7. Three Spades. Shows six clubs and five spades. Responder bids three no trump to play; four clubs invites game in clubs; four diamonds is a slam try in spades; four hearts is Blackwood; and four spades is to play.

8. Three No Trump. Shows six or seven clubs to the A K Q, and a distribution of 6-3-2-2 or 7-2-2-2, and a minimum of at least a king or a queen in two of the unbid suits. Incidentally, a five-club bid by responder during any of these auctions must be passed.

TWO CLUBS—TWO OF EITHER MAJOR SEQUENCE

Two hearts or two spades by responder are natural bids, non-forcing, that show at least five cards in the suit bid.

OPENER	RESPONDER
2 ♣	2 ♥ or 2 ♠

Any responses by opener over two of a major are natural. Opener should pass if he has a minimum and two- or three-card support. He should bid three clubs if he prefers his own suit, raise to game if he has four-card support, bid another five-card suit if he has one, or bid two no trump with 15 or 16 high-card points and the two unbid suits stopped.

TWO CLUBS—TWO NO TRUMP SEQUENCE

Two no trump is forcing. Responder will clarify with his next bid: whether two no trump shows 10 or 11 points, no major suit, and interest in three no trump; or a five card major with 12 or more high-card points.

OPENER	RESPONDER
2 ♣	2 no trump

If opener has a minimum two-club bid that would reject the 10- or 11-point hand responder might have, he signs off in three clubs. With 10 or 11 points, responder will pass. With the strong hand, he will bid his five-card major and opener will raise with three-card support or bid three no trump without it.

With more than a minimum two-club bid, opener can bid three no trump, or three diamonds to show six clubs and four or five diamonds, or three hearts or three spades to show three or four cards in the suit bid (holding both suits, opener should bid hearts first).

TWO CLUBS—THREE CLUBS SEQUENCE

Three clubs is a mild invitation to game in clubs and probably denies a four-card major.

OPENER	RESPONDER
2 ♣	3 ♣

Opener should introduce a five-card major if he has one. Responder will raise with three-card support. Any other bids by opener are natural.

TWO CLUBS—THREE OF ANOTHER SUIT SEQUENCE

A jump to three of a new suit shows a strong six- or seven-card suit and forces to at least game.

OPENER	RESPONDER
2 ♣	3 ♦ or 3 ♥ or 3 ♠

All subsequent bids by opener are natural.

TWO CLUBS—THREE NO TRUMP SEQUENCE

Three no trump shows a balanced hand, all suits well stopped, and no particular interest in playing a suit contract. Guarantees 15 or 16 high-card points.

OPENER	RESPONDER
2 ♣	3 no trump

Since responder's bid is a natural slam try, opener may pass or bid naturally if his hand warrants.

TWO CLUBS—FOUR CLUBS SEQUENCE

Four clubs is preemptive and virtually demands that opener pass. Usually this bid would show a Yarborough (no points) and three or four clubs.

OPENER	RESPONDER
2 ♣	4 ♣

Four clubs is used as a wedge to prevent the opponents from locating the correct contract.

TWO CLUBS—FOUR DIAMONDS SEQUENCE

Four diamonds, which we call Modified Roman Redwood, is an ace-asking bid.

OPENER	RESPONDER
2 ♣	4 ♦

Four hearts by opener shows 0 or 3 aces. Four spades shows 1 or 4 aces. Four no trump shows 2 aces. Five clubs shows 2 aces and an excellent club suit, including the queen. If after bidding four diamonds, responder bids five diamonds, it is a king ask and the responses are the same.

TWO CLUBS—FOUR OF A MAJOR
OR FIVE CLUBS SEQUENCE

Four hearts, four spades, or five clubs by responder are, without exception, the end of the auction.

OPENER	RESPONDER
2 ♣	4 ♥ or 4 ♠ or 5 ♣

If the opening bid of two clubs is overcalled by a suit bid through four spades, doubles by responder are negative and show strength and length in the unbid suits.

This completely covers the two-clubs opening bid sequence. There are other opening two-bids that need to be discussed.

TWO DIAMOND OPENING BID

Two diamonds shows any 4-4-4-1 distribution and 16 to 24 high-card points; or a weak two-heart bid, showing six hearts and 6 to 12 high-card points; or a very strong balanced hand of 26 or 27 high-card points, not rich in aces and kings, a bid which rarely occurs. Bids that have more than one meaning, of which two diamonds is an example, are becoming increasingly popular in expert circles. They cram additional meanings into the same initial bid and, while they are not immediately revealing to the opponents, partner can soon find out which kind of hand is held. In addition, several two-bids take pressure off the otherwise crowded one-club opening and provide more specific information.

Most frequently responder bids two hearts over two diamonds. Two hearts means responder is not strong enough to force opener to bid if opener's two-diamond bid was actually a weak two-bid in hearts. The weak two-heart holding, it should be added, is nine times more likely to occur than the strong 4-4-4-1 hand.

OPENER	RESPONDER
2 ♦	2 ♥

Opener must pass if he has the weak two-bid. With the strong hand, opener has one of eight bids.

1. Two Spades. Shows a singleton in one of the majors and 16 to 19 high-card points. To learn opener's exact distribution, responder bids two no trump. Opener bids three clubs to show 4-1-4-4, three diamonds to show 1-4-4-4 and 16 or 17 high-card points, and three hearts to show 1-4-4-4 and 18 or 19 high-card points.

2. Two No Trump. Shows a singleton club and 16 to 19 high-card points.

3. Three Clubs. Singleton diamond, 16 to 19 high-card points.

4. Three Diamonds. Singleton heart, 20 to 24 high-card points.

5. Three Hearts. Singleton spade, 20 to 24 high-card points.

6. Three Spades. Singleton club, 20 to 24 high-card points.

7. Three No Trump. A rare exception. Shows a balanced hand, 26 or 27 high-card points, with 9 or more points in queens and jacks.

8. Four Clubs. Singleton diamond, 20 to 24 high-card points.

Whenever opener has shown 16 to 19 high-card points, responder's cue bid of the singleton would ask opener to define his strength more precisely. The cheapest bid by opener shows 16 or 17 high-card points, the next cheapest shows 18 or 19. If the auction had shown a 16- to 19-point hand with the spade singleton, the point count range would be known within one.

OPENER	RESPONDER
2 ♦	2 ♥
2 no trump (club singleton)	3 ♣ (asks for strength)
3 ♥ (18 to 19)	

After defining the point count of the 16- to 19-point hand, or after receiving a 20- to 24-point response, a cue bid of the singleton asks for controls. Opener has five possible responses with the weaker hand: the cheapest response shows 4 controls; next, 5 controls; next, 6; next, 7; finally, 8 controls.

If opener has the 20- to 24-point hand, the cheapest bid shows 6 controls and the bids range progressively upward to 10.

OPENER	RESPONDER
2 ♦	2 ♥
3 ♣ (singleton diamond)	3 ♦ (asks strength)
3 ♠ (18 or 19 points)	4 ♦ (asks controls)
4 no trump (6 controls)	

OPENER	RESPONDER
2 ♦	2 ♥
3 ♥ (singleton spade, 20 to 24 high-card points)	3 ♠ (asks controls)
4 ♣ (7 controls)	

There are 12 controls in the deck, but the singleton king is never included in responses to the control ask.

After asking for controls, a further cue bid by responder asks for queens. With no queens, opener bids the cheapest no trump. With one or two queens, he bids the cheaper queen. With all three queens, he jumps to seven clubs. The queen in the singleton suit is not counted, and queen-asking sequences are always grand slam tries.

OPENER	RESPONDER
2 ♦	2 ♥
2 ♠ (singleton in either major)	2 no trump (asks singleton)
3 ♣ (singleton heart)	3 ♥ (asks strength)
3 no trump (18 or 19)	4 ♥ (asks controls)
5 ♣ (6 controls)	5 ♥ (queen ask)
6 ♣ (club queen, no spade queen)	

After a positive response to a queen-asking bid, yet another cue bid, or five no trump, whichever is cheaper, is a further queen-asking bid. Opener should bid his other queen. With no more queens he bids no trump or the cue bid, whichever is cheaper.

OPENER	RESPONDER
2 ♦	2 ♥
3 ♠ (singleton club)	4 ♣ (asks controls)
4 ♠ (8 controls)	5 ♣ (queen ask)
5 ♦ (queen of diamonds)	5 no trump (further queen ask)
6 ♣ (no more queens)	6 ♠ (ends auction)

A natural bid by responder at the six level is a sign-off. However, if the auction was such that a negative response to a second queen ask would be higher than the final contract, opener should bid seven with the trump queen.

OPENER	RESPONDER
2 ♦	2 ♥
4 ♣ (one diamond)	4 ♦ (control ask)
4 no trump (8 controls)	5 ♦ (queen ask)
5 ♥ (heart queen)	6 ♣ (sign-off)
7 ♣ (club queen)	

In the preceding auction, responder would have had to bid five no trump to ask for further queens. The negative response to this bid would be six diamonds, and the proper contract if opener does not have the queen is six clubs. Thus, responder signs off at six clubs, expecting opener to go to seven if he has the club queen.

Any time responder fails to go through an asking bid sequence, he is signing off. The only exception is a raise to four of a minor, which invites to game in that minor. Opener must have very good trump and a maximum hand to accept.

OPENER	RESPONDER
2 ♦	2 ♥
3 ♣ (singleton diamond, 16 to 19 high-card points)	4 ♣ (mild invitation to game in clubs)

There are other bids besides two hearts that responder can make over two diamonds, and all of them assume opener's bid showed a weak two-bid in hearts.

TWO DIAMONDS—TWO SPADES SEQUENCE

Two spades shows five or more spades, is forcing, and promises sufficient values to be trying for game opposite the weaker of opener's two meanings.

OPENER	RESPONDER
2 ♦	2 ♠

Opener may make the following bids:

1. Two No Trump. 4-4-4-1 with any singleton and 16 to 19 high-card points. Responder bids three clubs to learn the singleton, and opener bids three diamonds to show a heart singleton, three hearts to show a spade singleton, three spades to show a club singleton, and four clubs to show a diamond singleton. Control-asking bids and queen-asking bids are the same as previously discussed. The strength-asking bid is not needed or used.

2. Three Clubs. A weak two-bid in hearts with three or four clubs to an honor and more than a minimum in high cards. If responder bids three hearts or three spades, opener may pass; otherwise the auction proceeds to at least game.

3. Three Diamonds. Exactly the same as three clubs except it shows three or four diamonds to an honor.

4. Three Hearts. A minimum weak two-bid in hearts. Responder may pass or bid three spades, which opener may want to pass.

5. Three Spades. A weak two-bid in hearts with either three-card spade support or two spades to an honor (A, K, or Q).

6. Three No Trump. Shows 4-4-4-1, a singleton club, and 20 to 24 high-card points.

7. Four Clubs. A singleton diamond and 20 to 24 high-card points.

8. Four Diamonds. Singleton heart and 20 to 24 high-card points.

9. Four Hearts. Singleton spade and 20 to 24 high-card points. If responder bids four spades over four hearts, it is to play. Four no trump would ask for controls.

To Responses #6, 7, and 8, the control asks and queen asks are the same as already discussed.

TWO DIAMONDS—TWO NO TRUMP SEQUENCE

Two no trump forces opener to clarify his hand and usually shows balanced distribution.

OPENER	RESPONDER
2 ♦	2 no trump

Opener may bid as follows:

1. Three Clubs. Shows a weak two-bid with a very good suit, either six hearts headed by the K Q J, A Q J, A K J, A Q 10, or A K 10. If responder then bids three hearts, opener may pass if he has no additional values. Any other bid by responder forces to at least game.

2. Three Diamonds. Shows a maximum weak two-bid in hearts, and the hand can be either balanced or unbalanced. If responder bids three hearts, it is unconditionally forcing. Opener should bid three no trump with a balanced hand, or cue bid with an unbalanced hand.

3. Three Hearts. A minimum weak two-bid in hearts. The bid may be passed.

4. Three Spades. Shows 16 to 24 high-card points and a singleton club.

5. Three No Trump. A weak two-bid in hearts with six hearts headed by the A K Q.

6. Four Clubs. A singleton diamond and 16 to 24 high-card points.

7. Four Diamonds. Singleton heart and 16 to 24 high-card points.

8. Four Hearts. Singleton spade and 16 to 24 high-card points.

Over Responses #4, 6, 7, or 8, responder asks for controls by bidding the singleton. The cheapest response shows 4 controls, etc., through 10.

TWO DIAMONDS—THREE CLUBS SEQUENCE

Three clubs shows five or more clubs, usually six, and enough values to try for a game opposite the weak two-bid.

OPENER	RESPONDER
2 ♦	3 ♣

Opener may bid as follows:

1. Three Diamonds. A good weak two-bid in hearts and an honor in diamonds. Any response other than four clubs commits the partnership to at least game.

2. Three Hearts. A minimum weak two-bid in hearts. Can be passed.

3. Three Spades. Good weak two-bid in hearts with a spade control. Forces to game.

4. Three No Trump. Good weak two-bid in hearts with minimum of queen and one other in diamonds and spades.

5. Four Clubs. A weak two-bid in hearts and at least three clubs.

6. Four Diamonds. 4-1-4-4 and 16 or more high-card points.

7. Four Hearts. 1-4-4-4 and 16 or more high-card points.

8. Four Spades. 4-4-1-4 and 16 or more high-card points.

9. Four No Trump. 4-4-4-1 and 16 or more high-card points.

TWO DIAMONDS—THREE DIAMONDS SEQUENCE

Three diamonds shows five or more diamonds, usually six, and enough values to try for a game opposite the weak two-bid.

OPENER	RESPONDER
2 ♦	3 ♦

Opener may bid as follows:

1. Three Hearts. Minimum weak two-bid in hearts. Can be passed.

2. Three Spades. More than a minimum two-bid in hearts and an honor in spades.

3. Three No Trump. Good weak two-bid in hearts with minimum of queen and one other in spades and clubs.

4. Four Clubs. 4-1-4-4 and 16 or more high-card points.

5. Four Diamonds. Weak two-bid in hearts with three-card diamond support.

6. Four Hearts. 1-4-4-4 and 16 or more high-card points.

7. Four Spades. 4-4-4-1 and 16 or more high-card points.

8. Four No Trump. 4-4-1-4 and 16 or more high-card points.

TWO DIAMONDS—THREE HEARTS SEQUENCE

Three hearts is a preempt in hearts.

OPENER	RESPONDER
2 ♦	3 ♥

Opener must pass if he had a weak two-bid in hearts. Otherwise, he bids as follows:

1. Three Spades. 4-4-4-1 and 16 or more high card points.

2. Three No Trump. 4-1-4-4 and 16 or more high-card points.

3. Four Clubs. 4-4-1-4 and 16 or more high-card points.

4. Four Diamonds. 1-4-4-4 and 16 or more high-card points.

Peter and I do not use any sequences that begin two diamonds, three spades; two diamonds, three no trump; two diamonds, four clubs; or two diamonds, four diamonds.

TWO DIAMONDS—FOUR HEARTS SEQUENCE

Four hearts shows that responder wants to play the game in hearts opposite the weak two-bid.

OPENER	RESPONDER
2 ♦	4 ♥

Opener must pass if he had a weak two-bid in hearts. Otherwise, he bids as follows:

1. Four Spades. 4-4-4-1 and 16 or more high-card points.
2. Four No Trump. 4-1-4-4 and 16 or more high-card points.
3. Five Clubs. 4-4-1-4 and 16 or more high-card points.
4. Five Diamonds. 1-4-4-4 and 16 or more high-card points.

Occasionally the opponents will enter the bidding over two diamonds. If two diamonds is overcalled, a double by responder is for penalties. If opener doubles, he has the strong 4-4-4-1 hand and four cards in the suit he is doubling. If he has the strong hand with the singleton in the suit bid, he bids the next highest suit. Just such a hand arose in the Von Zedtwitz Double Knockout against Tom Smith and Steve Altman, two former teammates, and helped us win the match.

NORTH (Weichsel)
♠ K Q 10 5
♥ A K 6 3
♦ A J 8 4
♣ 7

WEST (Altman)
♠ A J 7
♥ Q 7
♦ K 6 5
♣ K Q 9 6 5

EAST (Smith)
♠ 9 8 4
♥ 9 5 2
♦ Q 10 7 3 2
♣ 10 2

SOUTH (Sontag)
♠ 6 3 2
♥ J 10 8 4
♦ 9
♣ A J 8 4 3

Neither side vulnerable. The bidding:

WEST	NORTH	EAST	SOUTH
	2 ♦	Pass	2 ♥
Double	Redouble	Pass	Pass
3 ♣	Pass	Pass	Double
Pass	Pass	Pass	

Altman entered the auction because he was afraid Peter's opening bid was a weak two-bid in hearts, and that he would pass my two-heart response. Altman doubled, and Peter's redouble showed the strong three-suit hand. Peter's pass after Altman's three-club bid showed the singleton club (with four clubs he would have doubled). I doubled and we set the contract four tricks.

TWO HEART OPENING BID

Two hearts shows one of two types of hand: 12 to 15 high-card points and 4-4-1-4 or 4-4-0-5 distribution; or 12 to 15 high-card points, four spades, five hearts, and any other minor suit distribution. Responder usually bids two no trump over two hearts.

OPENER	RESPONDER
2 ♥	2 no trump

Responder's two no trump is forcing and asks opener to define his distribution. Opener bids as follows:

1. Three Clubs. 4-4-1-4 or 4-4-0-5. Responder bids three diamonds to ask for further clarification. Opener may bid three hearts to show 4-4-1-4 and 12 or 13 high-card points; three spades to show 4-4-0-5 and 12 or 13 high-card points; three no trump to show 4-4-1-4, 14 or 15 high-card points, and a singleton A, K, or Q of diamonds; four clubs to show 4-4-1-4 and 14 or 15 high-card points; and four diamonds to show 4-4-0-5 and 14 or more high-card points.

2. Three Diamonds. 4-5-3-1.

3. Three Hearts. 4-5-2-2 and 12 or 13 high-card points.
4. Three Spades. 4-5-1-3.
5. Three No Trump. 4-5-2-2 and 14 or 15 high-card points.
6. Four Clubs. 4-5-0-4.
7. Four Diamonds. 4-5-4-0.

If opening bidder has 16 high-card points that are not particularly impressive, he could open with two hearts rather than one club if he chooses. The opening bid of two hearts might give a clearer description of his hand.

After opener has shown 4-5 in the majors, responder bids four of opener's short minor as a general slam try; four of opener's three-card minor is a natural slam try in that suit. Four hearts by opener is always a sign-off over these slam tries.

When responder knows opener's distribution and bids three of a major, it asks opener to pass.

Responder has other bids he can make over the two-heart opening. They are:

1. Pass. Wants to play two hearts.
2. Two Spades. No interest in game. Opener must pass.
3. Three Clubs. Invitational to game in no trump or clubs and shows a good six-card club suit.
4. Three Diamonds. Invitational to game in no trump or diamonds and shows an excellent six-card diamond suit headed by three of the top four honors.
5. Three Hearts. Invitational to game in hearts. Opener needs strong trump to accept.
6. Three Spades. The same as three hearts except the invitation is in spades.
7. Three No Trump, Four Hearts, Four Spades. Opener must pass.

TWO SPADE OPENING BID

Two spades shows 6 to 12 high-card points and exactly six spades. It is important to remember that weak two-bids in both hearts and spades deny a void and a five-card side suit, and generally opener has two of the top four honors in the long suit.

The most likely bid over two spades is two no trump.

OPENER	RESPONDER
2 ♠	2 no trump

Two no trump forces opener to clarify his weak two-bid. He may bid as follows:

1. Three Clubs. Shows an excellent six-card suit headed by K Q J, A Q J, A K J, A Q 10, or A K 10. If responder then bids three spades, opener may pass if he has no additional values. Any other bid by responder forces to at least game.

2. Three Diamonds. A balanced maximum weak two-bid. 6-3-2-2 distribution with any three-card suit. The spade suit is not as strong as it would be if opener bid three clubs. The first responsibility of the weak two-bidder is to show a strong suit.

3. Three Hearts. An unbalanced maximum weak two-bid. 6-3-3-1 distribution with any singleton, or 6-4-2-1 with any distribution in the remaining suits. Any bid by responder forces to at least a game.

4. Three Spades. Minimum weak two-bid. Responder may pass.

5. Three No Trump. Six spades to the A K Q.

6. Four Clubs. Six spades and four clubs to one of top three honors. Nine or more high-card points in the black suits.

7. Four Diamonds. The same as four clubs except the four-card suit is diamonds.

Responder has other bids he can make over the two-spade opening. For example, three clubs, three diamonds, and three hearts show five or more cards in the suit bid with enough other values to try for game opposite the weak two-bid. These bids are forcing. Opener rebids spades with a minimum weak two-bid and no fit with responder's suit; raises responder's suit with three-card support or two-card support headed by the A, K, or Q; bids three no trump with a high honor in each of the other two suits; or bids a new suit to show a good weak two-bid and a control in the suit.

Responder has five other bids he can make over the weak two-spade opening:

1. Three Spades or Four Spades. Must be passed.
2. Three No Trump. Must be passed.
3. Four Clubs. Asks in clubs. Opener bids four diamonds to deny first or second round control; four hearts to show a singleton or the king; and four spades to show the ace.
4. Four Diamonds. Asks in diamonds. Responses are the same as with four clubs except they are one notch higher.
5. Four Hearts. Asks in hearts. Responses are the same as with four clubs except they are two notches higher.

Whenever responder bids four no trump during one of these auctions, it is Blackwood.

TWO NO TRUMP OPENING BID

Two no trump shows a balanced hand with 24 or 25 high-card points. Responder has many bids he can make over two no trump:

1. Pass. Zero or one high-card point and denies a five-card major.
2. Three Clubs. Asks opener to bid a four-card major. If opener does not have one, he bids three diamonds. If responder then bids three of a major, he is showing five in the other major. The reason is so the strong hand can be declarer. If opener bids a major over three clubs, he bids the strongest one if he has both, and if responder wants to make a slam try in opener's major, he bids the other major. If responder bids four no trump after bidding Stayman, it is a natural slam try showing a balanced hand and about 8 high-card points.

OPENER	RESPONDER
2 no trump	3 ♣
3 ♦ (no major)	3 ♠ (five hearts)
4 ♥ (3 hearts)	

OPENER	RESPONDER
2 no trump	3 ♣
3 ♠ (at least four spades)	4 ♥ (slam try in spades)

3. Three Diamonds. Jacoby Transfer to three hearts. Shows 0 to 16 high-card points. Opener may bid more than three hearts with outstanding heart support. He may bid four hearts, or even a new suit—three spades, four clubs, four diamonds—which would be a cue bid showing the ace in the suit bid plus excellent four-card heart support and a top hand in aces and kings. Opener must bid three hearts if he has less than this strength. Responder's bid of a new suit on his second turn is natural and shows four or more cards in the suit bid. If opener accepts the transfer to three hearts, and responder then bids four no trump, it is a natural slam try showing 5 hearts, 7 or 8 high-card points, and a balanced hand.

4. Three Hearts. The same as three diamonds except the suit is spades.

5. Three Spades. Shows game or slam interest in both minor suits. Opener may reject by bidding three no trump, over which responder may still bid again. A major suit cue bid by responder would show a singleton or void in the suit bid. Responder may also bid a strong minor over three no trump.

6. Three No Trump. Ends the auction.

7. Four Clubs. Shows slam interest in one of the minors. Responder has 5 or more high-card points, and six or seven cards in one of the minors. Opener may bid in one of four ways: first, four diamonds, showing no slam interest in either minor; second, four hearts, showing slam interest if the suit is clubs; third, four spades, slam interest if the suit is diamonds; and fourth, four no trump, showing slam interest in both minors.

8. Four Diamonds. Modified Roman Redwood, an ace-asking bid. A response of four hearts shows 0 or 3 aces; four spades shows 1 or 4 aces; four no trump shows 2 aces.

9. Four Hearts and Four Spades. Slam try showing good six-card suit in suit bid. Opener may pass.

10. Four No Trump. Natural and a slam try.

This chapter has fully covered all of the opening two-bids in the W-S system. Because of some of these opening bids, the entire one-club structure has narrower and more precise meanings. For example, a player with 20 high-card points and 4-4-4-1 distribution would bid two diamonds rather than one club. Also, a player with 24 or 25 high-card points and a balanced hand would bid two no trump instead of one club. This has the effect of allowing the opening one-club bidder with balanced hands of 18 to 23 high-card points to define his point count within a two-point range.

Bidding should be as exact as scientific methods will allow. That is what Peter and I have tried to accomplish.

15

PROTECTING THE LEAD

B. JAY BECKER IS A LAWYER, LOOKS LIKE A BANKER, AND IS
known throughout the country as the nationally syndicated
columnist for King Features, a column he has written since
1956. Becker, "Mr. Becker" to everyone even in the informal
world of bridge, is like so many others the game has been
blessed with who span practically its entire history. Becker has
won seven Spingolds and seven Vanderbilts and at age seventy-
four is still even money to defeat anyone on the planet.

I met a fighter named Johnny Lombardo, who at age twenty-
five fought Sugar Ray Robinson to a dead heat. He staggered
Robinson twice but lost a split decision. At age fifty Lombardo
told me about the comeback he planned and everyone was
amazed and marveling that a person that old could be so
active and full of fire. I was not as impressed as the others.
B. Jay Becker played for the *World Championship* at age
sixty-nine. Waldemar Von Zedtwitz *won* a World Championship at age seventy-four. At ages fifty-seven, fifty-nine, sixty,

and sixty-one Oswald Jacoby won more Master Points than anyone on earth.

Jacoby, Von Zedtwitz, and B. Jay Becker give hope to people like me when we contemplate what to do in later years.

B. Jay Becker's partner was his son Steve, a slim, handsome, remarkably effective bridge teacher who ran the Boulevard Bridge Club which spawned and nurtured many of today's champions: Steve Altman, Joel Stuart, Gene Neiger, Andy Bernstein, Norman Kurlander, Mike Becker, Peter, and me.

It's fun to play against Steve and B. Jay. Steve respects his father, the two exude affection for each other, and there is never the danger of being caught in the crossfire of nasty and unpleasant recriminations.

Our bidding system enabled us on the very first hand to reach a virtually cold three no trump contract played from the correct side of the table with a minimum amount of information revealed to our opponents:

NORTH (Weichsel)	SOUTH (Sontag)
♠ 9 7 4 2	♠ K 5
♥ 9 8	♥ Q J 4
♦ A K 4	♦ Q 8 5
♣ K Q 4 2	♣ A J 9 6 3

Peter opened the north hand in first chair with one diamond. He had the absolute minimum, 12 high-card points and dull distribution. I made the game-forcing response of two no trump. Hearts were led and continued and I had an easy nine tricks. Because I had soft values—several queens and jacks—and a stopper in every suit, the two no trump response, rather than two clubs, was the proper course of action.

On the last two hands B. Jay and Steve bid a game that made and another that did not. For the round we were very slightly ahead, which is the minimum that should be aimed for by a partnership in the lead. A good partnership should not come back to the field. It should force the opponents to catch up.

"Wonderful," I said when Steve Sion and Marc Jacobus sat down to play.

Steve Sion, from Boston, was only twenty-four years old. His nickname is "Wonder," because of his youth and because he makes superficially silly moves at the bridge table that nearly always turn out to be inspired. His best plays are made without apparent thought, quickly, almost casually, which makes them doubly effective. Often when Peter and I make a good play it is telegraphed by a pause of several minutes to think.

Sion's girl friend, Mary Lou Cushner, attended the Calcutta. Mary Lou, known in the bridge world as Wonder Woman (her nickname is engraved on a gold chain she wears around her neck), is also an expert player. She is 5 feet 4, very attractive, slim, has sparkling green eyes.

Marc Jacobus, also from Boston, is an even faster player than Sion, but in his case the speed is often his downfall. He and Sion have won dozens of championships, but Jacobus's biggest victory came in the 1972 Life Masters Men's Pairs with Lou Hart as partner.

Steven Sion and Allan Cokin (a bridge professional in Florida) recently engineered a bridge teaching coup. They took an absolute beginner, Dr. James Sternberg of Fort Lauderdale, Florida, and turned him into a Life Master in less than one year. It was probably the first time in bridge history that this has occurred.

Peter and I bid a three no trump contract on the first hand with 24 high-card points. Peter had to guess which of two finesses to take. He guessed right and we had a whopping 140 additional IMPs.

Unbelievably, things got *better* on the next hand:

NORTH (Sion)
♠ J 9 5 3 2
♥ 8
♦ A 10 6 5 3
♣ 9 5

WEST (Sontag)
♠ K
♥ 9 7 6 5 4 2
♦ K Q 9 2
♣ 8 3

EAST (Weichsel)
♠ 10 8 7 6
♥ K 10 3
♦ J 7 4
♣ Q J 10

SOUTH (Jacobus)
♠ A Q 4
♥ A Q J
♦ 8
♣ A K 7 6 4 2

Neither side vulnerable. The bidding:

WEST	NORTH	EAST	SOUTH
			1 ♦ (!)
Pass	1 ♠	Pass	3 no trump
Pass	5 ♦	Pass	5 ♠
Pass	6 ♦	Pass	6 no trump
Pass	Pass	Pass	

Everyone knows about a slip of the tongue. Jacobus made a slip of the bidding box. He accidentally pulled out a card showing one diamond when he meant to bid one club. If he had immediately seen the error, it could have been corrected, but his hand was so strong that he was more concerned with his next bid after Sion's response. The one-diamond bidding error was caused by Jacobus playing too fast.

Speed at the bridge table can bring rewards. It puts the defense under pressure, especially on difficult hands, because they may get caught up in the action and carelessly misdefend by playing at declarer's tempo. Also, slow play may tip off potential problems and alert the defense.

I believe in playing fast, although Peter disagrees. I also believe the defense should be fast. Defenders can reveal valuable information to their opponents. The key to fast play is to think about what is to be done while the auction is in process. When a player hesitates, whether in bidding or during play or before making the opening lead, he is announcing that he has a problem, and the opponents often will be able to figure out what the problem is.

However, always doing the same thing can also be a tip-off. Good players have a filing cabinet in their brains and remember, years later, what a specific opponent bid. It behooves that opponent to vary his tempo and tactics in future encounters. Bridge players should not permit themselves to be a read-out at the table. The only information opponents are entitled to is what they can garner from the bidding and play. No extraneous information should be conveyed by emotions or the tempo of play.

Sion had no idea what was going on after the unlucky one-diamond bid by Jacobus and his subsequent jump to three no trump. Sion's bid of five diamonds supported the diamond suit he thought Jacobus had. The rest of the action was a confused jumble that ended at six no trump.

I led the king of diamonds and the contract was doomed. I knew that something was askance with their bidding because of my own strong diamond holdings. Jacobus played well but they went down two. Plus 180 IMPs.

"I'm sorry," Jacobus said to Sion.

"Forget it," Sion said.

"I pulled the wrong bid and didn't notice."

"It's okay."

This was a remarkable, if not spectacular, display of maturity, and it came from the youngest partnership in the field in terms of combined age. Many championship pairs would have disintegrated over even a lesser error.

Sion and Jacobus bid an excellent part-score contract against us on the third hand and made it. Plus 65 IMPs for them.

My own filing cabinet for the future added a "D" for dangerous for Sion and Jacobus. All bridge players are going to make mistakes. A partnership that can function smoothly after a mistake is one to reckon with.

We were halfway through the third session of the Calcutta, and unless some partnership was enjoying unheard-of success we still had the lead and probably had lengthened it.

No partnership in the Calcutta was any stronger than our next opponents, Bob Hamman and Kyle Larsen. Their $8,000 auction price, and impeccable credentials, clearly had made them one of the pre-tourney favorites.

The World Bridge Federation (WBF) has ranked the great players of the world and Number One among Americans is Bob Hamman, right behind the top six Italians, all members of the Blue Team. Hamman, thirty-nine, an original member of the Dallas Aces, was World Champion in 1970, 1971, and 1977. He also won the World Open Pairs in 1974, the Vanderbilt in 1964, 1966, 1971, and 1973, the Reisinger in 1962 and 1970, the Spingold in 1969, and the Grand Nationals in 1975 and 1977.

Hamman is a huge man, 6 feet 2 inches and 215 pounds, and his only "fault" is that he is too modest. I watched Hamman play a hand flawlessly in the 1976 Reisinger in Pittsburgh, but he went down an unavoidable one trick. After the session another kibitzer, who obviously did not know he was questioning one of the game's great players (even Oswald Jacoby and Charles Goren can walk down a crowded street without being recognized), figured that Hamman could benefit from some advice.

"You could have made that one no trump contract," the kibitzer said, "if you'd played a diamond to dummy's jack."

Actually, this play would have led to down three.

Hamman smiled. "I didn't think of that," he said.

"Well, it occurred to me instantly. I'm not the best player, although I'm considered pretty good where I come from, but I do know that against these sharpies you have to figure every angle."

"Where are you from?"

"Madisonville, Kentucky. We play for money there."

"Really?" Hamman seemed genuinely impressed.

At this point someone like Broadway Billy Eisenberg would have been suggesting a friendly set game to follow the evening session, but that was not Hamman's style.

"Well, you seem like a nice guy," the kibitzer said. "Just be more alert in the future."

"I appreciate your help."

"Glad to oblige. This game isn't as tough as it seems."

Kyle Larsen, Hamman's partner, is from San Francisco. Larsen was the youngest player ever to win both a national team championship and a national pairs championship at age eighteen. He was twenty-seven now and nearing the peak of his game.

Larsen dislikes losing more than anyone I know. I was his teammate in the 1976 Spingold, and when we lost in the Round of Sixteen he returned to our hotel room and started to bang his head against the floor. I grabbed him and stopped it. I thought he would seriously injure himself.

A person unfamiliar with the tension and pressure inherent in championship bridge might think that many top players were candidates for an analyst's couch. Maybe they are. But at the highest level the game requires a single-mindedness that is both mental torture and mental pleasure, and the uninitiated person probably has not experienced these clear, sharp, depressing/exhilarating sensations. With Ira Rubin as a partner in a national championship, Kyle Larsen, caught up in a nightmarishly complex hand, suddenly burst into a loud and unexpectedly on-key version of a popular rock and roll song. Play came to a halt and many kibitzers snickered and shook their heads. The veteran Rubin smiled approvingly.

On the first hand Peter and I bid and made a three no trump contract that was routine. The second hand was not routine:

NORTH (Weichsel)
♠ A K 2
♥ A Q 10 8 5
♦ Q 8 6
♣ A 2

WEST (Hamman)
♠ Q 10 5 4 3
♥ K J 6 3
♦ 2
♣ K 9 5

EAST (Larsen)
♠ J 9
♥ 7 4 2
♦ 10 5 3
♣ J 7 6 4 3

SOUTH (Sontag)
♠ 8 7 6
♥ 9
♦ A K J 9 7 4
♣ Q 10 8

Neither side vulnerable. The bidding:

WEST	NORTH	EAST	SOUTH
	1 ♣	Pass	2 ♦
Pass	2 no trump	Pass	3 ♣
Pass	3 ♦	Pass	4 ♦
Pass	6 ♦	Pass	Pass
Pass			

My two diamonds was positive and showed five or more diamonds. Peter's two no trump showed hearts. My three clubs showed less than 4 controls and no three hearts to the A, K, or Q. Peter's three diamonds asked in diamonds. My four diamonds showed six diamonds to two of the top three honors. Because Peter had the Q, he knew I had the A K, and he also knew I had no other king because I had shown less than 4 controls. He now jumped to six diamonds. He knew that at the worst the slam depended on establishing the heart suit.

Hamman led a club and I had no trouble taking thirteen tricks. Less than half the field bid this slam (playing Standard American and holding only 29 high-card points, many partnerships had difficulty realizing their slam potential), and we scored about 100 IMPs.

On the third hand Hamman and Larsen bid four hearts and we could not defeat them. They scored 75 IMPs on the hand.

I was sure we were still far ahead. Such a position in the late-middle stages of an important bridge tournament is quite rare, and it can be a dangerous position to occupy: players in any sport tend to *let up* when they are leading by a wide margin, or, the opposite side of the coin, they tend to *give up* when they are far behind.

Peter and I have a solution that usually works: even if it is the 724th and final deal of the Grand Nationals, and we are ahead by 100 IMPs on the last hand, we try to play as if we are behind by one IMP. We *pretend*. It makes the game more exciting, and helps us play better.

CHAPTER

16

OPENING BIDS AT THE THREE AND FOUR LEVEL

THREE-LEVEL AND FOUR-LEVEL OPENING BID SEQUENCES

THREE CLUBS BY OPENER SHOWS ANY SEVEN-CARD SUIT headed by the A K Q with at most an outside queen. Although the bid occurs rarely, it carries a very valuable negative inference: the preemptor on other auctions does not have a seven-card suit to the A K Q. If a person had a solid seven-card suit and an outside king or more, he would open the bidding with one of the strong suit and jump in the suit at his next turn.

Frequently, responder will be able to know what suit opener has. When he does not know the suit, however, he bids three diamonds.

OPENER	RESPONDER
3 ♣	3 ♦

Opener bids the suit he has, and responder should be able to gauge whether to pass, go to game, or try for slam.

If responder introduces a new suit over opener's solid suit, it is an ask in the suit bid. Opener makes the cheapest bid with no void or singleton; next cheapest, a singleton; finally, a void.

OPENER	RESPONDER
3 ♣	3 ♦
3 ♠ (spade suit)	4 ♦ (asks in diamonds)
4 no trump (void)	7 ♠

Here is how the hand would look:

OPENER	RESPONDER
♠ A K Q 9 8 5 3	♠ 7 2
♥ 10 6 4 2	♥ A 5 3
♦ Void	♦ Q 10 8
♣ 9 5	♣ A K Q J 2

Whenever responder bids opener's suit, opener must pass. Whenever responder bids a new suit other than diamonds (which is unconditionally forcing) over three clubs, opener should raise if he has support, or retreat to his own suit if he has less than two-card support.

THREE DIAMONDS, THREE HEARTS, THREE SPADES OPENING BID SEQUENCES

Three diamonds, three hearts, and three spades are preemptive bids that generally show seven-card suits with little outside strength. The opening preemptor, when deciding whether to bid, must evaluate the quality of his long suit and take into consideration his vulnerability. Preemptive bids, whether very strong or very light, should be agreed upon in advance by the partnership.

All game bids over these preempts are natural and to play. Opener must pass. All new suit bids, with the exception of four clubs, that are below the game level are natural and forcing and ask opener to raise if he has support.

OPENER	RESPONDER
3 ♦, 3 ♥, or 3 ♠	4 ♣

Four clubs asks in trump. Opener has five responses if he is not vulnerable:

1. Four Diamonds. No A or K in long suit (6 or 7 cards).
2. Four Hearts. A or K in six-card suit.
3. Four Spades. A or K in seven-card suit.
4. Four No Trump. Two of top three honors in six-card suit.
5. Five Clubs. Two of top three honors in seven-card suit.

Opener has three responses to four clubs if he is vulnerable:

1. Four Diamonds. No A or K and a seven-card suit.
2. Four Hearts. A or K in seven-card suit.
3. Four Spades. Two of top three honors in a seven-card suit.

If after bidding four clubs responder bids a new suit, it asks in that suit. The cheapest response by opener shows no first or second round control; next cheapest, a king or a singleton; next, the ace or void.

OPENER (vulnerable)	RESPONDER
3 ♠	4 ♣
4 ♥ (A or K in seven-card suit)	5 ♦ (asks in diamonds)
5 ♠ (king or singleton)	

THREE NO TRUMP OPENING BID SEQUENCE

Three no trump shows an eight-card club or diamond suit with little outside strength. Generally denies the ace in the long suit. Responder may bid as follows:

1. Four Clubs. Wants to play four of opener's minor.

2. Four Diamonds. Wants to play four diamonds if that is opener's suit, or five clubs.

3. Four Hearts. To play.

4. Four Spades. To play.

5. Four No Trump. Asks opener to bid a small slam if his suit is very strong—K Q or A Q. Opener rejects slam try by bidding five of his minor. He accepts by bidding five no trump to show clubs, and six clubs to show diamonds.

6. Five Clubs. Opener passes with clubs, or bids five diamonds if he has diamonds.

7. Five Diamonds. To play.

8. Five No Trump. Grand slam force. Opener must bid seven of his suit if he has two of the top three honors.

Responder, of course, may pass three no trump if that is what he wants to play.

FOUR CLUBS OPENING BID SEQUENCE

Four clubs shows a very good seven- or eight-card heart suit (including the trump king), less than 16 high-card points, eight or nine playing tricks, and there is at least second round control in two of the three outside suits. Responder may bid as follows:

1. Four Diamonds. Asks opener to name the suit he has two quick losers in. Opener bids four hearts to show no suit the opponents can take two quick tricks in, and a non-solid heart suit; four spades, five clubs, and five diamonds would show the suit bid to contain at least two quick losers; and four no trump would show no suit with two quick losers and a solid heart suit.

2. Four Hearts. Shows no interest in heart slam.

3. Four No Trump. Blackwood.

FOUR DIAMONDS OPENING BID SEQUENCE

Four diamonds shows a very good seven- or eight-card spade suit (including the trump king) and the same requirements as the four-club opening bid. Responder's bids are also the same except one level higher.

FOUR HEARTS AND FOUR SPADES OPENING BID SEQUENCES

These bids show a weak preempt in the suit bid. Opener should have an eight-card major, or perhaps 7-4 distribution (K Q J 8 5 4 2 of spades, void in hearts, Q J 5 4 of diamonds, and 9 2 of clubs).

Four no trump is Blackwood, and any new suit bid by responder is natural and to play. Five of opener's major by responder is a natural slam try asking opener to bid a small slam if his suit is strong enough to play for one loser opposite two small cards in responder's hand.

FOUR NO TRUMP OPENING BID SEQUENCE

Four no trump is Blackwood.

This completely covers opening bids at the three and four level. They are all even more potent played in conjunction with the three-club opening bid and its negative inferences.

17

STEAK OR WATERCRESS

GAYLOR KASLE IS THE MOST SUCCESSFUL BRIDGE PROFESsional in the United States. He is inexhaustible. He plays 51 weeks a year (jokes abound about what he does that free week), all over the earth, and he pushes himself because he makes a good living and the demand for his services is enormous.

Gaylor lives in Tucson, Arizona, but calling him there is a waste of money. More likely he will be in Canada, Mexico, Europe, even Asia or Africa. Gaylor is a special teacher. He listens to people (which is what many bridge students really want), is understanding, patient, agreeable; he explains the game without a trace of paternalism; and most important he is a social animal who really enjoys other humans.

Many people "teach" bridge. Dozens of colleges carry the game as part of their curriculum. But the best teacher is a playing professional like Gaylor Kasle who can compete at the highest level and instruct at the most elementary.

If Gaylor has a fault, it is that he lacks the so-called killer instinct. He is different from Peter and me in this respect. When someone is on the canvas, Peter and I would stomp on him to keep him there. Gaylor would help him up.

Harold Guiver, "The Squeezer," was Gaylor Kasle's partner. Guiver is 5 feet 2, fifty-two years old, walks with a cane because of a hip operation, and is one of the top players on the West Coast.

One of the strong points of a club system is that a player can open the bidding with less values than is permitted by Standard American. Peter and I can open the bidding with as few as 10 high-card points with a distributional hand, something that cannot be done with Standard American. The first hand against Kasle and Guiver illustrated the point:

NORTH (Weichsel)	SOUTH (Sontag)
♠ A K 4	♠ Q 5 3 2
♥ A Q 10 6 5 4 3	♥ Void
♦ 10	♦ K J 8 2
♣ K 4	♣ A J 9 7 5

NORTH	SOUTH
	1 ♦
2 ♥	3 ♣
3 ♥	3 no trump
Pass	

My light opening bid caught Peter with a strong hand. He jump-shifted in hearts, and his heart rebid showed that hearts was his only suit. My three no trump bid was an attempt to end the auction. It showed a spade stopper and no desire whatever to play in hearts. Peter passed.

When light opening bids are permissible, responder must be very careful. Only when there is a fit should hands be bid with confidence.

We made three no trump.

Kasle and Guiver made a vulnerable four-heart contract on the second hand, and Peter and I scored a part-score on the third. We lost a few IMPs on the round, but time was zipping past and we were nearing the homestretch with a reasonably comfortable lead. I was ravenously hungry and decided to ask Peter when the session ended if he wanted to go out for a thick steak, compliments of me. The "compliments of me" was a hope that he would agree, a bribe. I should have anticipated his reaction ("At this point of the tournament? Are you crazy? You'll have a bloated belly and no brain"), and also the watercress salad that would have to last until well after midnight.

But for now the problem was Paul Trent and Judy Radin. Trent, "The Little Beast," is a lawyer, and expert at both bridge and backgammon. He is 5 feet 3 inches and extremely bright, has an enormous vocabulary, and makes *The Times* crossword puzzle seem like child's play. Trent was a teammate of mine in 1971 when I won my first national championship.

Judy Radin was twenty-seven and one of the three or four best women players in the country. Judy is a bridge professional and a winner, which is why people like to play with her. Judy, paired with Kathy Wei, would later win the Women's World Pair Championship.

On the first hand against Trent and Radin I held the following cards: 7 of spades; K 8 7 6 4 3 of hearts; K 10 8 2 of diamonds; and A 8 of clubs.

I made a light opening bid of one heart and Trent overcalled with one spade. Peter made a negative double, Judy raised to four spades, Trent and I passed, and Peter doubled.

We had caught them speeding. Trent had overcalled with only four spades and Judy had gone to game with five-card support and a good hand. We set them two tricks. The key was my light opening bid. If I had been forced to pass, the hand probably would have been passed out, which is what happened at many tables. Also, although many partnerships were playing weak two-bids, a suit headed by the K 8 is not good enough to justify such a bid.

Trent and Radin were quarreling. Judy said that Paul should not have overcalled one spade, and Trent said they were victims of bad luck. I had to agree with Judy.

Trent opened the bidding with one no trump on the second hand (16 to 18), Judy bid two clubs (Stayman), Paul bid two hearts, and Judy bid the final contract of four hearts.

Peter held the following cards:

♠ A 10 8 6 4
♥ 8 4
♦ K 8
♣ 7 6 5 3

Only one opening lead would defeat the contract, and Peter found it.

The king of diamonds.

It is most unusual to lead an unsupported king into the strong no trump opening bidder. Peter and just one other player in the field found the lead.

I had the ace of diamonds. Peter's king won, he continued a diamond to my ace, ruffed the diamond return, and cashed the ace of spades.

We bid and made a part-score on the third hand, but the big victory was Peter finding that opening lead. He knew the trump would break well for declarer (either 2-2 or 3-2) and his clubs seemed hopeless. Although the king of diamonds might give Trent and Radin an overtrick, it seemed like a good chance to take.

Bridge players come in all sizes. Our next opponents were Jim Linhart (6 feet 10) and Ken Gorfkle (5 feet 9). Linhart grew up in the San Francisco Bay area and played basketball against Bill Russell, the great center for the Boston Celtics.

Peter and I joke a lot with Linhart, but there is some truth in what we say. A tall man has an obvious advantage in basketball but, if he is so inclined, he also has an advantage at bridge: unless the cards are handled very carefully, he can see an opponent's hand.

I do not consider it cheating to look at another player's cards if he is careless enough to show them. It *is* cheating to go out of your way in any manner to see them. In any case, Linhart bends in the other direction not to take advantage of his height.

Ken Gorfkle deals in options on commodities in New York. At the time of the Calcutta he was advising his friends and clients to buy copper. It seemed too much like gambling to me. I will gamble on myself at cards, I have some control over what happens, but the commodities market is more like Las Vegas than Las Vegas. Fortunes can be made and lost in a few hours.

Peter and I made a part-score on the first hand against Linhart and Gorfkle. I was now counting down to the end of the session. Only five hands to go. Unless absolute disaster struck, we should have a nice lead at the three-quarters mark of the tournament.

Linhart and Gorfkle bid four hearts on the second hand and made an overtrick. It was a normal result. If every hand went like this one—and of course they would not—we could not be beaten.

We bid an aggressive game contract on the third hand:

NORTH (Gorfkle)
♠ A Q 4 3
♥ 7 6 4 3
♦ 7 3
♣ K 10 3

WEST (Gontag)
♠ 10 6
♥ 5 2
♦ A Q
♣ A Q J 9 6 4 2

EAST (Weichsel)
♠ K 8 7
♥ K J 10 8
♦ K J 6 4 2
♣ 7

SOUTH (Linhart)
♠ J 9 5 2
♥ A Q 9
♦ 10 9 8 5
♣ 8 5

Neither side vulnerable. The bidding:

WEST	NORTH	EAST	SOUTH
2 ♣	Pass	2 ♦	Pass
3 ♣	Pass	3 no trump	Pass
Pass	Pass		

My opening two-club bid showed 11 to 16 points and a long club suit. Peter's two diamonds asked for distribution. Over two diamonds, I could have bid either two spades (a minimum two-club opening and no four-card major) or three clubs (a maximum two-club opening and no four-card major). Because I had a strong seven-card suit I elected to show a maximum. I wanted to induce Peter to bid three no trump if he could.

With a normal spade lead by Linhart, the contract would have gone down two tricks. However, Jim gambled with a highly imaginative opening lead, the heart queen. Now the defense could no longer beat us. We made eleven tricks.

Our final opponents of the third session were Mike Moss and Bart Bramley. I was eager to get at that steak which I should have known Peter would veto, and I had to mentally urge myself to concentrate for just three more hands.

The success of the Cavendish Calcutta, one of the most important events in the world despite having been played only twice before, can be credited to Mike Moss. The event has become so popular that many of the best players in the world have to be turned away for lack of room.

Bridge players are an egocentric lot. The better ones believe that no one is as good at the game as they are. To have the chance to play against the best players, in a grueling four-session event, with money at stake, is something no great player can resist. Mike Moss recognized this and established the Cavendish Calcutta on a par with any other event in the world.

Moss had been the auctioneer the Friday night before the tournament began. He was excellent in the role. He is an extrovert with a winning personality. Or a losing one, depending on how you feel. Moss loves practical jokes and telling tall stories and making unusual deals. A favorite deal of Mike's is to offer a person one hundred dollars with the proviso that any time, in the person's lifetime, Mike can ask for and receive whatever change the person has in his pockets. I don't know how Mike has done with these arrangements.

Bart Bramley, Moss's partner, is a computer programmer. Bramley is a graduate of M.I.T., is extremely intelligent, and not surprisingly adopts a very scientific approach to the game. Bramley is quite thin, and his exceptional mental agility is occasionally disguised by his tortoise-like play.

On the first hand we bid a cold three no trump and scored two overtricks. On the second hand they bid three spades which went down two tricks. On the final hand of the session we finished the way we would have hoped:

NORTH (Moss)
♠ A 9 3
♥ J 7 2
♦ K 5 2
♣ Q 9 6 2

WEST (Sontag)
♠ 8
♥ Q 10 9 8 4
♦ J 9 8
♣ K 8 4 3

EAST (Weichsel)
♠ K Q J 10 5 4 2
♥ Void
♦ A Q 10
♣ J 10 5

SOUTH (Bramley)
♠ 7 6
♥ A K 8 5 3
♦ 7 6 4 3
♣ A 7

East-West vulnerable. The bidding:

WEST	NORTH	EAST	SOUTH
		4 ♦	Pass
4 ♠	Pass	Pass	Pass

Peter's four diamonds shows a strong four-spade opening bid but less than 16 high-card points. My four-spade bid was forced unless I was interested in slam. Peter was a little light for a vulnerable four-diamond bid; the jack of clubs should have been the queen.

The opening lead was the club two and Bramley won with

the ace and returned the seven, which I took with the king. I now was in my hand for the last time.

I tried a diamond finesse by leading the jack from my hand and playing dummy's ten under it. When it won, I finessed again. It was then a simple matter to drive out the ace of trump and make the contract. Bringing home four spades vulnerable and with only 19 high-card points was quite a plus score for us.

"I'll buy you a steak," I said to Peter.

"At this point of the tournament?"

"I need nourishment."

"Are you crazy?"

"Have a heart, Peter. I'm really starved."

"You'll have a bloated belly and no brain."

So we ate watercress salad and reviewed the afternoon session. We did well against Jim Jacoby and Dave Berkowitz; we lost a few IMPs against Blau and Ginsberg; we had a good round against Vic Mitchell and Bill Roberts; we had slightly the best against Steve and B. Jay Becker; we scored heavily against Sion and Jacobus; we won a few IMPs from Hamman and Larsen; we lost IMPs to Kasle and Guiver; we trounced Trent and Radin; we won IMPs from Linhart and Gorfkle; and we defeated Moss and Bramley.

When we returned for the final session that evening, the results for the three-quarter mark were up:

POSITION	PARTNERSHIP	COUNTRY	IMPS
1.	Weichsel-Sontag	U.S.A.	1,951
2.	Blau-Ginsberg	U.S.A.	1,692
3.	Cohen-Walvick	U.S.A.	1,203
4.	Sharif-Yallouze	Egypt-France	1,140
5.	Blair-Levin	U.S.A.	911

The $3,000 first place session prize went to Jim Jacoby and Dave Berkowitz. The $2,000 second place prize was won by Mike Becker and Alan Greenberg. Prizes of $1,000 went to Bob Hamman and Kyle Larsen and to Ahmed Hussein and Gail Moss.

Except for the tenacious Blau and Ginsberg, I did not think any partnership had a realistic chance of catching us. This was hardly a healthy attitude, as events would later show.

Nevertheless, this was the fourth session of a fatiguing event, and both Peter and I were in good physical shape. I thought certain other partnerships might not be. The pressure of the tournament, and the understandable discouragement of those partnerships not in contention, had to work in our favor.

Or so I thought. I did not consider the possibility that every partnership we met in the final round would put out a little harder against us because we were leading. Also, even the last place partnership was not going to relax when the possibility existed of winning that $3,000 session prize.

SESSION IV

CHAPTER

18

THE DOWNHILL SLIDE

THE CAVENDISH WAS PACKED TO BURSTING. PEOPLE HAD come from all over New York and even from out-of-state to see the finale of the world's richest bridge tournament. It was as noisy as Madison Square Garden for a Knicks game and as smoke-infested as a small town arena on fight night. The exquisite Cavendish, for this night at least, belonged to the people.

"Which ones are Weichsel and Sontag?" I heard a woman ask her husband.

"I'm Sontag," I said cheerily. "That's Weichsel over there."

She looked me over and sniffed. "I don't believe you," she said. "My favorite players are Sam Stayman and Omar Sharif, and I don't think you two would be ahead of them."

I know I don't dress as well as Sam or Omar—I can't afford to—and I certainly don't look like Omar, but what does that have to do with bridge.

"I'm really Sontag," I said. I wondered why it mattered.

"Maybe you are," she conceded. "But I think I'll go watch Mr. Stayman."

"An admirer of yours?" Peter asked a few moments later.

"She doesn't believe I'm Sontag," I said.

"Sensible woman," he said.

Our first opponents of this abbreviated final session (27 hands instead of 30) were Neil Silverman and Peter Pender. Silverman, only twenty-eight, is a fascinating character. He earns money in two highly unusual ways: he bets horses; and he finds lost heirs.

Neil lives in the same building I do, and I always check with him before an excursion to the racetrack. He always prefaces advice with "It's not a sure thing, but . . ." which so far has meant that it is a sure thing.

But life is not all roses and the winner's circle for Neil. He located the heir of an unclaimed estate and figured the two of them would live happily for a while: she on her unexpected inheritance, he on his finder's fee. However, she was a member of an outfit called the Zodiac People who refused to let members take anything from the "outside" world.

Silverman's partner, Peter Pender, is from San Francisco and is a former ice-skating champion. He was forty-one, thin and distinguished and tall with salt and pepper hair, a mustache, and the assurance people often have when they are born into a wealthy family. The great English player, Jeremy Flint, came to the United States in 1966 and, playing with Pender, became a Life Master in just eleven weeks. Of course, Flint was already a world-class player at the time.

Peter and I were able to show off our bidding system on the very first hand against Silverman and Pender.

NORTH (Weichsel)
♠ A 10 6 5 2
♥ A 5
♦ A 10
♣ K Q 4 2

WEST (Silverman)
♠ K Q 4
♥ 8 6 3 2
♦ Q 7 5 2
♣ 8 7

EAST (Pender)
♠ 7 3
♥ Q 10 7 4
♦ J 6 3
♣ A 10 6 5

SOUTH (Sontag)
♠ J 9 8
♥ K J 9
♦ K 9 8 4
♣ J 9 3

Neither side vulnerable. The bidding:

WEST	NORTH	EAST	SOUTH
	1 ♣	Pass	1 no trump
Pass	2 ♣	Pass	2 ♠
Pass	2 no trump	Pass	3 ♦
Pass	3 ♣	Pass	4 ♣
Pass	Pass	Pass	

My bidding showed 9 to 11 high-card points with 4-3-3-3 distribution and a four-card minor. When Peter finally bid three spades to introduce his five-card suit, I raised to four. We made five.

They bid two good part-scores on the second and third hands and made them. The round was just about a push. I thought about Blau and Ginsberg, second and straining (or were they second and holding on?—second was worth a lot of money and few people had expected them to be so high), and how there were only twenty-four hands to go.

We changed tables to play Joe Silver and Fred Hoffer. We had to walk the width of the room and scattered people shouted encouragement or patted our backs. It reminded me of scenes I have watched on television when spectators encourage the leader of a major golf tournament as he walks from the fifteenth to the sixteenth tee. I felt good.

A number of my friends, and Peter's too, were in the Cavendish this night. They knew this was very special and wanted to share it with us. Peter's parents were proud as peacocks. My friends Bobby and Triinu were nervous and pulling so hard for us that they were expending more energy than we were. It is surprising to me how many people you can think of as friends actually secretly cheer against you. But there are others, real friends, who are for you, and they make it worthwhile.

I had a bet with Joe Silver on the Calcutta. We bet a good bottle of champagne on which partnership would finish higher. He knew he owed me the champagne, which meant he would do everything to stop me from enjoying it.

Joe Silver is a Canadian lawyer who represented that country in the 1974 World Pair Olympiad, the same year he won the Vanderbilt. Silver is spunky and self-confident, a thirty-six-year-old who is in excellent physical shape.

Fred Hoffer is a Montreal merchandiser, forty years old, a good bridge player but not quite in the same league as Silver. I met him for the first time at the auction two nights before when I was making the champagne bet with Joe Silver, and he did not see why we had to spice up the action when already there was so much at stake.

Silver and Hoffer bid four hearts on the first hand and made five, a good result for them because several pairs bid a small slam that depended on little more than the location of the diamond ace and went down.

Twenty-three hands to go, I thought.

They bid four spades on the second hand and we set it one trick by maneuvering to get a club ruff. We scored a few IMPs.

Twenty-two hands to go.

They also bid four spades on the third hand, but this time it was a poor risk:

NORTH (Silver)
♠ A K 10 5
♥ 8
♦ A Q J 10 5 4
♣ J 10

WEST (Sontag)
♠ 8 6 4 2
♥ A K 10 4 3
♦ Void
♣ A 9 4 2

EAST (Weichsel)
♠ 9 3
♥ J 7 6
♦ 9 7 6 2
♣ K 8 7 3

SOUTH (Hoffer)
♠ Q J 7
♥ Q 9 5 2
♦ K 8 3
♣ Q 6 5

East-West vulnerable. The bidding:

WEST	NORTH	EAST	SOUTH
		Pass	Pass
1 ♥	2 ♦	Pass	2 no trump
Pass	3 ♠	Pass	4 ♠
Pass	Pass	Pass	

I deviated from our system by bidding one heart instead of two hearts because Peter was a passed hand, we were vulnerable, my heart suit was good and the spade suit was virtually nonexistent. It turned out to be a good decision because they ended up in four spades and Peter's opening lead was the heart jack. Silver covered with the queen and I won with the king. I then led the ace and Silver had to ruff. He was now playing a 3-3 fit and I had four trump. We set them four tricks.

Their auction was okay until the final call. To bid four

spades with only three-card support was a mistake, Peter and I would have bid a contract of either three no trump or four diamonds. Four diamonds is cold, and three no trump can be made against a weak defense (at most it goes down one trick).

We changed tables again—the guide card called for us to change after each opponent during the final session—and sat down to play Lou Bluhm and Larry Gould.

Bridge is a game where a partnership may do nothing wrong and still be demolished because the opponents play brilliantly. That is what happened to us against Bluhm and Gould, starting with the very first hand:

WEST (Gould)	EAST (Bluhm)
♠ A K J 8 5	♠ 6 3
♥ A 10 5 3	♥ K 2
♦ A 9 3	♦ K Q 10 8 7 2
♣ 7	♣ Q J 10

WEST	EAST
1 ♠	2 ♦
2 ♥	3 ♦
6 ♦	Pass

It was a fast, effective auction, although not particularly scientific. Peter and I would have bid as follows:

Weichsel	Sontag
1 ♣	2 ♦
2 ♠	2 no trump
3 ♥	3 no trump
4 ♦	6 ♦
Pass	

Six diamonds was cold. The problem was that more than half the field did not bid it. We lost a ton of IMPs.

Bluhm and Gould were equally inspired on the second hand:

WEST (Gould)	EAST (Bluhm)
♠ Void	♠ Q 10 9 7 4 3 2
♥ K 7 4 3 2	♥ A 10
♦ A K 7	♦ 9 7 2
♣ J 10 9 7 2	♣ Q

WEST	EAST
1 ♥	1 ♠
2 ♣	2 ♠
Pass	

Bluhm made a sensational underbid of two spades and Gould wisely passed. There was no way we could beat this contract. Most all other East-West partnerships climbed to the three-level and went down. We lost half-a-ton of IMPs on this hand.

On the third hand we could not avoid going down one trick in a part-score.

I had the worst kind of feeling: helplessness. There was no one to be angry with, not even myself. We had done nothing wrong, yet Bluhm and Gould had picked us clean.

"It will be all right," Peter said. "Just play your game."

Right, I thought. I thought about Kyle Larsen banging his head on that hotel room floor, and another player in the World Championship who was so unhappy with his results that he quit the game entirely, and even Peter, normally the soul of equanimity, who once in a fit of depression over bridge considered suicide, and I did not want to lose this tournament and be tempted to tell him to go ahead.

CHAPTER

19

ONE-BID SEQUENCES

ONE DIAMOND OPENING BID SEQUENCE

ONE DIAMOND IS THE CATCHALL BID IN OUR SYSTEM. IT IS made on all hands deemed worth an opening bid from 12 to a poor 16 high-card points. It can be made with as few as one diamond.

ONE DIAMOND—ONE HEART
OPENING BID SEQUENCE

One heart is a natural response showing four or more hearts and 6 or more high-card points. However, on occasion it could be right to respond to one diamond, one heart, or one spade opening bids with zero high-card points as a bluff. Partner's opening bid has probably shown less than 16 high-card points and it might be unwise to sit idly by while the opponents merrily bid their hands.

The opening one-diamond bidder, over the one-heart response, raises to two hearts with four trump; bids one spade with four spades but not four hearts; bids one no trump with a balanced hand and 12 to a poor 15 high-card points; bids two clubs to show five clubs and four or more diamonds; bids two diamonds to show five or six diamonds; bids two spades to show two of the top three honors in hearts, three hearts, and an excellent six-card diamond suit; bids two no trump with 15 high-card points, a very good six-card diamond suit, and stoppers in spades and clubs; bids three clubs to show 14 to 16 high-card points and at least 5-5 distribution in clubs and diamonds with good suits; bids three diamonds to show a very strong six- or seven-card diamond suit with 14 or 15 high-card points; bids three hearts to show four hearts, 14 to 16 high-card points, and probably an outside singleton —this bid is never made with 4-4-3-2 distribution; bids three spades to show a singleton or void in spades, good four-card heart support, 15 or 16 high-card points (they must be quality points); bids four clubs to show the same as three spades except the short suit is clubs; bids four diamonds to show a six card diamond suit headed by the A K Q and four hearts to at least one of the top three honors; and four hearts to show four very good trump or five trump to at least one high honor and a good six-card diamond suit.

Responder has a good picture of opener's hand after opener's rebid. If responder now jumps to two no trump, three hearts, or three spades (if opener has bid a spade), it is game invitational and opener may pass. If responder jumps to three diamonds, game must be reached. Jumps into new suits at the three level are natural, force to at least game, and show a strong 5-5 distribution. If responder bids the fourth suit, it is unconditionally forcing for one round.

OPENER	RESPONDER
1 ♦	1 ♥
2 no trump (15 high-card points, very good six-card diamond suit, stoppers in clubs and spades)	3 ♦ (must be passed)

OPENER	RESPONDER
1 ♦	1 ♥
1 no trump (balanced hand, 12 to a poor 15 high-card points)	2 ♣ (check-back Stayman)

In the second auction responder is looking for three-card heart support. Opener bids two hearts with three hearts, two diamonds with two hearts and a minimum, and two no trump with two hearts and a maximum. Any bid suit by responder at his next turn, except three clubs (which should be passed), is unconditionally forcing to game.

OPENER	RESPONDER
1 ♦	1 ♥
1 no trump	2 ♣ (check-back Stayman)
2 ♦ (two hearts and a minimum)	3 ♥ (game-forcing)

ONE DIAMOND—ONE SPADE OPENING BID SEQUENCE

One spade shows four or more spades and 6 or more high-card points.

OPENER	RESPONDER
1 ♦	1 ♠

Most of the auctions in this sequence are exactly the same as with one diamond, one heart, with the following exceptions:

1. One No Trump. Shows 12 to a poor 15 high-card points but opener may have a singleton spade. Responder bids two

clubs as check-back Stayman. Opener's responsibility is to show three-card spade support or a four-card heart suit.

2. Two Hearts. Shows five or six diamonds, four or five hearts, and is non-forcing.

3. Three Hearts. Shows two of the top three honors in spades but only three spades, and an excellent six-card diamond suit.

ONE DIAMOND—ONE NO TRUMP
OPENING BID SEQUENCE

One no trump by responder shows 6 to 10 high-card points and denies a four-card major.

OPENER	RESPONDER
1 ♦	1 no trump

Opener may bid as follows:

1. Two Clubs. At least four diamonds and four clubs, non-forcing.

2. Two Diamonds. Five or six diamonds, non-forcing.

3. Two Hearts. Five or six diamonds and four hearts, non-forcing.

4. Two Spades. Five or six diamonds and four spades, non-forcing.

5. Two No Trump. Strong six-card diamond suit, 15 or 16 high-card points, and stoppers in at least two of the other three suits.

6. Three Clubs. At least five diamonds and five clubs, both suits are very good, and the bid is highly invitational but not forcing.

7. Three Diamonds. Very good six- or seven-card diamond suit, probably an unbalanced hand, non-forcing.

8. Three Hearts. Five hearts and six diamonds, forcing.

9. Three Spades. Five spades and six diamonds, forcing.

10. Three No Trump. To play.

ONE DIAMOND—TWO CLUBS
OPENING BID SEQUENCE

Two clubs shows five or more clubs, 10 or more high-card points, and both opener and responder are forced to bid at least once more.

OPENER	RESPONDER
1 ♦	2 ♣

Opener bids naturally over two clubs: two diamonds would show at least five diamonds; two hearts or two spades would show four cards in the suit bid plus four or more diamonds; two no trump would show a minimum, balanced hand; three clubs would show at least three clubs to a high honor or any four clubs; three diamonds would show an excellent diamond suit; three hearts or three spades would show five of the suit bid and six diamonds; and three no trump would show a balanced hand, 14 or 15 high-card points, and stoppers in the major suits with a five- or six-card diamond suit.

If responder now bids three clubs or two no trump, the auction may end. Otherwise, at least game must be reached.

ONE DIAMOND—TWO DIAMONDS
OPENING BID SEQUENCE

Two diamonds shows 10 or more high-card points, four or more diamonds, and is forcing. Usually denies four-card major.

OPENER	RESPONDER
1 ♦	2 ♦

Opener may bid as follows:

1. Two Hearts. Shows a stopper in hearts. Usually looking for three no trump. Two no trump or three diamonds by responder may be passed.

2. Two Spades. The same as two hearts except the stopper is in spades.

3. Two No Trump. Balanced minimum hand. May be passed. If responder bids three diamonds, opener must pass.

4. Three Clubs. Exactly five clubs and only one or two diamonds. May be passed. If responder bids three diamonds, opener must pass.

5. Three Diamonds. Three or more diamonds, a minimum in high cards, and some distribution such as a singleton or doubleton. May be passed.

6. Three Hearts. Singleton or void in hearts with four or more diamonds.

7. Three Spades. The same as three hearts except the shortness is in spades.

8. Three No Trump. Balanced hand with 14 or more high-card points and stoppers in the other suits.

9. Four Clubs. Singleton or void in clubs with five or more diamonds.

Whenever either partner bids two no trump or three diamonds, the auction may end. Otherwise, the partnership is usually forced to three no trump or four diamonds. The only exception is a one diamond, two diamonds, three clubs sequence.

ONE DIAMOND—SINGLE JUMP SHIFT OPENING BID SEQUENCES

A single jump shift by responder shows (in the suits) 16 or more high-card points, a strong suit in the suit bid, and is a slam try. These bids never show a second suit unless it is diamonds.

OPENER	RESPONDER
1 ♦	2 ♥, 2 ♠, 3 ♣, or 3 ♦

Opener, over these jump shifts, should make the most natural bid possible. He should make the minimum bid in no trump with a balanced hand and 12 to 14 high-card points; he should rebid diamonds with a five-card suit and one of the top three honors; he should bid a strong four-card suit if he has one; he should jump in a new suit to show a fit with responder (three or four cards to a high honor) and a singleton or void in the suit bid; and he should raise responder's suit if he has one of the top three honors, even doubleton.

Remember, when the auction goes one diamond, three diamonds, diamonds is responder's suit, not opener's.

A jump shift by responder to two no trump shows a balanced hand, 12 to 15 high-card points, and no four-card major; or it shows 18 or 19 points and a balanced hand.

OPENER	RESPONDER
1 ♦	2 no trump

Two no trump is forcing to at least game. If responder jumps to four no trump at his second turn, he is showing the 18- or 19-point hand.

Opener bids naturally over two no trump. Of course, since responder does not have a four-card major, opener will only bid a major over two no trump to show a diamond suit and a singleton or void in the suit bid. 4 hearts or 4 spades shows 6 diamonds and 5 in the major bid.

ONE DIAMOND—THREE HEARTS, THREE SPADES, OR THREE NO TRUMP SEQUENCE

Three of either major over one diamond is a natural preempt showing seven cards in the suit bid, almost no strength in the outside suits, and the long suit is headed by the Q J or K J.

OPENER	RESPONDER
1 ♦	3 ♥ or 3 ♠

Three no trump by responder shows a balanced hand with 16 or 17 high-card points.

OPENER	RESPONDER
1 ♦	3 no trump

ONE DIAMOND—FOUR DIAMONDS SEQUENCE

Four diamonds shows seven or eight diamonds and very little outside strength.

OPENER	RESPONDER
1 ♦	4 ♦

ONE DIAMOND—FOUR OF A MAJOR SEQUENCE

Four of a major must be passed.

This entirely covers the important one-diamond opening bid sequences, the most frequent opening bid in the W-S system. When using this bid, it is important to know how to handle interference from the opponents. If the opening bid of one diamond is doubled, responder may pass, bid one heart or one spade to show five or more in the suit bid (forces opener to bid again), bid one no trump to show a balanced hand with 7 to 9 high-card points, bid two clubs to show five or six clubs and less than 10 high-card points (nonforcing), bid two diamonds to show the same as two clubs except the suit is diamonds, bid two hearts or two spades to show a good six-card suit in the suit bid and 4 to 7 high-card points, bid two no trump to show five clubs and five diamonds and 7 to 9 high-card points, three clubs or three diamonds to show six or seven cards in the suit bid and 7 to 9 high-card points, and redouble to show 10 or more high-card points.

If the opponent overcalls a suit, all doubles by responder

are negative; one no trump is natural, 7 to 9 high-card points; two no trump is forcing to game with their suit well stopped, 12 or more high-card points; all suit bids except two diamonds are forcing; all jumps in new suits show 5 to 8 high-card points and six or seven cards in the suit bid, non-forcing; and a cue bid of their suit shows either the ace and a small card, or the king or queen and two small cards, and indicates a desire to play three no trump from the opening bidder's side.

ONE OF A MAJOR OPENING BID SEQUENCE

One heart and one spade show five or more cards in the suit bid and 11 to 16 high-card points. In the third or fourth chair opener may bid a strong four-card major.

ONE OF A MAJOR—ONE NO TRUMP
OPENING BID SEQUENCE

One no trump shows 0 to 12 high-card points and is forcing if responder is an unpassed hand. Responder may have a fit with opener's major.

OPENER	RESPONDER
1 ♥ or 1 ♠	1 no trump

Opener may bid as follows:

1. Two Clubs. Shows five of the major and three or more clubs. Responder may pass; correct to the major with two or more of the major and 0 to 6 points; bid a new suit at the two level to play; bid two no trump to show 10 to 12 points, a balanced hand, and less than three of opener's major; bid three clubs to show five or more clubs and 9 or 10 points;

bid three diamonds to show 9 or 10 points and ten cards in clubs and diamonds; and three of opener's major to show a balanced hand, 10 to 12 points, and three card support.

2. Two Diamonds. The same as two clubs except opener has three or more diamonds. If opener has a five-card major and both three clubs and three diamonds, he would bid two clubs.

3. Two Hearts. If opener had hearts, this would show a six-card suit and probably no good four-card suit. If opener had spades, this shows four or five hearts. Responder may pass; correct to two spades if that is opener's suit; bid two no trump or three of opener's major to invite game; or three of a minor to show a six- or seven-card suit which asks opener to pass.

4. Two Spades. If opener had spades, this shows six spades and probably no good four-card suit. If opener had hearts, this shows exactly six hearts and four spades. Responder bids the same as with two hearts.

5. Two No Trump. Strong six-card major, 15 or 16 high-card points, and a balanced hand. Responder may pass; bid three no trump to play; bid four of the major to play; or sign off in three of the major or in three of a minor.

6. Three Clubs. Non forcing. Shows a very good five card major and five good clubs.

7. Three Diamonds. The same as three clubs except the second suit is diamonds.

8. Three Hearts. If opener originally bid spades, this shows a strong 5-5 in spades and hearts. If opener bid hearts, it shows six or seven hearts, less than 16 high-card points, and an unbalanced strong playing hand.

9. Three Spades. If opener bid hearts, this shows six hearts and five spades and a strong playing hand. If opener bid spades, it shows six or seven spades, and a strong unbalanced playing hand.

10. Four of Opener's Major. To play. Responder must pass.

ONE OF A MAJOR—TWO OF A MINOR
OPENING BID SEQUENCE

Two clubs or two diamonds shows five or more cards in the suit bid and is unconditionally forcing to game unless responder rebids his minor suit on his next turn. Opener would then be allowed to pass. Of course, if responder was a passed hand, two of a minor would not be forcing.

OPENER	RESPONDER
1 ♥ or 1 ♠	2 ♣ or 2 ♦

Some sample auctions will suffice to explain these sequences:

OPENER	RESPONDER
1 ♠	2 ♦
2 ♥	2 ♠ or 2 no trump (game-forcing)

OPENER	RESPONDER
1 ♠	2 ♣
2 ♦	3 ♠ or 3 no trump (natural slam tries)

OPENER	RESPONDER
1 ♥	2 ♦
2 ♥	4 ♥ (shows strong diamonds and hearts)

OPENER	RESPONDER
1 ♥	2 ♣
2 ♦	3 ♥ (slam try showing three or more hearts and 15 or more high-card points) or 4 ♥ (strong diamonds and hearts, no first or second round control in unbid suit)

ONE HEART—ONE SPADE
OPENING BID SEQUENCE

One spade shows five or more spades.

OPENER	RESPONDER
1 ♥	1 ♠

Opener must raise with any three-card support. If opener started with four spades and six hearts, he should jump to three spades or bid four clubs or four diamonds to show a singleton in that suit and a maximum in high cards.

OPENER	RESPONDER
1 ♥	1 ♠
2 ♣	3 ♠ (non-forcing)

OPENER	RESPONDER
1 ♥	1 ♠
2 ♣	3 ♥ (forcing)

ONE SPADE—TWO HEARTS
OPENING BID SEQUENCE

Two hearts unconditionally forces to game unless responder bids three hearts on his second turn.

ONE OF A MAJOR—SUPPORT BY
RESPONDER OPENING BID SEQUENCE

If responder raises opener's major to the two level, he is showing three or more trump and 7 to 9 high-card points. With less than 7 points, responder should first bid a forcing no trump and bid two of opener's major at the next opportunity. The reason is that game is unlikely because opener did not bid one club.

Opener may make a game try over responder's raise by bidding a new suit to ask if responder has help in the suit, or by raising his own suit to the three level which asks responder to bid the game if he has good trump.

If responder raises opener's major to the three level, he is showing 10 to 12 high-card points and four or more trump. Opener may pass, cue bid for slam, or bid game. If opener bids three no trump, he is asking responder to bid a singleton. Responder bids the singleton if he has one, or bids four of the major if he does not.

If responder raises opener's major to three no trump, it shows a strong preemptive raise to four of the major, excellent trump, an outside singleton or void, and no more than an outside king.

Four clubs or four diamonds by responder shows a singleton or void in the suit bid, four or more cards in opener's major, and a good 11 to 13 high-card points.

A jump to four hearts over a one-spade opening bid shows a singleton or void in hearts and the other requirements for a bid of four clubs or four diamonds.

A jump to three spades over one heart shows a singleton or void in spades and otherwise is identical to four clubs or four diamonds.

When responder jumps to four of opener's major, opener must pass.

ONE OF A MAJOR—THREE CLUBS
OPENING BID SEQUENCE

Three clubs is a strong raise in opener's major. It guarantees a minimum of four trump to the jack and the hand may contain a singleton.

OPENER	RESPONDER
1 ♥ or 1 ♠	3 ♣

This is an excellent convention, one of the highlights of

the W-S system. It was originally invented by Al Roth. Opener has one of four bids over three clubs:

1. Three Diamonds. Shows a singleton or void, not necessarily in diamonds.
2. Three Hearts. Two of the top three honors in opener's major and no singleton or void.
3. Three Spades. The A or K in opener's major, no Q, and no singleton or void.
4. Three No Trump. No A or K in opener's major and no singleton or void.

After any of these responses, the partnership's primary obligation is to discover the honor strength of opener's major.

OPENER	RESPONDER
1 ♥ or 1 ♠	3 ♣
3 ♦	

Responder may make the following bids:

1. Three Hearts. Shows two of top three trump honors. Opener bids three spades if he has the other honor, and responder should bid three no trump to ask opener to name his short suit. If over three hearts opener bids three no trump, he is denying the other trump honor. Responder can still ask for the short suit by bidding four clubs. Opener may bid four of a minor over three hearts to deny the other honor and cue bid for slam. Opener may bid four of his major to deny the trump honor and indicate a weak hand with no interest in slam.

2. Three Spades. Shows the A or K of trump but not the Q. Opener bids three no trump to show the other two top trump honors. Responder may bid four clubs to ask for the singleton. Four clubs or four diamonds by opener over three spades is a natural cue bid looking for slam and denying one of the other trump honors. Four of the original major over three spades is a sign-off.

3. Three No Trump. No A or K of trump. If opener bids

four of either minor over three no trump it is a natural cue bid looking for slam. Four of a major by opener ends the auction.

OPENER	RESPONDER
1 ♥ or 1 ♠	3 ♣
3 ♥ (two of top three honors)	

Responder may make the following bids:

1. Three Spades. Shows the other trump honor. The auction then follows a logical cue bidding pattern to slam.
2. Three No Trump. Denies other trump honor but is still interested in slam.
3. Four Clubs or Four Diamonds. Denies other trump honor and is a cue bid showing slam interest.
4. Four of a Major. Sign-off.

OPENER	RESPONDER
1 ♥ or 1 ♠	3 ♣
3 ♠ (the A or K of trump)	

Responder may bid as follows:

1. Three No Trump. Shows the other two top trump honors. The auction then follows a logical cue bidding pattern to slam.
2. Four Clubs or Four Diamonds. Shows an expected trump loser but is still interested in slam.
3. Four of a Major. Sign off.

OPENER	RESPONDER
1 ♥ or 1 ♠	3 ♣
3 no trump (no A or K in trump)	

Responder may bid as follows.

1. Four Clubs or Four Diamonds. Cue bid. Still interested in slam.
2. Four of a Major. Sign-off.

A failure to go through the trump picture auction is an ask in the suit bid, because trumps are assumed to be solid.

OPENER	RESPONDER
1 ♥ or 1 ♠	3 ♣
4 ♦ (asks in diamonds)	

Responder bids as follows:

1. Four Hearts. No first or second round control.
2. Four Spades. Second round control.
3. Four No Trump. First round control.

If responder is a passed hand and then bids two clubs over opener's major, it shows 10 to 12 high-card points and guarantees at least three of opener's major. If opener rebids two diamonds, he shows a full opening bid with at least a five-card major. Two of either major by opener denies the values of a first or second chair opening bid. This is called Reverse Drury.

When there is an overcall or a double after opener bids one of a major, the entire structure is the same as with one diamond with two exceptions:

OPENER	OVERCALLER	RESPONDER
1 ♥	2 ♣	3 ♥ (10 to 12 high-card points, four trump, invitational)

OPENER	OVERCALLER	RESPONDER
1 ♠	Double	2 no trump (the same as 3 hearts in the previous auction)

Responder bids two spades or three diamonds over a one-heart opening to show a strong hand with 16 or more high-card points and the suit bid. The auction then proceeds normally.

Responder bids three diamonds or three hearts over a one-spade opening to show the same as the previous paragraph.

Responder bids two no trump over one of a major to show a balanced hand with 13 to 15 high-card points. Opener bids naturally over two no trump.

ONE NO TRUMP OPENING BID SEQUENCE

One no trump shows 15 to 17 high-card points, a balanced hand, and may contain a five-card major. Responder may bid as follows:

1. Pass. Zero to 7 high-card points and probably denies a five-card major or six-card minor.

2. Two Clubs. Forcing Stayman. Asks opener to bid a major suit if he has one, and with both majors opener bids hearts first. If responder bids a new suit after bidding two clubs, it is natural, shows at least five in the suit, and forces to game. If responder bids two no trump after bidding two clubs, he is showing 8 or 9 high-card points and may not have a four-card major.

3. Two Diamonds. Jacoby Transfer (forces opener to bid at least two hearts). Shows five or more hearts and any point count. Opener usually bids only two hearts, but on some rare hands may want to show he has maximum high-card strength and excellent heart support. He would do this by bidding three hearts, which shows four trump and 4-3-3-3 distribution. Opener might also bid two spades, three clubs, or three diamonds, which would show four trump and a doubleton in the suit bid. Two no trump by opener would show an excellent 17-point hand and three good hearts.

4. Two Hearts. Jacoby Transfer and identical to two diamonds except the long suit is spades.

5. Two Spades. Forces opener to bid two no trump and responder will clarify his hand on the next bid in one of four ways: (1) three clubs, showing no game interest and at least

5-5 distribution in the minors—opening bidder either passes or chooses three diamonds; (2) three diamonds, shows game or slam interest and at least 5-5 in the minors and 10 or more high-card points; (3) three hearts or three spades, showing 5-4 distribution either way in the minors, a singleton in the suit bid, and 10 or more high-card points; or (4) three no trump, showing 5-4 distribution either way in the minors, two weak doubletons in the majors, and 10 to 13 high-card points.

6. Two No Trump. Forces opener to bid three clubs. Responder will clarify on next bid in one of four ways: (1) pass, wants to play three clubs; (2) three diamonds, wants to play three diamonds; (3) three of a major, showing 8 or more high-card points, a void in the suit bid, and four in the other major plus 5-4 distribution either way in the minors; or (4) three no trump, showing 5-4 distribution either way in the minors, two weak doubletons in the majors, and 14 or 15 high-card points.

7. Three Clubs. Shows 4-4-4-1 with a black suit singleton and 9 or more high-card points. Opener bids three diamonds to ask for the singleton. Three hearts shows a spade singleton, three spades shows a club singleton. If opener cue bids the singleton he is asking for controls. The cheapest bid by responder shows one or two controls, the next cheapest, three controls, etc.

8. Three Diamonds. The same as three clubs except it shows a red suit singleton. Three hearts by opener asks for the singleton. Three spades shows a diamond singleton, three no trump a heart singleton. Control asks are the same.

9. Three Hearts. Shows a strong six- or seven-card club suit, no other four-card suit, and indicates slam interest.

10. Three Spades. The same as three hearts except the long suit is diamonds.

11. Three No Trump. To play.

12. Four Clubs. Gerber, asking for aces.

13. Four Diamonds. Texas Transfer to four hearts. If responder next bids four no trump, it is Blackwood.

14. Four Hearts. Texas Transfer to spades.

15. Four No Trump. Shows 15 or 16 high-card points and

4-3-3-3 distribution with any four-card suit. Bid is non-forcing.

There are five additional auctions after a one no trump opening bid that are worth discussing.

OPENER	RESPONDER
1 no trump	2 ♦ (Jacoby Transfer)
2 ♥	2 ♠ (five hearts and five spades, 4 to 6 high-card points, non-forcing)

OPENER	RESPONDER
1 no trump	2 ♥ (Jacoby Transfer)
2 ♠	3 ♥ (five spades and five hearts, forcing to at least game, 10 or more high-card points)

OPENER	RESPONDER
1 no trump	2 no trump (forces to 3 clubs)
3 ♣	4 ♣ or 4 ♦ (five cards in the suit bid, 15 or 16 high-card points, and 3-3-2 distribution in the other suits)

OPENER	RESPONDER
1 no trump	2 ♣ (Stayman)
2 ♥ or 2 ♠	Jump in a New Suit (a fit with opener's major, singleton or void in suit bid, and a slam try)

OPENER	RESPONDER
1 no trump	2 ♦ or 2 ♥
2 ♥ or 2 ♠	Jump in a New Suit (a good six- or seven-card major, no four-card suit, singleton or void in suit bid, and a slam try)

This completely covers all the opening one-bids. All that remains to be discussed are several special auctions and how to handle interference over the one-club opening bid.

20

WE LOSE THE LEAD

THE SIMILARITY BETWEEN LARRY BLUM'S LAST NAME AND Lou Dlulm's seemed to me to augur no good. Sadly, my worst fears would be justified, and once again it was something we could not prevent.

Larry Blum is an old-time rubber bridge player, a veteran money player who knows all the ropes. He is not particularly fond of duplicate bridge. He judges the merit of a bridge player by how he does head-to-head for money against top-flight competition, not by mopping up mediocre competition in meaningless duplicates. When he plays in duplicates, which is rare, it is only in major team events. Other tournaments merit his scorn. He is a purist, above the petty race for Master Points, and only the lure of this big money Calcutta justified compromising his principles.

Dr. Sam Marsh, Larry Blum's partner, is a medical doctor with a thriving practice in Queens. He was responsible for turning one of my infrequent vacations into a busman's holiday. The team I was on had just been eliminated in the semi-finals of the 1974 Spingold and I flew to Puerto Rico for some sun. No sooner had I arrived than I ran into Dr. Marsh, and I ended up locking horns with him in marathon rubber bridge sessions.

The first hand against Blum and Marsh was a continuation of our roller coaster slide down from the lead:

NORTH (Dr. Marsh)
♠ Void
♥ J 8 7 4 3
♦ K Q 8 6 2
♣ K 3 2

WEST (Sontag)
♠ A J 9 8 7
♥ 9 5
♦ J 10 7
♣ A J 6

EAST (Weichsel)
♠ Q 10 5 2
♥ K Q
♦ 9 4
♣ Q 9 8 7 5

SOUTH (Blum)
♠ K 6 4 3
♥ A 10 6 2
♦ A 5 3
♣ 10 4

Both sides vulnerable. The bidding:

WEST	NORTH	EAST	SOUTH
			1 ♦
1 ♠	2 ♥	3 ♥	Pass
3 ♠	4 ♦	Pass	4 ♥
Pass	Pass	Pass	

Everyone seemed to have a good hand if the bidding was to be believed, which often happens when high-card points are equally distributed. The bid that set everything else up was Blum's light one-diamond opening. Peter and I could have taken a vulnerable four-spade sacrifice that would have gone down only one trick, but we elected to defend with our 20 high-card points.

They made five hearts. We lost two tons of IMPs on this hand because it was passed out at 15 of the 20 tables. It was a horrendous result for us.

My friends laugh when I tell the story, but I really did have an attack of vertigo. When the room stopped whirling I looked at Peter and saw a ghost. He was sickly white and I could see the bones in his face pressing against his skin. There was nothing he could say to encourage me, and I could not think how to help him.

Somehow we got through the second hand against Marsh and Blum. We even scored a few IMPs when we set their aggressive three no trump contract by two tricks.

The second hand was a feeble, rote effort to get up off the floor, but on the third hand they clubbed us down again:

SOUTH (Blum)
♠ K Q 5 3
♥ J 10
♦ Q J 7 4 3
♣ K 6

Peter opened the bidding with four hearts and it was passed out. There was only one opening lead that Blum could make to beat us and he found it: the club king. Marsh had the ace and two other clubs and he gave Blum a ruff and later cashed the ace of diamonds. Only one other South player found that opening lead.

I knew we were not in front any more. Indeed, a later check of the scores at this point revealed that Blau and Ginsberg were now leading, and Sharif and Yallouze were closing in on us for second. We had gone into the final session leading by 259 IMPs, 748 over third place, and now we might just disappear from the board.

Peter and I walked to the kitchen and stood in a corner drinking coffee. We did not say a word. After a while I laughed, and he did too.

We walked over to our next assignment, 650 pounds of bridge players: John Lowenthal (The Stripe-tailed Ape, 225 pounds) and Paul Heitner (The Whale, 425 pounds). Lowenthal is so named because he advocates an unusual double. When the opponents are on their way to slam, he believes in doubling them at the game level before they get there in the hope that they will pass. A doubled game, of course, counts for less than a slam. If, however, the opponents redouble, Lowenthal's solution is "to run like a stripe-tailed ape."

Paul Heitner earned his nickname for an obvious reason.

Heitner and Lowenthal use their own club system—called the Canary Club—and Heitner especially is a bridge theorist. As early as 1965 Heitner wrote in *The Bridge Journal*, "The main virtue of a one club system is the limitation thus achieved for other opening bids. Playing a strong one club bid, one never has to open with a nonforcing bid on a very strong hand and hold one's breath, hoping that *someone* will keep the bidding open." Heitner also pointed out that responder over bids of other than one club is "free to use his judgment and intuition to do nasty things to his opponents." The responder can jump to game on good or bad hands because he knows the limits of opener's strength. In addition, "Opener is free to raise a response to the limit of his playing strength without fear that responder will expect great high card strength."

Heitner and Lowenthal bid and made three diamonds on the first hand and we lost a few IMPs. I was no longer counting down. I wanted the Calcutta to go on and on, at least until we regained the lead, but in reality it would end in just fourteen hands.

We made an overtrick on the second hand in a no trump part-score. I wondered what Blau and Ginsberg had done.

Heitner and Lowenthal bid one spade on the third hand and made an overtrick: a few more precious IMPs lost.

We were behind at this point. We sensed it, *knew* it, but

"dammit, Alan," Peter said, "we can't lose."

I had been wanting to watch Ron Blau and Marty Ginsberg, but I made up my mind to watch myself. The Calcutta, I determined, would be won or lost at our table on the last twelve deals.

Gail Moss is a friend of mine and I did not even say hello.

"You got it locked up?" she asked.

"We're behind," I said.

Gail Moss is one of the five best women players in America, and one of the five best in the world. She is married to Mike Moss and they have four children.

Gail's partner, Ahmed Hussein, is an Egyptian who lives in New York City and is a mathematical engineer with a doctorate in engineering and a Master's in math. He has taught at Brooklyn Poly and the University of Cairo.

Ahmed was a former student of mine. I gave him several playing lessons in New York City tournaments and he learned quite well. He now holds his own in high-stakes rubber bridge games against people like Ira Rubin, Howard Schenken, Phil Feldesman, Mike Becker, Paul Trent, Jeff Westheimer, and Jimmy Cayne.

Gail and Ahmed bid a vulnerable four spades on the first hand and made an overtrick. It was an absolutely routine result, but now only eleven hands remained to play catch-up.

They bid a part-score on the second hand and made it. I thought of Blau and Ginsberg, grinning devilishly, burying opponent after opponent. But the truth was they could not know they had passed us. Ten hands left.

At last! The third hand against Gail and Ahmed was one where we had at least a measure of control over our destiny:

NORTH (Gail Moss)
♠ A Q 9 4
♥ A Q 6 2
♦ 6
♣ A 10 6 4

WEST (Sontag)
♠ 10 3
♥ 5 4
♦ A Q 8 7 3
♣ J 9 7 2

EAST (Weichsel)
♠ J 8 7 6
♥ K 10 8 7
♦ K 10
♣ K 8 5

SOUTH (Hussein)
♠ K 5 2
♥ J 9 3
♦ J 9 5 4 2
♣ Q 3

Neither side vulnerable. The bidding:

WEST	NORTH	EAST	SOUTH
	1 ♣	Pass	1 ♦
Pass	1 ♥	Pass	1 no trump
Pass	2 no trump	Pass	Pass
Pass			

We reached down and pulled out a professional defense. My opening lead was a diamond from the strong five-card suit and Peter won with the king. He returned the ten, covered by declarer's jack, and won by my queen.

Dummy was squeezed. Ahmed had to discard from a strong four-card suit, and after a considerable length of time he pitched the club four.

Now I had to consider for a while. I realized it would be wrong to cash the diamond ace because it would set up Ahmed's nine. Ahmed's club discard marked Peter with an honor in clubs; furthermore, I knew from the bidding that Peter had at least four cards in each of the major suits (otherwise, Ahmed would have raised Gail's one heart to two, or bid a spade over one heart); therefore, I had two purposes in mind when I led the nine of clubs. First, I wanted to deceive Ahmed. The proper play with a four-card suit to an honor is usually the fourth best card. Second, I wanted to protect Peter if he had the queen and Ahmed played low from the dummy. Ahmed did play low and Peter won with the king.

Peter returned the five of clubs, another deception. Since he originally held three clubs, it was correct to lead back the second highest club to give the proper count. But that was exactly what we were trying not to do.

Ahmed tried a heart finesse which lost to Peter's king. Peter returned a club. Ahmed cashed the heart jack, the heart ace, and the ace and king of spades. This was the end position:

NORTH (Dummy)
♠ Q 9
♥ 2
♦ Void
♣ Void

WEST (Sontag)
♠ Void
♥ Void
♦ A 8
♣ J

EAST (Weichsel)
♠ J 8
♥ 10
♦ Void
♣ Void

SOUTH (Hussein)
♠ J
♥ Void
♦ 9 5
♣ Void

If Ahmed had known the actual end position, it would have been easy for him to make the contract. He would have led the heart two from dummy and Peter would have been forced to win with the ten. Peter would then have to lead from his J 8 into dummy's Q 9. But because of our deception Ahmed was sure Peter had the jack of clubs, the ten of hearts, and one spade. He led the queen of spades and Peter cashed the last two tricks. Down one!

We were behind just a few IMPs going into the last nine hands. It was incumbent for the last 75 minutes that we play the best bridge of our lives.

21

SPECIAL SEQUENCES

ONE CLUB—ONE DIAMOND— TWO HEARTS SEQUENCE

ONE WAY TO PLAY THIS SEQUENCE (AS A STRONG TWO-BID IN hearts) has already been described. But we have experimented with a new meaning that readers might find worthwhile: two hearts in this context shows 19 or more high-card points with at least 5-4 distribution either way in the minors.

OPENER	RESPONDER
1 ♣	1 ♦
2 ♥	

Opener could have the following cards:

OPENER
♠ A 5 2
♥ 4
♦ A K Q 6 5
♣ A Q 7 3

Opener has a problem with this hand. The hand is not strong enough to jump to three diamonds over the negative response, but two diamonds is a dangerous underbid: if responder had five clubs to the king, game or even slam might be possible yet the auction could end at two diamonds. This new convention is designed to handle such an awkward bidding hand.

Responder can make the following bids over two hearts:

1. Two Spades. Shows 6 to 8 high-card points and asks opener to make a natural rebid. Opener bids two no trump to show 5-4 either way in the minors, 2-2 in the majors, and 19 or 20 high-card points; three clubs to show five clubs, four diamonds, 3-1 either way in the majors, and 19 or 20 high-card points; three diamonds to show five diamonds, four or five clubs, 2-1 or 3-1 either way in the majors, and 19 or 20 high-card points; three hearts to show three good hearts, a singleton or void in spades, and nine or ten cards in clubs and diamonds, and 19 or more high-card points; three spades to show the same as three hearts except spades is the stronger suit; and three no trump to show 5-4 in the minors, a balanced hand, and 20 or 21 high card points. If responder bids four of a minor over any of these bids, it is invitational to game in that suit and may be passed.

2. Two No Trump. Shows 6 to 8 high-card points with most or all of the strength in the majors.

3. Three Clubs. A weak hand with no interest in game. Opener should pass.

4. Three Diamonds. The same as three clubs.

5. Three Hearts. Natural and forcing. Shows a good five- or six-card heart suit.

6. Three Spades. The same as three hearts except the suit is spades.

7. Four Clubs. Invitational to game in clubs. Not many high cards but a good fit.

8. Four Diamonds. The same as four clubs except the suit is diamonds.

9. Four Hearts. Slam try in clubs.
10. Four Spades. Slam try in diamonds.

If players decide to use this convention, another bid must be found to replace the strong two-bid in hearts. The following sequence could be substituted:

OPENER	RESPONDER
1 ♣	1 ♦
1 ♥	1 ♠
3 ♥ (strong two-bid in hearts)	

Here is another special sequence that requires discussion:

OPENER	RESPONDER
1 ♣	1 ♦
1 ♥	1 ♠
2 no trump	

Two no trump unconditionally forces to game, shows a balanced hand packed with controls. Responder can bid Stayman, transfer to a major, show interest in both minor suits by bidding three spades, show interest in one of the minors by bidding four clubs, or bid three or four no trump.

Opener can have one of the following two hands for his two no trump bid:

♠ A K;   ♥ A 8 4;   ♦ A K Q 7 2;   ♣ K Q 5.
or
♠ A K 3;   ♥ K 6;   ♦ A K 7 4;   ♣ A K 9 5.

Opener would have started the bidding with two no trump (24 to 25 high-card points) instead of one club with the following hand:

♠ K Q J; ♥ A Q 5; ♦ A Q 9 2; ♣ A K 7.

INTERFERENCE OVER BLACKWOOD

If interference occurs over Blackwood at the five level, double by responder shows no aces, pass shows one ace, and any bid shows two aces (DOPI—double none, pass one).

If interference occurs over Blackwood at the six level, double by responder shows zero, two, or four aces, and pass shows one ace or three aces (DEPO—double even, pass odd).

INTERFERENCE OVER ASKING BIDS

The double of an asking bid (trump ask, control ask, etc.) allows responder to redouble with the worst holding, pass with the next worst, make the cheapest bid with the third holding, the next cheapest with the fourth holding, etc.

If the opponents bid over the asking bid (except double), responder doubles to show the worst holding, passes to show the next worst, etc.

FOUR NO TRUMP BIDS

Four no trump has a variety of meanings, depending on how the auction has proceeded.

It is a natural invitational raise whenever it is bid directly over a no trump call:

OPENER	RESPONDER
1 ♥	2 ♣
2 no trump	4 no trump

OPENER	RESPONDER
1 no trump	4 no trump

Four no trump is Blackwood when it is jumped to over any other bid but no trump, or when a suit has been agreed upon in a non-cue bidding auction:

OPENER	RESPONDER
1 ♣	2 ♥
4 no trump (Blackwood)	

OPENER	RESPONDER
1 ♠	3 ♥
4 ♥	4 no trump (Blackwood)

Four no trump is a sign-off when no fit has been agreed upon, or when the possibility of a high-level contract has been explored:

OPENER	RESPONDER
1 ♠	2 ♥
3 ♦	3 no trump
4 ♦	4 no trump (sign-off)

OPENER	RESPONDER
1 ♣	2 no trump
3 ♣	3 ♥
4 ♣	4 no trump (sign-off)

Four no trump can show continued interest in slam with an inability to cue bid when a suit has been agreed upon and cue bidding has taken place at the four level:

OPENER	RESPONDER
1 ♠	2 ♦
3 ♦	3 ♠
4 ♥ (cue bid)	4 no trump (forcing slam try)

OPENER	RESPONDER
1 ♣	2 ♣
2 ♥	3 ♥
4 ♦ (cue bid)	4 ♠ (cue bid)
4 no trump (forcing slam try)	

INTERFERENCE OVER ONE
CLUB OPENING BID

This is the last major portion of the W-S system that needs to be discussed, and is extremely important. Detractors of club systems allege that their main weakness is their susceptibility to preemption. Peter and I have worked for a long time to learn how to circumvent these disruptions, and even to turn them to our advantage. Whenever Peter and I play against anyone, we immediately ask them what they bid over our strong one-club opening. Under the rules of bridge they are required to answer. Frankly, Peter and I enjoy playing against these opportunistic sharpshooters.

After a one-club opening bid, if the opponent doubles to show a good hand or as a take-out, responder may bid as follows:

1. Pass. Shows 0 to 5 high-card points.

2. Redouble. Strong 9 or more high-card points and forces to game.

3. One of a Suit. Natural, non-forcing, 5 to 8 high-card points, five or more cards in the suit bid.

4. One No Trump. Natural, balanced hand, non-forcing, and 6 to 8 high-card points.

5. Two Clubs. Same as one of a suit except responder is showing clubs.

6. Two Diamonds, Two Hearts, Two Spades. Game-forcing, 9 or more high-card points, five or more cards in the suit bid.

7. Three of any Suit. Excellent six- or seven-card suit that will play for only one loser.

8. Four of any Suit. Six or more cards in the suit bid headed by the A K Q.

The opponent may double one club to show clubs. If so, except for Responses #2 and 5, responder bids the same. A redouble would show 9 or more high-card points and at least four clubs to one of the three top honors. Two clubs forces to game and shows a singleton or void.

The opponent may overcall one club at the one or two level in a natural suit. Responder may bid as follows:

1. Pass. Shows 0 to 5 high-card points or the responder may have a penalty double of the overcaller's suit. Opener will reopen with a double whenever he is short in the overcaller's suit.

2. Double. Shows 6 to 9 high-card points initially. If responder bids a new suit after doubling, it forces to game and shows five or more cards in the suit bid and 9 or more high-card points. If responder bids their suit after doubling, it shows 9 or more high-card points, forces to game, and usually is looking for game in no trump. When opener bids a new suit over responder's double, responder must bid again even if he has only 6 high-card points and no fit—his weakest bid would be to raise opener's suit.

3. Any Non-Jump New Suit Bid. Non-forcing, 5 to 8 high-card points, five or more cards in the suit bid.

4. One No Trump. Natural, non-forcing, 6 to 8 high-card points, balanced hand.

5. Cue Bid. Game-forcing, shows 9 or more high-card points, a singleton or void in suit bid, and either 4-4-4 or 5-4-4 distribution in other suits.

6. Two No Trump. Game-forcing, 9 or more high-card points, balanced hand, and at least two stoppers in their suits.

7. Jump Shift to Two or Three Level. Game-forcing, 9 or more high-card points, and six or seven cards in suit bid.

8. Double Jump to New Suit. Game-forcing, 9 or more high-card points, excellent six or seven cards in suit bid.

The opponent may make a preemptive overcall of two spades or higher over the one-club opening bid. Responder bids as follows:

1. Pass. Shows 0 to 6 high-card points. May also have a strong holding in their suit. Opener is obliged to reopen the bidding with a double if he is short in their suit.

2. Double. Shows 7 or more high-card points. The same principle applies as in the double in the previous auction.

3. New Suit at Three Level. Game-forcing, usually shows a six-card suit.

4. Three No Trump. To play, shows 10 to 12 high-card points.

5. Jump Shift into New Suit. Excellent six or seven cards in suit bid.

6. Two No Trump. Invitational, shows 7 or 8 high-card points and their suit double-stopped.

The opponent may make an overcall that shows a specific two-suit hand, such as double to show the majors, and one no trump to show the minors. Responder bids as follows:

1. Pass. Shows 0 to 5 high-card points.

2. Double. Penalty oriented. Shows length and strength in at least one of their suits. If the opponent had doubled, responder would redouble to show the same hand.

3. Cheapest Cue Bid. Shows 6 to 9 high-card points, length in the other suits, and promises to bid at least once more.

4. Most Expensive Cue Bid. Game-forcing, 9 or more high-card points, length in the other suits.

5. One No Trump. Natural, non-forcing, 6 to 8 high-card points.

6. One of a New Suit (not theirs). Natural, non-forcing, 5 to 8 high-card points, at least five cards in suit bid.

7. Two No Trump. Natural, forcing, at least 9 high-card points.

8. Jump in Any Suit. Forcing, 9 or more high-card points, six or seven cards in suit bid.

9. Double Jump in Any Suit. Forcing, 9 or more high-card points, excellent six or seven cards in suit bid.

The opponent may make an overcall over one club to show shortness in the suit bid (Exclusion Overcall). Responder bids as follows:

1. Double. Shows 9 or more high-card points, and four cards in the overcalled suit.

2. One No Trump. Shows 6 to 8 high-card points and four or five cards in the overcalled suit.

3. Cue Bid. Shows 9 or more high-card points, forcing, and five or more cards in overcalled suit.

4. Any New Suit. Natural, non-forcing, 5 to 8 high-card points, at least five cards in the suit bid.

5. Pass. Shows 0 to 8 high-card points. Double by responder at his next opportunity shows 6 to 8 high-card points.

The opponent may overcall in a suit over one club to show the next highest suit (Jacoby Transfer Overcalls). Responder bids as follows:

1. Pass. Shows 0 to 5 high-card points.

2. Double. Six to eight high-card points.

3. Bidding Their Suit. Game-forcing, 9 or more high-card points.

4. One No Trump. Non-forcing, stopper in their suit, 6 to 8 high-card points.

5. Any New Suit Except Their Promised Suit. Non-forcing, 5 to 8 high-card points, at least five cards in suit bid.

6. Two No Trump. Shows 9 or more high-card points, game-forcing, and at least two stoppers in their suit.

7. Jump in Their Suit. Game-forcing, singleton or void in their suit, and at least four cards in each of the other three suits.

8. Jump in New Suit. Shows 9 or more high-card points and six or seven cards in the suit bid.

9. Double Jump in New Suit. Shows 9 or more high-card points and a very strong six or seven cards in the suit bid.

The opponent may overcall one club with a system called CRASH (Color, Rank, and Shape) in which a double shows either both black suits or both red suits, one diamond shows either both majors or both minors, and one heart shows either spades and diamonds or hearts and clubs. Machiavellian maneuvers like CRASH are in reality tributes to the power of the one-club opening bid. They show the lengths experts will travel to impede the one-club auction. But systems like CRASH can be neutralized. Responder bids as follows:

1. Double or Redouble. Double over one diamond or one heart, and redouble over double, shows 9 or more high-card points and a balanced hand. Any future doubles by opener or responder are for penalties.

2. Any New Suit Bid. One diamond, one heart, one spade, and two clubs—over double—or one heart, one spade, two clubs, and two diamonds—over one diamond—or one spade, two clubs, two diamonds, and two hearts—over one heart— all show 9 or more high-card points, five or more cards in the suit bid, and force to game.

3. Pass. Shows 0 to 8 high-card points, and forces the opening club bidder to keep the auction alive.

The opponent may overcall after the bidding has gone one club, pass, one diamond. Opener bids as follows:

1. Pass. Minimum, balanced hand, or length in their suit.

2. Double. Take-out double. Shortness in overcaller's suit.

3. One No Trump. Natural, 19 to 21 high-card points, and a stopper in overcaller's suit.

4. Jump in Another Suit. Forcing, at least five cards in suit bid, and 21 or more high-card points.

5. Cue Bid. Game-forcing, shows very strong two-suit hand.

The opponent may double after the bidding has gone one club, pass, one diamond. Opener bids as follows:

1. One Heart. Forcing. Could show either a heart suit or a strong balanced hand.

2. Redouble. Good defensive hand with strength in the doubler's suit or suits.

3. All Other Bids (with one exception). Natural, as if there had been no double. The exception is that if the double showed diamonds, then two diamonds by opener is a game-forcing cue bid, usually showing two suits.

Whenever responder takes any action except passing after an overcall, doubles by opener are always for *penalties*.

This concludes the instruction portion of the book. The W-S system has been presented in its entirety.

W-S works for experts and nonexperts alike. The system has proved itself numerous times in national and international competition, but it can be just as valuable to the average player.

I would suggest that most partnerships not try to learn the system all at once. At first play parts of the system. The partnership that plays part of it will soon want to play it all.

22

THE LAST HARD PUSH

No room for error remained. The Calcutta was too close and there was too little time.

Our opponents were Michael Rosenberg from Scotland and Zia Mahmoud from Pakistan, a dangerous partnership. Rosenberg was a recent winner of the *London Sunday Times Invitational*, and Mahmoud was a tough customer who made his living playing rubber bridge for high stakes.

The Cavendish was noisier even than before. Bridge audiences are different in this respect from people who follow any other mental game. Attend a chess or backgammon tournament and you can hear the pieces move and the dice rattle. At bridge tournaments, including the most important, spectators feel they have a right, even a duty, to offer advice during the event. At the 1976 Vanderbilt a kibitzer leaned over Peter's shoulder after he had gone down in a part-score and told him how he should have played the hand.

"Could you imagine," Peter asked, "how Arnold Palmer would react if someone rushed up to him on the seventeenth tee to tell him why he had hooked his drive?"

Still, bridge audiences are fun and golf galleries are not,

perhaps because bridge is more democratic. The rawest bridge beginner can enter virtually any tournament he desires and find himself facing Oswald Jacoby or Alan Truscott, which might project for him an exaggerated picture of his own expertise. The average person in a golf gallery will never play Arnold Palmer.

Anyway, the noise did not bother me. It is something every tournament bridge player accepts.

Rosenberg and Mahmoud bid and made one no trump against us on the first hand. We lost IMPs on this hand even though we played strong defense. They had 25 high-card points and we held them without an overtrick. The problem was that many partnerships bid three no trump and went down one.

It seemed that we had run into a horrendous streak of bad luck. Our sole recent good result had been the last hand against Gail Moss and Ahmed Hussein, and even that modest swing in our favor had required several extraordinary defensive plays.

It did no good to dwell on luck or the lack of it.

On the second hand I had to make a decision that I knew might win or lose the Calcutta for us. I held the following cards:

WEST (Sontag)
♠ Q J 9 7 6 4 3
♥ Q 8
♦ 10 4
♣ Q 5

Both sides were vulnerable and this was the bidding:

WEST	NORTH	EAST	SOUTH
		1 ♦	Double
2 ♠	3 ♥	Pass	Pass
?			

I had to decide whether to pass or bid three spades, and I took my time. Peter's opening one-diamond bid and my seven-card suit made it tempting to bid three spades. But Mahmoud's double and Peter's pass, coupled with my two queen doubletons (perhaps more valuable for defense than offense), militated against three spades.

More time went by. There was no chance of being rushed. Peter would want me to take forever if it meant making the right choice, and Mahmoud and Rosenberg knew we were playing for the championship and would never consider trying to speed things up.

I passed and it turned out right. We set them two tricks, but would have gone down two tricks if I had bid three spades. The hand enabled us to win back the IMPs we lost on the first deal, and 85 more!

I believed we had recaptured the lead. There were seven hands to go.

They bid three no trump and made it, a normal result.

Six hands to go.

I loved what was happening. What good bridge player wouldn't? There was great competition, we were in the running in the deep homestretch, we might never again have the opportunity to win back-to-back Calcuttas, and the prize in this prestigious event was more than glory or Master Points.

Peter and I, in dozens of strategy sessions, have worked out how we should play in just such a situation: no reckless or wild deviations from our system, but aggressiveness should be favored over timidity. We sat down to play:

Lou Reich and Jay Merrill.

Reich and Merrill bid three no trump on the first hand and we set them one trick.

Plus 75 IMPs for us.

Five hands to go.

Reich and Merrill bid four hearts on the second hand and we set them two tricks.

Four hands to go.

We bid five clubs on the third hand and made six with only 25 high-card points.

Plus 105 IMPs for us.

Three hands to go.

The final hand against Reich and Merrill, a large swing in our favor, succeeded because of our bidding methods:

WEST (Sontag)	EAST (Weichsel)
♠ K 8 4	♠ A 9 5 2
♥ A 7	♥ 6
♦ 9 6 2	♦ K J 10 8
♣ A K J 8 5	♣ Q 10 7 3

WEST	EAST
1 no trump	3 ♦ (red singleton)
3 ♥ (asks singleton)	3 no trump (heart singleton)
4 ♣ (natural and forcing)	4 ♠ (shows ace)
5 ♣ (sign-off)	Pass

Half the field bid three no trump with these cards, and a heart opening lead destroyed them. Here is the way most partnerships bid the hand:

WEST	EAST
1 no trump	2 ♣ (Stayman)
2 ♦	3 no trump

We made one last walk through the crowd. I could not remember the only partnership we had not played.

Bobby Wolff (former World Champion) and Jim Hooker.

Peter and I bid four spades on the first hand in a faultless auction but a great opening lead by Wolff-Hooker gave them a trump trick and we were down one. Wolff-Hooker took 90 IMPs from us.

Two hands to go.

We had played 115 hands in the tournament and I was still not sure we had shaken Blau and Ginsberg (we hadn't) or Sharif and Yallouze.

I held the following cards on the second hand:

WEST (Sontag)
♠ 8 7 6 5
♥ Q J 3
♦ Q 8
♣ A K Q J

and opened one diamond. I did not open one no trump because I had a poor 15 high-card points and 10 of these were
in one suit. Peter, a passed hand, jumped to two no trump
with only 10 high-card points and we ended in three no
trump which Peter made.

Plus 95 IMPs.

Many pairs also bid three no trump, but with West as the
declarer, and could not make the contract.

One hand to go.

"Are we playing this last hand against the champions?"
Bobby Wolff asked.

"We don't know," Peter said.

"Then we'd better play real hard," Wolff said.

The last hand was a teeter, one in which a fortune of IMPs
could be won or lost:

NORTH (Wolff)
♠ J 4 2
♥ K Q J 5 4
♦ A 9 7
♣ 8 3

WEST (Sontag)
♠ A 3
♥ 2
♦ Q 10 8 6
♣ Q J 10 9 6 4

EAST (Weichsel)
♠ K Q 10 8 7 6
♥ 7
♦ K 5 3
♣ K 7 2

SOUTH (Hooker)
♠ 9 5
♥ A 10 9 8 6 3
♦ J 4 2
♣ A 5

East-West vulnerable. The bidding:

WEST	NORTH	EAST	SOUTH
	1 ♥	1 ♠	3 ♥
Double	Pass	4 ♠	5 ♥
Pass	Pass	Double	Pass
Pass	Pass		

Wolff started the auction with a light opening bid. Hooker invited to game over Peter's overcall and I doubled to show values and length in the minor suits. Peter's four-spade bid was aggressive and well reasoned and we would have made it. Hooker went to five hearts because he had strong six-card support for his partner and believed correctly that we could make four spades. Peter doubled because he knew we had half the deck in high cards.

We set them three tricks and scored 110 IMPs.

Peter's chin dropped to his chest. He was wrung out, drained. I was hardly in shape to start the tournament over, either.

It took an hour for the final results to be posted. A French television director asked me how we had done. The cameras were filming. I told him first or second.

We compared results with Blau and Ginsberg. Peter was sure we had won. In the past he had always been right, but there was no way he could be sure until the scores of every partnership had been compared on each hand against one another.

The scores were posted at 1 A.M.:

POSITION	PARTNERSHIP	COUNTRY	IMPS	MONEY
1.	Weichsel-Sontag	U.S.A.	1,892	$50,400
2.	Blau-Ginsberg	U.S.A.	1,612	$36,000
3.	Sharif-Yallouze	Egypt-France	1,242	$21,600
4.	Cayne-Eisenberg	U.S.A.	1,029	$14,400
5.	Cohen-Walvick	U.S.A.	905	$ 8,640
6.	Blum-Marsh	U.S.A.	863	$ 5,760
7.	Blair-Levin	U.S.A.	861	$ 4,320
8.	Mike Becker-Greenberg	U.S.A.	855	$ 2,880

Peter saw the scores first and he punched my arm. Then we were talking to the French television director again and crowds of players and kibitzers waited to offer congratulations.

All the time invested with Peter, the work endured on the system, endless effort, it all seemed worthwhile in this moment of triumph.

Omar Sharif walked up to shake hands.

"Let's go out tonight," he said.

"And have a big steak and drink," I said.

We went to a discotheque, Le Cocu, and stayed until the sun came up.

"Why," Sharif asked late in the morning, "did you two win?"

"System," Peter said.

ABOUT THE AUTHOR

ALAN SONTAG was born in New York City in 1946 and attended Queens College. He has won many national and international bridge championships, including the Vanderbilt, the Reisinger, the Life Masters Pairs, the Life Masters Men's Pairs, the *London Sunday Times* Invitational twice (the most important pairs tournament in the world), the Cavendish Calcutta twice (the biggest money tournament in the world), and numerous regional and sectional championships. He writes, with Oswald Jacoby, a nationally syndicated bridge column. In between traveling to various tournaments around the world, Alan Sontag makes his home in New York and enjoys an occasional game of backgammon.